the book of

all about **ecstasy**

the book of e

all about **ecstasy**

push & mireille silcott

Cover designed by Pearce Marchbank, Studio 20
Picture research by Nikki Lloyd

ISBN: 0.7119.7519.1
Order No: OP 48107

Exclusive Distributors:
Book Sales Limited,
8/9 Frith Street,
London W1V 5TZ, UK.

Music Sales Corporation,
257 Park Avenue South,
New York, NY 10010, USA.

The Five Mile Press,
22 Summit Road,
Noble Park,
Victoria 3174, Australia.

To the Music Trade only:
Music Sales Limited,
8/9 Frith Street,
London W1V 5TZ, UK.

Typeset by Galleon Typesetting, Ipswich
Printed by CPD Wales, Ebbw Vale

A catalogue record for this book is available from the British Library.

Visit Omnibus Press on the web at www.omnibuspress.com

Contents

Foreword   vii

Acknowledgements   ix

1   Ecstasy At The Saint Disco, New York City by **Mireille Silcott**   1

2   Ecstasy F.A.Q.   7

3   Ecstasy At The Starck Club, Dallas, Texas by **Mireille Silcott**   14

4   Merck: The Origins Of E by **Push**   22

5   1972–1985: In Therapy And In Court by **Push**   27

6   Alexander Shulgin: A Personal Perspective by **Myron Stolaroff**   36

7   Ecstasy And The UK Press I   40

8   August 1988: What We're On Is Happiness   44

9   From Ibiza To The Summer Of Love: A First Person Account   47

10   Busts, Raids And Clampdowns: A Policeman's Lot by **Push**   52

11   E Is For England: Ecstasy And Football by **Push**   62

12   Manchester: Diary Of A Club Owner   64

13   Scotland The Rave: Hanger 13 And Hardcore Excess by **Mireille Silcott**   68

14   Song Lyrics: Ebeneezer Goode   79

15   Ecstasy And The UK Press II   82

16   Ecstasy And Raving America I: San Francisco, California by **Mireille Silcott**   87

17   Ecstasy And Raving America II: Orlando, Florida by **Mireille Silcott**   98

18   The Rise And Fall Of The Chill-Out Ideal by **Mireille Silcott**   107

19   Nicholas Saunders: A Personal Perspective by **Dr Karl Jansen**   109

20   Script I: Snowball   112

21   Script II: Coronation Street   116

22   Interview: Paul And Janet Betts by **Push**   118

23 "I Done 12 One Night, Y'know What I Mean?" by **Push**   126

24 Agitation And Legislation: The CJA And Beyond by **Push**   130

25 Editorial I: "Press The Panic Button"   137

26 Editorial II: "Ecstasy – Editorial Comment"   139

27 Harm Reduction And Safer Dancing by **Push**   142

28 Leaflet: Chill Out   152

29 E Testing by **Push**   154

30 Beyond The Gateway I: Ketamine, GHB, 2C-B And
Methamphetamine   162

31 Beyond The Gateway II: Legal And Prescription Drugs   169

32 Ecstasy And The UK Press III   176

33 Q&A: Dealers And Manufacturers   181

34 Superclubs And The Mainstreaming Of E Culture by **Mireille
Silcott**   184

35 Ecstasy And Other Drugs On The American Gay Circuit by
Mireille Silcott   189

36 The Drug Czar And "A Better Britain" by **Push**   198

37 Report From The Research Lab by **Push**   204

38 Gatecrasher Kids And Candy Ravers by **Mireille Silcott**   212

Bibliography   225

Internet Resources   241

Foreword

When we first conceived this book, in late 1998, one of the questions we kept getting asked was "Why another book about ecstasy culture?" There was no denying that several books along such lines were already on the shelves. It was a question we had needed to ask ourselves, too.

Our answer was that we wanted to write something which wasn't a history of dance culture or a 'decade of acid house' book in which E played a supporting role. Others had already tackled that task, and admirably.* Instead, we wanted to author a text in which the drug itself – among the most popular and controversial illegal substances of the 20th century – was the driving topic, more than the music and the nightlife styles it helped spawn. We wanted to focus on both Britain and America. We wanted to show both pros and cons. We also wanted to include a few of what we felt were little-explored aspects of ecstasy's past and present.

It was a pretty tall order. Especially if, as we'd originally intended, we were going to write a fluid history, the kind which goes from A to B with few deviations into other letters in between. So, about a month into our work, we gave up on fluidity and split up writing duties.

One of us – the one with a heavier social conscience – wanted to create a book which would be practical to the current E user. A functional book containing easy-to-access information about the legal issues surrounding the drug, the politics of the drug, what the drug does in the brain and what kind of research has been done on it. The other wanted to write about the historical positioning of ecstasy in youth culture. About how the "love drug" fits into the lives of all the different types of people who choose to use it – be it at raves or clubs, in stadiums or hotel rooms.

For a time, we rammed our heads together. And then, what came out was the idea of a compilation. A loosely chronological anthology about ecstasy that is practical as well as unpredictable, here-and-now as well as retro-gazing, full of hard facts as well as special stories. A big, fat compendium in which the kaleidoscopic realities of E – the zillion and one truths that are all equally valid – could be told in many different ways.

We agreed this kind of collage would be a good way to reflect the

---

* For further reading, see Matthew Collin's *Altered State*, Simon Reynolds' *Energy Flash* [*Generation Ecstasy* in the US] and Sheryl Garratt's *Adventures In Wonderland*.

hall-of-mirrors nature of the ecstasy experience. In *the book of e: all about ecstasy*, then, you will find everything from cultural overviews to straight-forward information. Everything from reprints of E safety pamphlets, to interviews and oral histories, song lyrics, excerpts from television dialogue and film scripts – all of which deal with the drug.

It's estimated that over a million ecstasy tablets are consumed in Britain every weekend. There may be close to that number consumed in America. Every single person who takes E has an opinion about the drug, as do many of the people who have never tried it. We have endeavoured to present as many of these opinions as possible. We encourage you to start reading at whichever chapter, whichever point of view, you find most interesting. And we hope that, embedded in all these words about one little pill, you can locate your truth about it, too.

Acknowledgements

This book was possible only because the following people agreed to take time out to share their knowledge with us or to assist us in any number of other ways. We owe an enormous debt of gratitude to all of them.

Push would like to thank:

Herman-Louis Matser at the Adviesburo Drugs in Amsterdam; Paul and Janet Betts, for their warmth; Ciaran O'Hagan at Release in London; Dr Karl Jansen for steering both of us through lots of medical jargon; Rick Doblin and the crew at MAPS; Ken Tappenden for the encouragement as well as for information; Dr George Ricaurte and Cammille Bentley at Johns Hopkins University; and James McQueen, for sitting up to his neck in newspaper cuttings.

Additional thanks to: Colin Angus, Stephen Ashurst, Jeff Barrett, Calvin Bush, Shane Collins, Caroline Coon, Charles Cosh, John Derricott and Kirsteen at Hit in Liverpool, David Donald, Claire Eaves, Dave Fowler, Mike Goodman and Rosie Sorrell at Release, Maria Jefferis, Jackie Keer, Mike Linnell at Lifeline, Eugene Manzi and Juliette Sensicle at London Records, Pat O'Hare, Charles Overbeck, David Pearce, Dr Ingunn Possehl and Silke Muenk at Merck, Harry Shapiro at the Institute for the Study of Drug Dependence, Joe Shepherd and Denise Hart at the Cabinet Press Office, Liz Simon, Mark Sutherland, Steve Sutherland, Brian Sweeney, Nick Taylor, Helen Trafford and Joel Orme at Granada TV, Ben Turner, Lindsey McWhinnie, Mark White, and Wiz.

Also, oodles of thanks to all my family and friends. Special thanks for keeping me almost sane to the Brentford Triangle posse: Sam Dodson, Ruth Rollason and Adam 'Spider' Dodson at the Salmonroof Fax Bureau; Rat Scabies, Mrs Scabies and the rest of the Scabies clan, and honorary Triangle member Lord James Clayton.

Mireille Silcott would like to thank:

Kerry Jaggers, who gives just about the best interview in all of Gayland, U.S.A.; the ever-eloquent Wade Hampton for his encyclopedic remembrances of the Starck; Jon Campbell for turning Scotland rave inside out for me; Matt Hays and Robert Vézina for their years of schooling on the politics of the circuit; AK 1200, Eli Tobias and Bevin O'Neil in Orlando; Malachy O'Brien, Dianna Jacobs, and the Wicked boys in San Francisco; and Aim-E and all the LA candy rave massive.

Additional thanks to: Steven Baird, Stace Bass, Kid Batchelor, Daniel Boulanger, Mike Cadger and all the folks at Crew 2000, Dave Canalte, Caroline and Charles, Jayne Casey, Bonnie Clark and Ricky McGowan at Colours/Street Rave, Bethan Cole, Bettina Costanzo, DJ Icey, DJ Remark, DJ Sandy, DJ Spice, Duane at Amato, D-Xtreme, Kurt Eckes, Chris Hand, the Hardkisses, Andy Hughes, Karl Jansen, Ian Kronish, Joe in Texas, Dave Liddel at the Scottish Drugs Forum, Fraser MacIntyre, John Mancini, John Marsa, Doc Martin, Claire Mead, Mark Moore, Mr. C, Marc Nicholson, Martin O'Brien, Ben Parsley, Andy Pemberton, Rod 'Disco Grandad' Roderick, Rich Rosario, Ira Sandler, Simone at *The List*, Nick Spiers, Myron Stolaroff, Sunshine and Moonbeam at Dubtribe, Tommy Sunshine, Ben Turner, Jason Walker, Tom Wilson, and Tony Wilson.

I am grateful to all my family, especially my grandparents Beatrice and Maurice and my parents, for their tireless support. To Mike Kronish for his big love and for slipping food under the door every so often, and to Alana Klein for being my lifelong editor and best friend. Massive shout out to my bro' Jonathan Handel for being the coolest fifteen year old in all of North America, and for being a constant inspiration.

Both authors also wish to express their king-sized gratitude to Mark Wernham (formerly Mark Roland) for introducing the two of us to each other; to Lucy Olivier and Omnibus' Rob Dimery for having faith from the get-go; to our editor Chris Charlesworth for having patience later on; to Helen Donlon for her extra-curricular support; and to Ian McGregor for going well beyond the call of book jacket design duty.

1

Ecstasy At The Saint Disco, New York City

MDMA – ecstasy – was not the only drug at the Saint. No, there was also MDA, which was popular, too. There was K – ketamine – which was just debuting and quite fashionable. There was cocaine, which most members could afford. And poppers. And tiny, shining crystals of methamphetamine. There were rags doused with ethyl chloride from a spray bottle. People would dance with those bunched around the corners of their mouths, spraying and sucking with every new song mixed in by the DJ.

Blonde hash, skunk weed, dull grey speed. Quaaludes, Xanax, Valium. THC, PCP, LSD: at the Saint disco, everything was readily available. Except alcohol. Everyone was readily available. Especially on the balconies. It was probably one of the most, if not *the* most, impressive gay nightclubs that ever existed in New York City. Built in the old Fillmore East concert venue on 2nd Avenue and 6th Street in 1980, with a price tag of six million dollars and the capacity to hold 7,000 patrons, it was still what you would call a disco – but a second-wave disco, where the music was Euro and electronic and what was soon increasingly called hi-NRG (first Boney M, later, 'So Many Men, So Little Time', by Miquel Brown, and the entire *oeuvres* of Frankie Goes To Hollywood and Hazell Dean). It was mainly white, it was private, it wasn't cheap, and it was men-only.

The Saint existed at the end of the golden age of gay nighteries. At the tail of the high disco era, where gay sex and clubs, and gay sex in clubs, became legitimate signs of a new, carefree liberation. The Saint seemed hundreds of years away from the pre-Stonewall drag-run piano bars and basement grottos of the Sixties. It seemed many futures beyond even the clubs it directly superseded: glitzy dance boutiques like the Flamingo. Or less flash all-hours homo-discos like the Anvil, Crisco Disco and 12 West, places with brick walls with naive skyline murals painted on them, where coloured cardboard and balloons were the main materials with which to decorate for special events.

Everybody who went to the opening of the Saint in 1980 said it felt like a new era, a new world even. You passed through the unmarked metal

1

doors on 2nd Avenue. Crossed into the formidable marble vestibule. Then went through the towering video screens, twinkling copper, crystal, and mirror of the front bar. Walking up the grand staircases, you would start hearing the rumble of bass and the thick hum of thousands of men dancing. Saint patrons said it was then, at that exact point, that it felt like you were entering into a universe too big to fit into any city, even New York.

It was when you reached the dancefloor that you *knew* you had reached a new world. The creator and owner of the Saint, Bruce Mailman – who also owned the most beautiful and celebrated gay bathhouse in New York, the Saint Marks Baths – said he wanted his disco to be a place where all time, space and limitations evaporated. An area where lights and immense sound became time and space itself. There were no columns or harsh corners anywhere in the club and its dancefloor, which fitted almost 3,000, was perfectly round. Round, and covered by the largest planetarium dome on the East Coast at that time, rising up from the floor on one side of the dancefloor. It was at about 4am every night, when the 'sleaze music', the sultry, pretty morning music (like The Police's 'Every Breath You Take', Kenny Rogers & Dolly Parton's 'Islands In The Streams', Bonnie Tyler's 'Total Eclipse Of The Heart') would start, that the cosmos was projected onto the skin of the dome. You were surrounded by all the stars of the universe – people said it felt like you were dancing in outer space. That you couldn't even feel the floor when the sky came on. Everything belonging to real life just melted away, until you left the Saint early the next afternoon.

Kerry Jaggers was a prototypical Saint member. A beautiful, sandy-haired, blue-eyed, well-built, gay man of middle-class background, he came to New York in the late Seventies from his native Texas, the state where he had launched a spate of successful discotheques as a DJ, a lighting designer and a consultant. Jaggers' lifestyle was jet-setting and glamorous. He knew Grace Jones intimately and, back in Texas, often played host to visiting celebrities looking for decadent nights out. He vacationed on gay resort Fire Island in the summers, and his Rolodex was thick with numbers of other 'A-list' men from all over the world.

Like other Saint members, Jaggers wore bandannas, fashionably ripped t-shirts and Levi's 501s tucked into Converse high-tops when he went to the disco. When he danced, he would take off his shirt like everyone else, and loop it into the waistband of his jeans. The rule was comfort and maleness, no flamboyant queeny stuff. Some people would even dance in pyjama bottoms, sweatpants or gym shorts. Anything that would let you move and sweat freely.

Like other Saint members, Jaggers lived for the pristine lines, clean studio techniques and the fast, repetitive, electronic beats of the NRG electro-disco then coming out of Europe. He liked the way that music could be easily mixed into a seamless flow, the way Saint DJs like Roy Thode, Robbie Leslie or Michael Fireman could "take you on a head trip" with it, building and building the beats per minute into an exhilarating speed-peak.

Like other Saint members, Jaggers liked the way you could just drop yourself into the middle of the club's dancefloor and immediately feel 'as one', somehow intrinsically connected and in love with everyone else there.

Jaggers never referred to any of these things – comfortable clothing, repetitive electronic beats, mass-identity, one-love – as being part of an emerging 'ecstasy culture', the way people would eight years later when the drug hit the UK and acid house exploded. He never considered himself part of any meaning-doused drug movement when he mixed his four measures of legal MDMA powder – procured from one of the Saint's two immovable in-house dealers – into his beverages. He just did it.

"And so did everyone else I knew," says Jaggers. "But the drug was never the main focus, the drug – legal, remember – was no more controversial than baby powder. Men were the focus, sex was the focus . . . every Saturday, at any given time, there were over a thousand men writhing together, having open, beautiful, sex on the Saint's balcony. Ecstasy is something that takes down your inhibitions; many at the Saint were pretty uninhibited to start with. You can imagine what it was like."

MDMA, acquired from labs in Texas and California, was all over New York's gay circuit by the early Eighties. Celebs and glamour-amours sampled it at Studio 54, but coke was generally preferred at that club. It found its way into gay bathhouses, but the men there usually favoured one of MDMA's chemical cousins – MDA. It was easier to sustain an erection on MDA and it felt, as former Saint party organizer Rod Roderick puts it, "less lovey, more hardcore fucky". You could also get ecstasy at the Paradise Garage, says Roderick, a man now known on the circuit as 'Disco Grandad', "but then you could get anything at the Garage, 36 different flavours . . . and all that mattered to them [the Garage patrons] was their R&B-disco-soul music. It was a black crowd, it was more music-oriented, drugs were *whatever*."

After 1988, when house culture had grown old enough to develop its own standardised lore and mythology, the Paradise Garage (which closed in 1987, the same year as the Saint) was the New York club that became known as the 'seminal club'. The 'legendary' place of DJ Larry Levan that house-lovers began name-dropping when playing authenticity matches. In the same context, the Saint fell into semi-obscurity, a memorable club for 'fag culture' maybe, but just a pretty, inconsequential superdisco to the history of house culture at large.

It's safe to say that the Saint's hi-NRG music evolved much less illustriously than the proto-house disco-soul of the Paradise Garage. But if one is to consider ecstasy to be an important, even indispensable factor in the construction of present-day house culture, then the historical exclusion of the Saint is a very big blip. "There were, of course, many drugs at the Saint," says Kerry Jaggers. "But I still think you could say it was the first 'ecstasy club' in Manhattan – the first nightclub where there were lots and lots of people on it, reacting to it."

Jaggers remembers ecstasy arriving at the Saint sometime in 1981. "Through one person, I believe. He was getting it from this circuit of therapists who were experimenting with it. He supplied all the dealers in the club with thousands of pills.

"At the beginning, people didn't quite know how to take it [the drug]. People tried to smoke it, people tried to shoot it, people tried to put it up their bums. Some snorted it at the beginning, because everyone was used to snorting things – but it was so caustic, it would hurt, and make you cry, and it did some major damage to your nasal passages.

"The Saint had free coffee. The thing that soon caught on was putting three or four carefully measured coke-spoon scoops of the pure powder into a cup of coffee. Maybe five if you were really hardcore. It would make your coffee bitter, so you sweetened it a whole lot. And you'd chase it all down with a bar of chocolate, which was also given out for free at the club. Everybody at the Saint thought caffeine was a catalyst, that it made MDMA hit faster."

The effect ecstasy had on the Saint club may sound familiar to those who have experienced the drug in the house era: "You'd pass through the front bar, where there was all this big, carpeted box seating," says Jaggers. "And the vision was all these men with their shirts off, grinning at the air, with huge, dilated pupils.

"The dancefloor was indescribable. There is a word in German called *gesellig*, it's a word that the English dictionary can't translate. As I understand it, it means, like . . . okay, imagine Munich at Oktoberfest, thousands of people in every direction, clinking their beer steins and indulging in this very convivial, tribal, ancient thing, like they've known each other forever. When I became a card-carrying ecstasy user at the Saint, I thought of that word – *gesellig* – a lot. Ecstasy gave us that – a deep feeling of acceptance in ourselves and the people we were surrounded by.

"Nobody thought about it, or talked about it, but as the drug became more and more popular, I watched it change the Saint," continues Jaggers. "Change from being a buncha guys who were 'sexually liberated', yes, but underneath that still *scared* of their sexuality. *Scared* of being found out. *Scared* of each other. Those people blossomed and bloomed. I had never seen anything like it. It was magical."

But the magic was cut short.

In early 1982, the acronym AIDS had not yet been invented. Many in the gay community called it 'gay cancer', as the mysterious illness was still generally thought to be the fixed property of homosexual men. In the medical community it was referred to as GRID: Gay Related Immune Deficiency. In New York City, from where over half of the 300 American GRID cases reported by March 1982 emanated, one oft-used moniker for the disease was 'the Saint Disease'. At the time, the illness seemed to almost exclusively strike the type of gays who went to that club: those who had glamorous weekends of drugs and multiple partners, long memberships at both the Saint and the Saint Marks Baths, and shared beach houses with friends and lovers on Fire Island in the summer. The 'A-list' gays.

By the summer of 1982, a palpable fear was building in gay Manhattan and on Fire Island. "People still didn't know it was a sexually transmitted disease, even doctors didn't really know," says Jaggers, who was diagnosed HIV positive in 1990. "It was commonly thought that this *thing* – this horrible set of symptoms killing people – could have come from some environmental cause. Was it poppers? Was it bad air in the club? Could you get it off the toilet seats? From mixing drugs? From MDA? From ecstasy?" Some researchers at the Center for Disease Control in Atlanta, were still seriously questioning whether a 'bad batch' of poppers or another popular club drug could have been the culprit behind this disease that struck so many nightclubbers. "Everything was so unclear. People were beginning to be afraid. All we had to go on was the odd rumour or announcement."

It was a couple of years before the question mark of GRID became the understood reality of AIDS, a sexually transmitted disease, and the Saint's decline sharpened rapidly. Bruce Mailman, the owner of the club, was one of the first New York gay business owners to take a marked interest in the fight against AIDS, raising money and often giving up the club for fundraisers. "But by 1984, 1985, people were dropping like flies," says Jaggers. "Some blamed Bruce Mailman, because people went to the Saint or the Saint Marks Baths to have sex. He was looked down upon as killing people's friends, and the club became the centre of a very hairy dispute."

Kerry Jaggers wasn't living in New York when the ecstatic magic of the Saint had evaporated. In 1984, he had received a call from Grace Jones.

She said she was involved in a new club in Dallas, Texas, a place freshly designed at great cost by hot French industrial designer Philippe Starck. Jaggers says he remembers the conversation perfectly: " 'Daaahrling,' she said to me. 'It's called the Starck Club. We've lost our DJ. Pack your bags and come home to Texas. We will arrange for a first class ticket and a limo.' " Jaggers immediately gave up his flat in New York. He stayed with his friend Rick, "an ecstasy-lover and ecstasy dealer", for a couple of days before departing. As a gift, Rick gave Jaggers a Ziplock bag filled with fluffy ecstasy to take back to Texas with him – New Yorky club drugs may be hard to come by in Texas, thought Jaggers. He travelled to Texas with the bulging baggie of ecstasy in his suitcase, "no more controversial than baby powder".

(MS)

2

Ecstasy F.A.Q.

What is ecstasy?
The chemical name for ecstasy is 3, 4 methylenedioxymethylampheta-
mine. Which is a right royal bastard to type as well as read. Thankfully, it's
generally known in scientific and medical circles as MDMA. Many users
simply call it E. During the early days of the drug in the US, it was also
often called X or XTC.

MDMA belongs to a family of drugs known as phenethylamines. Chemically speaking, it's closely related to another phenethylamine, MDA (3,
4-methylenedioxyamphetamine), and to mescaline. MDMA is also described as an hallucinogenic stimulant, or a psychedelic amphetamine. This
a bit misleading, though, as there are very few reports of pure MDMA
causing the sort of hallucinations prompted by, say, LSD (d-lysergic acid
diethylamide, better known as acid).

It's worth noting early on that what is sold as ecstasy is not always
MDMA. Occasionally it's MDA, a more classically psychedelic substance
which leads to a longer and stronger high than MDMA. More commonly
it's a third phenethylamine, MDEA (3, 4-methylenedioxyethylampheta-
mine, also known as MDE), the effects of which generally only last a
couple of hours. Other ecstasy pills may contain a huge range of substances, including ketamine and added amphetamine (speed), while some
have no illegal drug content whatsoever. There have been persistent
rumours of pills containing heroin, but there's absolutely no evidence to
suggest this is anything more than one of the many myths surrounding
MDMA. For a start, it would make no economic sense. Nevertheless, the
fact that MDMA can be cut with anything from LSD to caffeine means
users can never be sure of what they're getting.

The pure form of MDMA is a white crystalline powder. Although it's
increasingly sold as powder in a plastic bag, it's traditionally and more
widely available as either a pressed tablet, often branded with a symbol of
some sort, or a capsule. The active oral dose of the drug is at least 75mg,
with most pills containing 80-120mg. The exact nature and strength of the

effects doesn't just depend on the dose, though. The body weight, tolerance levels, and general physical health and mental state of the user all have parts to play. So do the circumstances under which MDMA is taken. While it's best known as a dance drug and the most popular place to take it is at a club or a rave, some people pop pills at home. Without moving the furniture back, either.

What does ecstasy do in the brain?
MDMA acts on a brain chemical called serotonin (5-hydroxytryptamine, also known as 5-HT), a neurotransmitter which transfers messages across the synapses (or gaps) between adjacent neurons (nerve cells). Serotonin is thought to play an important part in shaping mood, thought processes, sleeping patterns, eating patterns, reaction to external stimuli and control of motor activity. Many medical experts believe that low levels are associated with depression. The chemical is produced by one neuron and released into the synapses, transmitting information to another neuron before being absorbed back into the first in a process known as reuptake. MDMA causes a flood of both serotonin and dopamine (another neurotransmitter) into the synapses and also disrupts the serotonin neurons' reuptake process.

What does ecstasy feel like?
An MDMA pill takes effect after 30 to 45 minutes, starting with little rushes of exhilaration. These are sometimes accompanied by feelings of nausea and disorientation. Some users also find their stomach starts churning. Others experience a mild panic, especially if they're unfamiliar with the drug. Such uncomfortable effects don't usually persist for long, though. The peak effects of MDMA are felt 60 to 90 minutes after ingestion and last for two to four hours, followed by a gradual comedown.

MDMA enhances physical sensations. The sense of touch is heightened, food may smell and taste different to normal, and many people say that music sounds better. There's more awareness of the moment and more contentment with whatever that moment might be. People feel positive about both themselves and the wider world around them (a state sometimes known as 'entactogenesis', from the Latin word meaning 'to touch within'). Inhibitions are loosened, egos are softened and people experience a close emotional bond with others (empathogenesis). Everyday social defences are weakened and communicating with strangers is no longer taboo. Hence all that 'unity' and 'one love' stuff.

In short, MDMA produces an overall sense of well-being, a feeling of happiness edging on euphoria. No wonder E culture hoisted the smiley symbol up its flagpole. The drug doesn't *create* happiness, though - it doesn't create anything. It merely unlocks feelings which are already present but held in check on a day-to-day basis. While the effect of MDMA on serotonin levels means these are generally positive, this isn't universally so and a few people encounter sadness. There is, however, a consensus among users that, whatever the exact shape of the experience, it is usually controllable.

The sense of well-being generally associated with MDMA can last for days, weeks and even months after taking the drug. For some people, it seems to help them to deal with enduring problems in their lives, such as understanding their sexuality, calming their aggression or coping with a childhood trauma. For others, it simply makes them feel better about themselves. In other words, it helps them come to terms with who they are, with many accounts of vastly improved personal relationships as a result.

Does the drug have any unpleasant effects?
Yes. For a start, MDMA can cause a loss of body temperature regulation, leading to a rise in body temperature or perhaps a fall. Or first one and then the other. There are changes in blood pressure and heart rate, too, usually upwards. Users may also find they have a dry mouth, blurred vision, wiggling eyes and the chills. Involuntary muscular activity and muscular tension sometimes occurs, resulting in twitches and cramps. The lower face muscles are especially prone to this, causing jaw clenching and teeth grinding. This 'gurning' effect has long been a joke in clubland. Gurners don't realise they've morphed into gargoyles, though, because MDMA also has what is known as a paradoxical relaxation effect, which means that users are unaware of what is happening to their bodies. This paradoxical relaxation effect also makes physical activity seem easier, with minor pains and fatigue not noticed.

Many people feel tired or depressed in the days immediately after taking MDMA. A lot of clubbers put the tiredness down to several hours of bal-listic behaviour on the dancefloor, but fatigue is also a common after-effect for those who take pills at home. People who suffer post-MDMA depression generally find that it peaks three or four days after they have taken the drug. This has led to a midweek blues syndrome within the weekend-focused club community. In a few cases, depression becomes a long-term problem, sometimes of a severe nature.

The blues are by no means all that users have to worry about. According to some research, the involuntary jaw clenching may cause damage to back teeth. More seriously, there have been numerous cases of MDMA-induced hepatitis and, more seriously still, liver failure. Those who repeatedly take the drug may also suffer from a range of post-MDMA psychological problems – paranoia, anxiety, panic attacks, insomnia and nightmares, to name just a few.

Does ecstasy cause long-term brain damage?

At the time of writing, the latest research into the neurotoxicity of the drug suggests that it decreases the density of serotonin neurons in the brain. Moreover, it seems that the extent of this decrease is linked to the extent of MDMA use. But while some medical scientists believe that this is proof of brain damage, others are not so sure. It is also presently unclear whether or not the effect on serotonin neurons is permanent, and how, in terms of functionality, the effect might be exhibited in users. Having fiercely debated MDMA neurotoxicity for a number of years, the medical world looks set to continue to do so well into the 21st century.

Can taking ecstasy kill you?

Taking MDMA can prove fatal. A few people are particularly chemically sensitive to the drug and just one dose may be enough to kill them. Some of those who have suffered liver failure have required liver transplants, but the transplants have not always been successful. Other fatalities associated with MDMA have been due to an overdose, the signs of which include vomiting, dizziness, head pains and strong muscle cramps. The most common cause of MDMA-related death, however, is due to the drug inducing a rise in body temperature to the point of hyperthermia (overheating).

The potential danger of hyperthermia is all the greater for clubbers. Part of the drug's appeal to clubbers is that the paradoxical relaxation effect, the unawareness ingredient, allows them to dance for a long time without feeling tired. But in doing so they are pushing their body temperatures up. The loss of body fluids through sweating and the often crowded environments of nightclubs or raves can be factors in body temperature rise, too. The result can be extreme heatstroke. To add another possible problem to the pile, the paradoxical relaxation effect also means that most of those in danger of overheating don't even realise it. In the same way that their legs don't seem to feel tired, they're oblivious to the normal warning signs that their temperature is soaring and their pulse is racing.

Some of those who have died of MDMA-induced hyperthermia have registered body temperatures as high as 43 degrees C (almost 110 degrees F). Normal body temperature is 37 degrees C (98.6 degrees F). As the body starts to overheat, small clots form in the bloodstream, leading to a condition called Disseminated Intravascular Coagulation (DIC). The clots cause a depletion of the blood's essential coagulation agent, which is normally used to stem internal bleeding from the hundreds of tiny cuts constantly present in body and brain tissue due to damage caused in the day-to-day running of the body. A depletion of coagulation agent can be extremely dangerous. If bleeding occurs in the brain, for example, it can lead to a stroke, or in worst case scenarios death. What's more, this whole process can occur in just a few hours.

Are there ways to make taking ecstasy safer?
Clubbers taking MDMA should replace body fluids lost through dehydration by drinking plenty of water. One pint every hour or so is a common guide, but it's better to sip small amounts regularly rather than gulp down a huge volume in one go. Be aware that you don't need to drink so much if you're not dancing and that drinking an excessive amount can lead to acute water intoxication, which can itself be fatal. Water is not an antidote to MDMA, it just helps combat dehydration and overheating, and a large intake can produce an imbalance in body fluids, including a dilution of the salt in the blood. Salt holds water in the blood system and, with a reduced level, water is lost into the surrounding body tissue. The tissue then swells. The brain is unable to swell, though, because of the skull. In some cases, the result is a dangerous compression of the brain. With this in mind, isotonic sports drinks are also recommended as they help to replace lost body salts. Alcohol, however, is best avoided because it can cause further dehydration.

Other advice is to take regular breaks away from the dancefloor (every 30 minutes, say) and wear light, loose clothes. Even if you own the funkiest woolly hat in history, it's perhaps best to stuff it in your pocket – you give out more heat at the extremities of the body. Keep in contact with your friends and tell them if you start feeling unwell or even just uneasy. And don't mix MDMA with other drugs. A fair few of the deaths associated with MDMA have involved another substance. New users should also consider taking half rather than a whole pill.

Almost all doctors would advise anybody with heart, liver, kidney or blood circulation problems to stay away from MDMA. The same goes for those suffering from hypertension, epilepsy, asthma, diabetes or glaucoma, anybody who is prone to panic attacks and anybody with a history of mental illness. Taking MDMA while on certain anti-depressants can also be dangerous. This is especially so of anti-depressants which are MAOIs (monoamine oxidase inhibitors), as the combination invites the risk of fatal hypertensive crisis. Combining MDMA and anti-AIDS drugs which are protease inhibitors is another potentially deadly mix. Popping a pill isn't a very clever idea if you're pregnant, either.

What is the drug's legal status?
Anybody not wanting to break the law should stay away from MDMA. The manufacturing, trafficking and possession of the drug are outlawed

pretty much worldwide. It is a Class A substance in the UK (under the Misuse Of Drugs Act) and Schedule I in the US - these categories being the most restrictive in their respective countries. In the UK, the maximum sentence for possession of a Class A substance is seven years in prison and an unlimited fine. The maximum sentence for trafficking is life in prison and an unlimited fine. Other Class A drugs include heroin, acid, cocaine and speed which has been prepared for injection.

Is ecstasy addictive?
MDMA is not addictive in the same way as, say, heroin. There are no heroin-type physical withdrawal symptoms. There have, however, been cases of users becoming dependent on the drug. But while it's perhaps only human nature that people often want to relive the good times they've had on MDMA by taking it again, frequent use results in a significant decrease in the loved-up 'ecstasy feeling' and an increase in the amphetamine-like effects. This is probably why most people who take MDMA say their first experiences were more enjoyable than later ones. It may also be why some users complain about the purity of ecstasy even during those times when police analyses indicate that a lot of unadulterated MDMA pills are in circulation.

The reason for the drug becoming less effective with continued use isn't clear. Some suggest it could be psychological, it could be that the novelty simply wears off. Others say it's physical, it's because of changes to the neurons in the brain caused by use of MDMA itself. One theory is that it's a result of some kind of unconscious self-defence mechanism acting to curb excessive use by depriving the drug of its more attractive features.

What are some common misconceptions surrounding ecstasy?
There are endless misconceptions surrounding MDMA - the one about it being a designer drug, for instance. A common misunderstanding is that this means it's chic and expensive. Another is that designer drugs are modelled to produce a particular set of effects – yet this could be said of any synthethic or part-synthetic drug. The original American definition of the term was a drug which has undergone molecular modifications to change its status from illegal to legal while retaining the psychoactive properties of the original compound. A chemical remix, if you like. Under this definition, then, no illegal drug can be considered as a designer drug. The confusion over the term in Britain is perhaps understandable given that the very practice of 'drug design' has long been effectively prohibited under UK law, which bans whole families of drugs rather than dealing with them one at a time.

There are countless myths about MDMA, too, including that it is an aphrodisiac. The earliest media reports on the drug said this was why ecstasy was popular with young people. However, although MDMA makes people more sociable and the enhancement of touch, taste and smell can give the sex act a few fresh twists, there's nothing to suggest users get their bells rung louder or more often than others. The reverse may actually be true, as a proportion of men experience erection problems with the drug – as much as 40 per cent according to some sources. Some men also find the size of their penis is sometimes reduced when on MDMA. Shrivelled willies are common among male speed freaks, so this effect could just be down to amphetamine-heavy tablets.

3

Ecstasy At The Starck Club, Dallas, Texas

In 1980 New York, at clubs like the Saint, gays were clubbing, sexing and drugging as both a celebration and a manifestation of an unprecedented amount of social freedom. In 1983 Texas, at clubs like the Starck in Dallas, people were clubbing, sexing and drugging as both a celebration and a manifestation of an unprecedented amount of green in their pockets. They'd struck it rich. It was party time.

At the core, Texas is a traditional, old boy state. Texas is a place where debutante balls are still written about grandly in the papers, where a slice of peach cobbler can still be the way to a man's heart. A place where politics are Republican, money is often as old as American cash can get, and cowboys still actually exist. But by 1984, the oil boom that had begun in the mid-Seventies had caught up with Texan society. New people were wealthy, not just from oil, but from anything. Designers and artists got benefactors, people with a bit of property suddenly found themselves sitting on real estate gold, entrepreneurs received funding in milliseconds, restaurants and boutiques spread into chains, universities swelled with private donations, plain farmers and ranchers turned, seemingly overnight, into eccentric millionaires. *Dallas*, the TV show, was not too far off the mark in its sequined day suits and gaggle of chauffeurs. Texas did feel that way – almost as if you could swipe the air in front of you and cash would flow out of the nothingness, like the atmosphere itself jangled with coins and promise.

The time was ripe, maybe over-ripe, for something like the Starck club to open up. A multi-million dollar danceteria with a list of 22 investors, including celebrities like Fleetwood Mac's Stevie Nicks, and expensively designed in black terrazzo and white marble by French designer Phillipe Starck. Starck – the most celebrated industrial designer of the Eighties, the man famous for making the household juicer into a spidery, stainless-steel mantelpiece accessory and toothbrushes into spermy-shaped 14 dollar objets d'art.

The hype precursing the Starck club was almost unbearable, building and building for months. By 12 May 1984, the night of the opening, half of the 'in-crowd' attending were already sceptical of the place. It couldn't possibly live up to the inflated promises: a Studio 54 type-club in the heart of Dallas, a place that mixed high-end with low-brow, gays and straights, country club and Culture Club. In Dallas, most straight clubs were rock venues, fratland booze-bins, or tourist traps with names like The Tijuana Yacht Club. Most gay haunts still had signs posted outside explaining that the establishment was gay and would not tolerate any "people who could not accept" that. And this new place, the Starck, had the audacity to use the words 'mixed club'? A mixed club with *unisex* bathrooms? The exclusivity of a Studio 54 was fine. The cross-cultural weirdness of New York – some Texans weren't sure if that would go over too well.

In the first few weeks of the Starck, it seemed these naysayers were right. The number of patrons at the club thinned out dramatically after the opening night gala featuring Grace Jones. French DJ Philippe Kreuchet had bailed, after finding himself on the French charts with a disco record. The club looked set for failure, it was already being leased out for private functions on weekends.

It was at his first meeting with one of the Starck investors that Kerry Jaggers, freshly flown in from New York to replace the missing DJ Kreuchet, was asked if he had ever heard about a drug called ecstasy. Maybe it was 'X-T-C', the investor wasn't sure. Whatever it was called, it was legal, and there was a buzz on it in Texas. Yes, replied Jaggers, he had heard of ecstasy, in fact he had brought some with him from New York, would the investor like to try it?

Within days, Jaggers was contacted again. The investor wanted more of this 'ecstasy' from New York, to sell over the bar at the Starck. Would Jaggers be able to hook up a connection? What neither Jaggers nor the investors knew, and would soon learn, was that ecstasy was already flooding into Texas, rolling in from California and New Mexico. Ecstasy was legal but, nonetheless, it was the underworld drug dealers, the same people who sold coke and speed in the clubs, from which the Starck soon started ordering the thousands of tablets with which to stock its bar. XTC: 15 dollars, plus tax, chargeable on your credit card. Within no time, there were crowds of 300 left standing outside a packed and glamorous Starck club every weekend.

One week Van Halen's David Lee Roth was flouncing across the club, strutting to New Order's 'Blue Monday' and Yaz's 'Situation'. The next week, teen-flick dreamboat Rob Lowe was guzzling champagne out of Starck's crystal flutes. One week Stevie Nicks was in surveying the premises. The next week, Grace Jones flew through with an entourage of beautiful lovers. It was all very hush-hush and discreet. Limos took stars from their hotels straight to the club, all arrangements smoothed out by a specially appointed concierge. Unlike Studio 54, where strobe lights competed with the flash of reporters' cameras, everything about the Starck was exceedingly private. The first floor was made up of white banquettes arranged in close-quartered cubicles, with white curtains that could close the whole way round each module. "When most curtains were closed – which was often – walking through that area was like walking through a sensual maze of white fabric, grazing this gleaming black terrazzo floor," says Kerry Jaggers. "It was almost as if the club was designed for that beautiful, hard-yet-soft *clarity* you reach with MDMA."

It was hard to get to the bars to buy the Starck's 100 per cent pure XTC pills. The crowds waving money at the barmaids were always four deep. There were free-floating dealers from whom it was usually easier to procure the drug. Some of the dealers wore t-shirts emblazoned with an 'X', or even ones proclaiming 'Buy My XTC'. Jaggers estimates that 70 per cent of those visiting the Starck did buy it. "Without any guilt or any stigma. It was not seen as other drugs were. It was seen as high class. Some of the same people who were worrying about their kids sampling pot were downing this stuff."

XTC did not change the amount of dancing that occurred in the Starck – always more of a schmooze-o-thon club. It probably did not change the magnums and magnums of champagne ordered. It did not change the standard habit of long-tailed shirts, rhinestone brooches, baggy Armani trousers, sequined dresses and the odd tuxedo. It did not erase elitism. If anything, the early only-those-in-the-know aura of the drug reinforced a terribly strict door policy, fixed on richesse (jet setters, celebrities, fashion or art world hipsters, yuppies) and a calculated peppering of streety style-tribe curiosities (a new wave eyeliner case here, a Mohawk haircut there, a Chinese goth girl on a leash, some drag queens).

But foreshadowing the UK in the late Eighties, ecstasy did erase many prejudicial hang-ups at the Starck – often hang-ups existing between people who all shared a similar economic stature. "There were rich kids, like preppy college dudes wearing Ralph Lauren in there: all hugging and chatting up these wealthy gays and male fashion models – people who they would've beat up behind the frat house a year before, if given the chance," says former Starck regular Wade Hampton. "I think that would later happen in England with ecstasy too, but with the lower classes . . . with those . . . waddaya call 'em – hoolies."

Wade Hampton III, now a record shop and label owner in San Francisco, was himself a rich kid. One of a growing mass of teens for whom the

Starck guest list was open. These were the offspring of Texas' sprawling Sloane set, equipped with their own American Express Gold cards, left to them by their parents who were always dashing off to homes in St Moritz, boats in Bermuda, political conferences in Washington or business in New York, Hong Kong, the Middle East . . .

These kids represent the beginning of a casual, friends-based dealing network that started connecting the dots between ecstasy and the campus. A network that would lead to the altogether surprising cases of trust fund teens, the sons of socialites, diplomats and millionaire ranchers being arrested for trafficking drugs in 1985 – after ecstasy was made illegal in the United States. "When we started going to the Starck, like 1983, it was all quite careless though," says Hampton. "People would give us pills at the club, just to see if we liked them, and if we wanted to buy some, like for our friends. We just sold them off, made a bit of extra money."

It was a few months before Wade Hampton and his friends decided to try the drug themselves. They booked a room at the Loewes Anatol Hotel, the most expensive hotel in Dallas. In the Starck's early era, the Loewes Anatol was dubbed the 'XTC hotel' by scenesters, because dealers would allegedly check in for months at a time, check out, and then check in again under a different name. Nobody asked any questions. "There was a great demand for ecstasy within the hotel," says Hampton. The Loewes Anatol was a five minute walk from the Starck. It contained its own luxurious club called Mistral, where the drug was also popular. "The Loewes had a restaurant in it, overlooking the Mistral club, called By The Ounce," continues Hampton. "The pun was totally intended – and this in a top-of-the-line Ritz Carlton-type hotel. It gives you a good idea of where Dallas people's heads were."

Hampton and his pack spent their first night on ecstasy "listening to Thomas Dolby's 'She Blinded Me With Science' in the hotel room for too many hours in a row." They pierced each others ears with a Loewes Anatol complimentary sewing-kit. After the 16-year-old heiress who put the room on her charge-card was sick all over the carpet, they began exploring the premises: the massive glass atrium, the chic mall built into the atrium, the Nana jazz club in one of the hotel's towers. "Nana was on the 28th floor. We just sat at a table, overlooking the whole city, breaking pills in half for hours. We were so dumbfounded that something could make you feel that way – like you wanted to screw a hole in the wall. But we never acted on the sexual energy. Rather, those who were there that night, we hung onto each other for a year as the best of friends, doing ecstasy over and over."

It was not long before Hampton's group were checking into the

17

Loewes Anatol every week. The 16-year-old heiress would book three $500 suites for weekends of fun between her and her friends and her friend's friends. The hotel would assign a security guard to the group, a discreet man who would follow them around on their ecstasy escapades late into the night, keeping tabs on the damage they did and the things they 'borrowed' from the premises. "I don't know how many times the Nana bar was broken into that year, with every bottle of alcohol taken out of it and brought up to [our] rooms. They knew it was us, they would just charge retail price for every single bottle onto our friend's credit card. The only person she had to report back to was a horse trainer who acted as her guardian, assigned to her by her family. It was one of those weird, rich kid family situations."

The blitz on ecstasy in the Dallas broad sheets began in 1984, when the US Drug Enforcement Administration (DEA) estimated that the number of ecstasy doses surging into Texas every month were edging 100,000. The *Dallas Morning News* was the most exhaustive in its coverage of the popular drug, erroneously categorising it either a "superamphetamine", an "hallucinogen" or, more commonly, a "designer drug" – a drug who's chemical make-up has been changed slightly to subvert illegality. Ecstasy was linked to other "legal killers" like a synthetic heroin called fentanyl, a drug the *Dallas Morning News* reported to be "3,000 times stronger than real heroin." This being the high era of MADD (Mothers Against Drunk Driving) and Nancy Reagan's mammy-ish 'Just Say No' campaign, the *Morning News'* reports usually came in the form of a general appeal to parents. Question: Do you know what your children are doing? Answer: Bad things.

"The drug problem is not something that went away after the psychedelic Sixties, or something happening in other cities in bad areas to bad families. It's here," stated a *Morning News* article on ecstasy entitled 'Drug Scene: How Bad?' on 3 March 1985. In the 12 May issue, the newspaper was well past the warning stage. " . . . Ecstasy will become the recreational drug of the Eighties," wrote reporter Pat Gordon.

Gordon was no soothsayer. Ecstasy was hardly an exclusive nightworld secret in Texas any more. The drug had reached non–clubbing high-schoolers and college kids by the winter of 1984. Newspapers ran stories of affluent 13 year olds burning out by taking a morning ecstasy every day before class, of dealers who stalked dangerously close to school yards. The successful career-folk at the Starck were of little or no concern to reporters; they were in fact at odds with the slant of the coverage taken in Texas (ecstasy as a seedy street drug; something that will ruin young lives and thwart futures). Yet that the drug was painted as a 'problem with youth' was not necessarily overactive broadsheet brouhaha. It *was* becoming a major problem. Especially with one segment of students – the ones training for government like their fathers had, the students at the terribly stiff-lipped and church-backed Southern Methodist University.

Wade Hampton draws a line between his group and students from SMU. "My friends and I were true nightclubbers by then, we respected the secrecy of the Starck and the scene," he insists. "The SMU students usually weren't connected to the club scene, so for them, ecstasy wasn't something with which to complement a fun night, it was a context-less thing to get fucked up on, beer-bash stuff. Watch SMU kids drink beer and you might understand – they are under pressure, they drink not for enjoyment but oblivion. You'd see the odd one careening into the Starck – taking five, seven, 10 pills in one go, overdoing it in a way that there was no *possibility* that the police and the newspapers wouldn't get involved. They were *obvious*, having to be rolled into hospitals in ridiculous states, having gone temporarily blind from overactive eyelid fluttering.

"And don't forget," continues Hampton. "They were *politicians'* kids. Their parents were all friends with George Bush [then Vice President of the US], for God's sake. They were the death knell for legal ecstasy, those kids."

In July 1984, the DEA announced a proposal to make ecstasy a Schedule I drug, the most restrictive drug category available in the United States. Measures were taken to curtail the usage of the drug while the proposal was being examined and processed: the sale of MDMA was made illegal. Although possession was still within the law. However, given the parentage of the SMU kids and their like, the heat was on to get MDMA's full scheduling through as quickly as possible.

In the months when it was still within the law to possess ecstasy but not to sell it, XTC lovin' Texans got creative in trying to outsmart the system. Throughout 1984, you could walk into trendy stores in downtown Dallas and buy a disposable plastic ballpoint pen for 25 dollars. They gave you a 'free' ecstasy pill with the pen.

Yet faced with illegality and increasingly being made (and dealt) by more underworldy sources, the quality of the ecstasy being sold became dubious. "The first total fakes came about this time, along with the first variation in types of so-called ecstasy you could buy," says Hampton. "I remember these pills called Turbos. They were supposedly 'enhanced', super-strong ecstasy. They came in a big, fat cap. But they were MDA." There was also a proliferation of a drug called Eve, which was MDEA, another one of Ecstasy's chemical cousins, a drug Texans believed legal.

On 31 June 1985, an exposé of ecstasy use on the SMU campus was published in the best-selling news magazine, *Life*. One day later, the

DEA proposal to make ecstasy a Schedule I was made effective – putting ecstasy in the same category as heroin or cocaine in the eyes of American justice.

In the months between the scheduling proposal of the summer of 1984 and the top-to-bottom prohibition of ecstasy in the summer of 1985, the Starck was going gangbusters. The place was on full-tilt, something of an extravagant storm, a last luxurious laugh, before an excruciating calm. Some nights would edge on the plainly loony, with patrons retiring to the Loewes Anatol atriums to fly remote-control toy helicopters inside them, something that had become a bit of a fad with the ecstasy set. "Everything was unravelling, and not just on the ecstasy level," says Hampton. "Texas oil was in big trouble – economically things were going downhill fast. Everyone at the Starck was in denial."

In 1985, international oil prices plummeted 50 per cent as a result of a market-flooding decision taken by OPEC, the international oil cartel (of which the United States is not part). Texas oil didn't have a fighting chance. Texans were losing entire fortunes within single days. Property value sunk 25 per cent in both Houston and Dallas. In Texas' major cities, incidence of arson had risen an astounding 20 per cent in 1985. The problem of people broiling their own properties had gotten so bad that premiere insurance company Aetna took out ads in Texas newspapers stating: "If you're thinking about burning down your home to collect the insurance money – think again. Aetna Life & Casualty is making arson a crime that doesn't pay."

"It's funny when you think about it now," says Hampton. "The economy falling through the floor and ecstasy drowning into illegality at the same time. I guess the only way the Starck could deal with it was through humour." On 30 June 1985, the night before the DEA made ecstasy Schedule I, the Starck organized a campy 'Farewell To Ecstasy' party. "It was a packed house," remembers Kerry Jaggers. "But a very melancholy crowd. Everybody was feeling very sad and kinda afraid, wondering what was going to happen . . ."

After that symbolic party, many older or more reputation-conscious patrons of the Starck stopped taking all ecstasy products. "But the banning affected young people more," says Hampton. "And while it degenerated the quality of the drug itself, it also did something quite positive – it created a counterculture. It was the first sign I ever saw of these pampered kids saying 'fuck the system' in a *big* way. The banning of ecstasy invested people with this drive to be elusive; to circumvent control and be their own thinkers. You can almost see it as a seminal point for what would become a defining aspect of the rave movement: the fight-the-power side, people thinking 'I'm doing the right thing, I'm doing it for my own reasons and I will do it by any means necessary'."

In September 1986, months after the Scheduling of MDMA, the Starck club was raided. Thirty-six people were arrested and a street value of almost $10,000 worth of drugs seized, mostly ecstasy and cocaine. The Starck had been under investigation for six months, after the police supposedly received numerous phone calls from patrons complaining of drugs being sold and used openly. "The raid made front-page headlines and a lurid, almost comical read," wrote Starck-supporter Russell Smith, music critic for the *Dallas Morning News*. "Lawmen described how their police dogs were supposedly slipping and sliding over drugs hurriedly ditched on the elegant sunken dance floor."

The Starck never quite recovered from the raid. After the police bust, it died a slow but sure death. When the club was on its last legs in 1988, its decor and musical policy seemed passé and its part in the story of ecstasy was quite finished. The house music percolating in Chicago, New York and Detroit within the very same years the Starck was kicking, had reached the UK. So had ecstasy. For all of the Starck's foreshadowings, it's safe to say nobody in America expected what was about to happen across the ocean, where XTC would become E, and get tagged with the very un-Starck big, yellow smiley as its new symbol.

(MS)

4

Merck: The Origins Of E

MDMA was first synthesised in 1912 by E Merck, a German pharmaceutical company founded by Emanuel Merck back in the mid-17th century. As Merck KGaA, the company is now one of the world's leading pharmaceutical corporations, rolling out a huge variety of prescription drugs, vitamin pills, reagents and pigments from bases in 23 different countries. Despite the grand scale of its current operations, with around 170 firms acting on its behalf across the globe, the controlling shareholders of the parent group are still all members of the Merck family circle.

How Merck came to synthesise MDMA is a mystery and will probably always remain so. Popular rumour insists that the drug was initially developed as an appetite suppressant, but there is absolutely no evidence to support this in Merck's massive historical and scientific archive, which is almost as old as the company itself and today boasts a staggering 700 shelf metres of material. Unfortunately, the Merck archive offers precious little information about MDMA at all, beyond the fact that the company filed for a patent for the substance on Christmas Eve, 1912. The patent was granted on 16 May 1914.

The patent itself is of no more help in trying to establish what Merck might have been doing with MDMA. It merely describes a series of chemical experiments with a variety of substances, suggesting that the drug was an accidental discovery rather than an intentional one. There's nothing in the patent about Merck putting MDMA through any kind of pharmacological tests and no clues as to whether the company had any particular use in mind for the drug. And if the company did have a use in mind, it would certainly have filed a patent for this as opposed to the purely chemical patent. Not to have done so would have made no sense. Furthermore, it's clear that MDMA was never marketed by Merck – either as an appetite suppressant or anything else – because it does not appear on any of the company's price lists which Dr Ingunn Possehl, the director of the company's archive, says are complete.

★   ★   ★

Within weeks of the MDMA patent being issued, Europe was hurled into the bloody chaos of the First World War. There was no respite from the slaughter for more than four years with the brief exception of the unoffical 1914 Christmas truce, when British and German soldiers famously emerged from their trenches to play football together in the sludge of no-man's land. It's been claimed that the reason for this sudden and short-lived outbreak of humanity was because the troops had been given doses of MDMA, making hugging and playing a much more attractive proposition than ripping each other's guts out with bayonets. It's undeniably a colourful image but almost certainly nothing more than what Matthew Collin calls "the most charming ecstasy myth of all" in his book *Altered State: The Story Of Ecstasy Culture And Acid House*.

Far from loving-up the trenches of the Western Front, MDMA seems to have spent the war years sitting on a laboratory shelf at the Merck factory in Darmstadt, a small city situated a few miles east of the Rhine between Frankfurt and Mannheim. The substance wasn't totally forgotten, though. Shortly after the First World War ended, Merck renewed their interest in MDMA, tinkering around with its properties and then filing for a second patent relating to the substance in July 1919. This was granted in March 1921. Like the first, the second patent concentrates exclusively on chemical matters, but its very existence proves that Merck's laboratory technicians believed there was something sufficiently intriguing about MDMA to continue experimenting with it.

Whatever that something was, it clearly wasn't intriguing enough for the company to pursue beyond 1921. By this point, the economic climate demanded that projects be more carefully prioritised: Merck wasn't the flourishing operation it had been in the decade leading up to the First World War, during which period it had doubled both its workforce and its output. The shortages of skilled manpower and raw materials which the war had brought to every area of German industry persisted long after the fighting stopped, and Merck was hit hard. Even if Merck had wanted to explore MDMA further, it may not have had the resources to do so. The result was that the substance was again consigned to the laboratory shelf.

There is no evidence of MDMA undergoing further tests, chemical or otherwise, for another 30 years. Merck was not responsible for these, though. Instead, it was the US Army, acting under the direction of the US Central Intelligence Agency (CIA), who conducted a series of experiments with the substance in the early Fifties.

Precisely how the Americans came to investigate MDMA is a matter of conjecture. The most logical suggestion is that they first learnt about it from Merck's 1914 patent. Patents are, after all, public information. Yet in this instance, it was also very limited information – the patent was only really a chemical recipe, it merely proved that MDMA existed, and this alone is unlikely to have been enough to spark American interest in the substance. Where, then, did this spark come from? And what use might the US military have had for MDMA anyway?

Clues to the possible answers lie in the Second World War and its aftermath. Darmstadt, the city Merck called home, suffered heavy Allied air raids in the latter stages of the conflict, leaving more than 12,000 people dead. The Merck plant itself did not escape the bombing, a raid in December 1944 reducing parts of the factory to rubble. A little over three months later, Allied land forces swept across the Rhine, with Darmstadt falling to American soldiers from the 90th Infantry Division of General George Patton's Third Army at the end of March 1945. The German Western Army was by now in tatters and resistance to the Allies in the Rhineland came mainly from diehard SS and Hitler Youth units, but the area around Darmstadt was captured relatively easily. The Merck factory was one of the sites immediately occupied by the US military, who assumed direct control of the company and remained at the plant until late September 1945.

With the final capitulation of Germany in May 1945, one of the first tasks of the victorious Allied forces was to investigate the covert activities of the nazi war machine. The Americans were especially keen to uncover details of the scientific, technical and chemical programmes initiated under the nazis. To this end, hundreds of German scientific and industrial sites were visited by US intelligence officers. Including Merck's Darmstadt factory. Ingunn Possehl, the Merck archive director, says employees of the company from this period have told her that they witnessed American soldiers seizing and removing production specifications and research documents from the plant.

Although it's not known if any of the seized information related to MDMA, this obviously cannot be ruled out. Perhaps the US military discovered something at the Merck factory which suggested that MDMA had some potential military use. Perhaps this is why there's now so very little information about the substance in the Merck archive – because it was all removed by the Americans.

Another possible scenario is that, at some point shortly after the Second World War, US military chemists simply synthesised MDMA themselves, independently of whatever had been found at Merck. In other words, the Americans could have discovered it from their own experiments.

If this were the case, their route to the substance would have started with the fact that it is related to mescaline. The main US intelligence agency at the time of the Second World War, the Office of Strategic Services (OSS), had first tested mescaline in 1942. Their experiments were part of the search for a 'truth drug', a drug which could be used to interrogate prisoners. By the end of the Second World War, though, the OSS had rejected mescaline and settled on a concentrated liquid extract of cannabis, a highly potent substance without colour, taste or smell which could be injected into food or cigarettes. The results were not always quite what the OSS wanted, but the cannabis extract worked well enough to be assigned the name 'TD' – a rather thin disguise for truth drug.

In 1947, the OSS was replaced by the CIA and a search for a new truth drug began. Much of the CIA's focus over the next few years fell on LSD, but mescaline was also now firmly back on the agenda. The revived interest in mescaline stemmed from discoveries made during the US intelligence sweep of post-war Germany. The nazis had also been hunting for a truth drug, a drug to "eliminate the will of the person examined" according to a report by the US Naval Technical Mission. At Dachau, the concentration camp near Munich, the medical wing of the Luftwaffe had tested the suitability of mescaline on 30 prisoners. With some success, too. In his history of LSD, *Storming Heaven – LSD and The American Dream*, Jay Stevens describes how the nazis gave the prisoners mescaline mixed with coffee or alcohol. The subjects were then interrogated. Although the doctors were unable to fully impose their will on the subjects, Stevens says they were able to "elicit the most intimate sort of personal details."

In the light of this, it would seem that the most likely reason for the US military investigation into MDMA was to test its suitability as a truth drug. This idea is further supported by the fact that it was actually one of eight mescaline-related substances examined by the US Army at the behest of the CIA in the early Fifties. Most of the MDMA tests took place at the Edgewood Chemical Warfare Services military base in Maryland, where the drug was given the code name EA (Edgewood Arsenal) 1475. Other experiments with MDMA took place at the University of Michigan in Ann Arbor.

By the beginning of the Fifties, with the Cold War now well underway, the Edgewood base was buzzing with activity. A wide range of different drugs were tested at Edgewood, but while there is plenty of surviving documentation on the military's LSD experiments, including film footage of soldiers collapsing into giggling fits on the base's assault course and parade ground, details of what was being done with MDMA are few and far between. The only military findings to surface to date are observations on the functional effects of MDMA on animals (which included muscular spasms, vomiting and breathing difficulties) and assessments on the drug's toxicity.

Although it's known that the US Army tested MDMA on a variety of animals, including rats, dogs, and non-human primates, there is no evidence of them ever giving the drug to human subjects. Ironically, if they had, they might have found its empathogenic effects yielded some interesting results in interrogation situations. In the event, though, the CIA decided MDMA was of no real use to them, particularly not after the onset of their MK-ULTRA programme in 1953.

MK-ULTRA – the MK standing for 'mind control' – saw the search for a simple truth drug shoved to one side as the CIA redirected their resources into unearthing a drug with more indiscriminate effects. A brainwashing drug, in other words. MDMA clearly didn't fit the bill for this and, like many of the substances tested at Edgewood in the years leading up to 1953, it was passed over in favour of the more obviously powerful LSD.

It seems ironic that the early history of MDMA, a substance later often described as a 'love drug', was largely determined by the dints of war, by men in uniforms and dark suits. The next time men in uniforms and dark suits took an interest in the drug, they were trying to put a stop to its use rather than trying to find a reason to start it.

(P)

5

1972–1985: In Therapy And In Court

The US Drug Enforcement Administration (DEA) first identified recreational use of MDMA in 1972, but it was another 12 years before they moved to make the substance illegal. Perhaps with good reason, too. There were approximately 2,400 DEA raids on clandestine laboratories in the US between 1972 and 1984, and only four of these labs were found to be in possession of the chemicals required to produce the drug. According to a 1976 DEA investigation, as few as 10,000 doses a year were then being sold on the black market in the whole of the US.

Although ecstasy is now closely linked with the club scene on both sides of the Atlantic, the first wave of American users took the drug at home. Some took it to attain greater spiritual awareness, others in a kind of self-psychotherapy. MDMA wasn't in particularly widespread usage until the early Eighties, though. Prior to this, it was far more common to come across its heavier cousin MDA – an occasional alternative to LSD for the Sixties West Coast hippy community and part of the pharmacopoeia of the American gay club scene throughout the Seventies.

MDMA's metamorphosis from a little-known substance on the fringes of the early Seventies psychedelic underground to the most culturally significant drug of the final years of the 20th century begins with Alexander Shulgin – Sasha to his family and friends. Shulgin served in the US Navy during the Second World War, when he was still only a teenager, and returned to his home city of Berkeley at the end of the conflict in 1945 to obtain a PhD in biochemistry at the University of California. He subsequently worked as a senior research chemist with the Dow chemical company, where he directed a variety of projects including the invention of a profitable insecticide. Shulgin's personal interest was in psychoactive drugs, though, which he preferred to test on himself rather than on animals. His first experience was with mescaline.

"That day is forever etched in my memory," he told British journalist Mark White in 1998. "I saw colours that had never existed in my world before. I heard music that carried a message of intense, joyful depth and

27

complexity. I viewed art that allowed me for the first time to truly understand the mindset of the artist. And – most important to me – I realised
that all of this richness, the seeing and the understanding, was not created
by a few hundred milligrams of a white solid. It was inside of me all the
time."

Shulgin left Dow by mutual agreement in 1965. With the development
of an underground counterculture fuelled by psychedelic drugs, most particularly LSD, the company had become increasingly concerned at the
nature of the chemist's main interest. At the same time, Shulgin was eager
to free himself from corporate constraints and he immediately set about
building his own laboratory in the garden of his home just outside
Berkeley. Here, during the course of the next 30 years or so, he experi-
mented with countless different psychedelics, inventing quite a few of
them himself along the way. Much of his work is detailed in two weighty
tomes, *PiHKAL: A Chemical Love Story* and *TiHKAL: The Continuation*,
published in 1991 and 1997, respectively. In *PiHKAL*, an acronym for
Phenethylamines I Have Known And Loved, Shulgin records the synthe-
ses and effects of 179 phenethylamine compounds, while in *TiHKAL* he
focuses on the tryptamine family of hallucinogenic drugs, which includes
DMT (dimethyltryptamine) and psilocybin mushrooms. Both books are
co-credited to Shulgin's wife Ann, whom he met in 1979 and married
three years later.

Alexander Shulgin was introduced to MDMA in the late Sixties and in
PiHKAL he assigns the drug number 109. His love of this particular
phenethylamine is obvious from the following extract from *PiHKAL*, in
which he details an experience with 120mg of the drug:

"The woodpile is so beautiful, about all the joy and beauty that I can
stand. I am afraid to turn around and face the mountains, for fear they will
overpower me. But I did look, and I am astounded. Everyone must get to
experience a profound state like this. I feel totally peaceful. I have lived all
my life to get here and I feel I have come home. I am complete."

MDMA didn't always evoke a positive response in Shulgin, though. On
another occasion, he took 100mg to see if it would act as a stimulant, to
raise him from what he called "a dull, uncaring tiredness". The result fell a
long way short of satisfactory: "I napped for a half hour or so and woke up
definitely not improved. The feeling of insufficient energy and lack of
spark that I'd felt before had become something quite strong, and might be
characterised as a firm feeling of negativity about everything that had to be
done and everything I had been looking forward to. So I set about my
several tasks with no pleasure or enjoyment and I hummed a little tune to
myself during these activities which had words that went: 'I shouldn't

have done that, oh yes, I shouldn't have done that, oh no, I shouldn't have done that, it was a mistake.' Then I would start over again from the beginning. I was stuck in a grey space for quite a while and there was nothing to do but keep doing what I had to do."

Despite such occasional negative experiences, Shulgin quickly became convinced that the benefits of the drug were way more than adequate compensation. He told the academic world so in numerous journals. His enthusiasm for the drug continues to this day, so much so that he's been called everything from "the father of MDMA" to "the stepfather of MDMA" to "the grandaddy of ecstasy". As a further indication of his standing with the E Generation, he was voted into the Top 10 of the "pre-millennial cultural aristocracy" alongside the likes of Oasis' Liam Gallagher and The Prodigy's Liam Howlett in a poll of 100 musicians, film-makers and novelists conducted by *Select* magazine in 1997.

But whatever the accolades, it's perhaps too simple to view Shulgin as being to ecstasy what Timothy Leary is to LSD. For a start, Shulgin's work was only possible by virtue of the fact he held a drug-handling licence from the DEA – although this was withdrawn following a raid on his home by around 30 federal and state law enforcement officers in 1994. The raid was almost certainly a delayed reaction to the publication of *PiHKAL*. Until then, he had friends in the DEA, some of whom attended his wedding to Ann, and officers would often bring confiscated substances to be tested at his laboratory.

The truth is that Alexander Shulgin has never seen himself on either one side or the other of the ecstasy debate. He merely conducted experiments and, with *PiHKAL* and *TiHKAL*, reported what happened. Although he has been drawn into the arguments over ecstasy in recent years, his interest is first and foremost chemical, not political.

Moreover, while not denying the importance of Shulgin's role in sparking up the pilot light, his part in the story is perhaps not as critical as that of his close friend, 'Jacob'. At least that's what he's called in Myron Stolaroff's 1996 book, *The Secret Chief: Conversations With A Pioneer Of The Underground Psychedelic Therapy Movement.* 'Jacob' was Leo Zeff, a highly respected elder statesman of the American psychology scene. Zeff's use of LSD and lesser known substances such as ibogaine in the treatment of many of his patients put him at the forefront of the psychedelic therapy movement during the Fifties and Sixties. By the mid-Seventies, when Shulgin introduced him to MDMA, he was close to retirement. But he became so convinced of the drug's therapeutic potential that he spent the next few years criss-crossing the country, introducing MDMA to several hundred American therapists and several thousand patients.

Zeff, who died in 1988, called MDMA 'adam'. It was under this name that an estimated half a million doses were administered to patients suffering from trauma, depression and other psychological conditions between 1977 and 1985. Adam wasn't a cure, not in the traditional sense anyway, but the therapists discovered the drug's empathogenic effects made patients, suffering from even the most difficult psychological conditions, communicate more easily and openly, thereby facilitating psychotherapeutic treatment.

Among those using MDMA in this way was Dr George Greer, who ran a private practice in New Mexico and was also employed part-time as a consultant psychiatrist at the state's main penitentiary. Assisted by his wife, Requa Tolbert, a psychiatric nurse, Greer began giving MDMA to patients in 1980 and continued to do so until 1985, treating a total of around 75 people with the drug during those five years. He was also responsible for what was then the most detailed medical report on the drug's effects on humans, *MDMA: A New Psychotropic Compound And Its Effects In Humans*, which he published himself in 1983. The basis of this was a study of 29 people given doses of 75 to 150mg of MDMA in a series of clinical sessions in Santa Fe, New Mexico, and San Francisco, California, between 1980 and 1983. The drugs for the sessions were synthesised at Shulgin's laboratory.

Greer reported that every one of the 29 subjects experienced some form of benefit from adam during their sessions. All noted a positive change in how they felt about themselves, as well as about others present and the world in general, and 22 of the subjects also said they could think more clearly and had greater insight into personal difficulties. Equally significantly, a questionnaire filled out by each patient some nine months after the last session suggested many of these positive effects were enduring. All except one claimed their personal relationships had improved since taking MDMA, and many also described positive changes in attitude (23 patients, with 11 of them specifically mentioning higher self-esteem) and mood (18 patients). In addition, six people reported drinking less alcohol in the months following the sessions, six said they decreased their cannabis intake and five decreased their caffeine intake. One subject claimed to be using less LSD than he had before.

Writing about the study in *The Journal Of Psychoactive Drugs* in 1986, Greer and Tolbert noted: "In general, it is reasonable to conclude that the single best use of MDMA is to facilitate more direct communication between people involved in a significant relationship. Not only is communication enhanced during the session, but afterwards as well. Once a therapeutically motivated person has experienced the lack of true risk involved in direct and open communication, it can be practised without the assistance of MDMA. This ability can not only help resolve existing conflicts but can also prevent future ones from occurring due to unexpressed fears or misunderstandings."

Although adam was never commercially available to the medical profession, lots of chemists were more than willing to manufacture the drug in the early Eighties. There was the escalating demand from therapists, for a start. There was also the fact that, while MDMA had effectively been outlawed in the UK since the 1971 Misuse Of Drugs Act, which banned all amphetamine-related substances, it remained completely legal in the US. And nobody there seemed to question that it should be otherwise.

The situation changed dramatically in 1984. With increased therapeutic use of the drug came increased recreational use. MDMA use rose from 10,000 doses per year in the mid-Seventies to an estimated 300,000 doses every month in the early Eighties. By 1984, this figure had rocketed to perhaps as many as two million doses a month. By now, too, DEA agents had reported that MDMA was available on the streets of 21 American states. Most recreational users knew the drug as ecstasy, but it was also sometimes called E, XTC or X. Alongside the usual suspect urban centres, such as New York City and Los Angeles, it was prevalent in college towns and on university campuses, especially those with traditions of progressive thinking. This is perhaps no great surprise, seeing as how many of those who had been producing the drug for therapeutic use were university chemists, some with experience in making LSD in the Sixties.

In July 1984, having decided that this could not be tolerated any longer, the DEA announced a proposal to clamp down on MDMA. They did so as heavily as possible by placing the drug into the Schedule I classification as laid down by the 1970 US Controlled Substances Act (CSA). Of the five Schedules available under the CSA, Schedule I is the only one to ban a substance completely, with manufacture, sale and use strictly forbidden. Severe constraints are also placed on any research involving Schedule I drugs, which are classified according to three conditions: "(a) the drug or other substance has a high potential for abuse; (b) the drug or other substance has no currently accepted medical use in treatment in the United States; and (c) there is a lack of accepted safety for use of the drug or other substance under medical supervision."

The proposal to classify MDMA as Schedule I horrified the hundreds of therapists who'd been using the drug. George Greer had seen it coming, though. He knew all too well about the spread in recreational use. He also knew that, as a result, the DEA would sooner or later exercise restrictions over the substance. He even agreed MDMA should not remain a completely uncontrolled drug, but he believed that the extent of any restrictions should be partly determined by its medical value and that it should be classed as Schedule III, allowing it to be available on prescription and for research purposes.

Greer's fear that the DEA wouldn't take the drug's medical potential into account in any scheduling decision was the chief impetus behind him making his experiences with the substance public in *MDMA: A New Psychotropic Compound And Its Effects in Humans*. He was also concerned that MDMA hadn't undergone any formal research and initiated moves to rectify this. He asked two American pharmaceutical companies for funding, but drew blanks with both. He next approached the US Food & Drug Administration for help, but again to no avail.

Enter Rick Doblin, then a 31-year-old student of psychedelic therapy. At the age of 18 Doblin, quite impressed with his own experiences with LSD, mescaline and hallucinogenic mushrooms, decided to pursue a career as a psychedelic therapist. He had refused to fight in the Vietnam War, and resisting the draft made him a criminal - as such, most professions were closed off to him. Psychedelic therapy was different, though. Not that Doblin was in any great hurry, which is why he spent much of the Seventies working as a builder – "getting a grounding in the material world" as he puts it. It wasn't until 1982 that he returned to his studies by enrolling in a workshop with Californian psychedelic therapy guru Stanislav Grof. It was at this point that he first came across MDMA. Like Greer and so many others before him, Doblin was immediately impressed with its therapeutic potential. But also like Greer, he realised it wouldn't be long before the authorities came down on the drug.

"It was inevitable," says Doblin, who is now president of the Multi-disciplinary Association for Psychedelic Studies (MAPS), a Florida-based research and educational organisation. "Knowing this, I helped to found the Earth Metabolic Design Laboratory, which supported efforts for MDMA research. We wanted to be able to say to the government, 'Here's a scientific study, here's some data, preserve this for the therapists at the very least.' The announcement of the proposed criminalisation of MDMA was followed by a 30 day 'comment period' and, within that period, I walked into the DEA's headquarters with petitions signed by the most prominent people willing to speak publicly about the medical value of the drug we could find. We then asked for a public hearing. If nobody had gone in over that period, MDMA would have been made illegal on Day 31."

Instead, the DEA's administrative law judge, Francis Young, agreed to the petitioners' request. He ordered three hearings to take place in Los Angeles, Kansas City and Washington DC between June and November 1985. During the months running up to the first of these, Greer, Doblin and Lester Grinspoon, professor of psychiatry at Harvard Medical School and a long-time proponent for the medical use of marijuana, gathered evidence, witnesses and money. The DEA were busy, too, even lobbying the World Health Organisation (WHO) in Geneva, Switzerland, and asking them to impose an international ban on MDMA in the certain knowledge that the US government would have to comply with this. Doblin promptly took a flight to Switzerland to argue against any such moves.

Doblin also spearheaded a media campaign to put over the challengers' case. The first major article about the drug appeared in *Newsweek* magazine in early 1985 under the title 'Getting High On "Ecstasy" '. It included a pro-MDMA quote from a Benedictine monk, Brother David Steindl-Rast, who claimed that "a monk spends his whole life cultivating the same awakened attitude it gives you", while Massachusetts therapist Dr Richard Ingrasci cited the case of a woman suffering from "a phobic dread of infections" who was cured after a single two-hour session with the drug.

"The American media were initially very sympathetic to MDMA," says Doblin. "Part of the reason for that was because people who didn't fit the stereotype drug user were willing to talk about the benefits they got from it. People like Brother David Steindl-Rast. There was positive publicity about MDMA on national TV, too, on the Phil Donahue show. We even had a couple of middle-aged women suffering from cancer who said that one dose of MDMA had helped them come to terms with their illnesses and that they'd want their children to take it if they were ever in a similar situation. Parents talking about how they wanted their kids to take a drug? It was incredible. It must have been extremely frustrating to the DEA."

Indeed it must. Part of the DEA's difficulty was that their attention had been completely focused on the recreational use of MDMA. They'd heard of 'ecstasy', of course, but they'd never heard of 'adam'. They had absolutely no idea that the drug was also being used by the medical community until Doblin walked into their offices with the psychiatrists' petitions. DEA pharmocologist Frank Sapienza admitted this was so in the *Newsweek* article. Nevertheless, the authorities remained steadfast in their determination to outlaw the substance, claiming it was now available on the streets of the majority of states.

What's more, by mid-1985, they were fully aware of the way that MDMA was being used as a dance drug in the bars and clubs of Texas, where they'd conducted undercover operations in February and March. They declared they would not wait for the outcome of the hearings before acting. Drawing upon a 1984 amendment to the CSA which permitted a one-year emergency scheduling of any new narcotic, the DEA ordered MDMA to be placed into Schedule I. The ruling was effective from 1 July 1985.

★   ★   ★

In the meantime, the hearings were underway, with Judge Francis Young taking evidence from more than a dozen psychiatrists. George Greer was the challengers' star witness and his testimony was supported by three other New Mexico psychiatrists, all members of the state's medical peer review committee. The most senior, Dr Rick Strassman, assistant professor of psychiatry at the University of New Mexico in Albuquerque, told Judge Young that Greer "has included the appropriate safeguards and has not experienced significant adverse reactions to this form of treatment". Not only that, but Strassman concurred with Greer's belief that all of the patients "experienced significant benefit" from MDMA. Dr Richard Ingrasci also took the stand, testifying that he had given the drug to some 100 patients with none of them suffering any apparent harm. Others lending their weight to the argument included Dr Norman Zinberg, an associate of Professor Lester Grinspoon at Harvard Medical School, and Dr Morris Lipton, deputy editor of the *American Journal Of Psychiatry*.

Bearing in mind the DEA had only recently learnt about the medical use of MDMA, it's not surprising that their lawyers, Stephen Stone and Charlotte Johnson, struggled to counter these testimonies. Their position wasn't helped by the fact that, to achieve their aim of making the drug Schedule I and banning it outright, proving the CSA conditions of "no currently accepted medical use" and "a lack of accepted safety . . . under medical supervision" were much more important than proving "a high potential for abuse". The latter was a condition of Schedule II as well as of Schedule I, while the two medical considerations were only pertinent to the Schedule I classification. And as far as the DEA was concerned, if MDMA was made anything other than Schedule I, it might as well be available from vending machines on every street corner.

In the event, Stone and Johnson had just one central line of attack open to them. Much of it came down to semantics. It revolved around the fact that MDMA had not been approved as a commercial drug by the US Food & Drug Administration (FDA), which the DEA lawyers claimed was required under the US Food, Drug & Cosmetic Act (FDCA) of 1938. No approval by the FDA, they argued, meant "no currently accepted medical use", the key words here being "currently accepted". By the same logic, "no currently accepted medical use" meant there must be "a lack of acceptable safety . . . under medical supervision". It was as simple as that, case closed. Although not in Judge Young's books.

"There is no denying that such a situation would greatly simplify the scheduling task of the DEA staff," he noted in his report, which was published in May 1986. "It provides a quick solution to the problem for the DEA. It provides a certain answer. But it is wrong."

Young's report went on to declare that the FDA's remit did not extend to establishing what was or was not "accepted medical practice". Moreover, the FDCA wasn't designed to impose legislative restrictions on physicians. Both the FDA and the FDCA were merely concerned with the trading procedures of a commercially available product and the fact that, in the words of the DEA, "there is no legitimate commercial manufacturer of MDMA in the US" was of no importance, said the judge. If it was, he added, "use by physicians is reduced to being determined by, and therefore equated with, a businessman's or corporation's determination of the economic feasibility of mass production." What was and was not "accepted medical practice" could only be established by physicians themselves, he ruled.

Balancing the legal ponderings and neat semantics of the DEA against the medical profession's eight years of experience with MDMA, Young declared that the drug did not meet the conditions for Schedule I. He didn't accept the bulk of the fragmented evidence for "a high potential of abuse" which the DEA had presented, either. The fact that MDMA was a phenethylamine with a similar chemical structure to several Schedule I drugs, most notably MDA, didn't establish any degree of abuse potential. Eight other phenylethylamines hadn't been placed into any Schedule at all. It was similarly irrelevant that the drug was classed as a central nervous system stimulant. So was caffeine. Young also cast doubt on the testimony of the DEA's witness from the Haight-Ashbury Free Medical Clinic in California, who said the clinic was currently treating three to four people with MDMA-related problems a month. According to the judge, this figure was "unreliable". As were claims that the drug was associated with two deaths, one in Seattle, Washington, and the other in Santa Monica, California. After studying the toxicology reports, he ruled that the involvement of MDMA in these deaths was "questionable".

Judge Francis Young's report concluded that, not only should MDMA not be classed as a Schedule I substance, but it shouldn't be considered Schedule II, either. Instead, Young agreed with George Greer and recommended the drug be placed into Schedule III.

There was to be very little cause for celebration for Greer, Doblin and Grinspoon, though. After all, the judge's recommendation was only a recommendation. As such, as far as the DEA were concerned, it could easily be ignored. And ignoring it is precisely what they did. In November 1986, six months after the publication of Young's report, the DEA ordered the temporary placement of MDMA into Schedule I to be revoked in favour of a permanent placement into the very same classification. It has remained a Schedule I substance ever since.

(P)

35

6

Alexander Shulgin: A Personal Perspective

The following is an essay on Alexander Shulgin, the oft-called 'father of MDMA', written by Myron Stolaroff. Stolaroff – author of the book The Secret Chief: Conversations With A Pioneer Of The Underground Psychedelic Therapy Movement *– is a director of the Albert Hofmann Foundation, an organisation devoted to furthering the investigation of psychedelic substances.*

I have been very blessed to have two outstanding teachers in my life. In many ways, they are very much alike. They are both very bright, quick-witted, sensitive, intuitive, delighted with life, full of good cheer and laughter, and wonderful storytellers. They both offer unending support and good will.

One of them is the world-renowned chemist Alexander Shulgin, affectionately known as Sasha, who I first met in 1963, plus or minus a year. The other is my Tibetan Buddhist meditation teacher, Alan Wallace, the translator of many important Tibetan texts into English. Over time, I enjoyed weighing in my mind which I would rank as the most important. At first, Sasha Shulgin was my choice, as I found the psychedelic world provided the most powerful and rapid learning tools available to man, and I benefited from Sasha's personal teaching and guidance enormously. But as time went on, I found the extraordinarily outstanding psychedelic experiences difficult to preserve in ordinary daily activities and I would sink back into strongly formed old habits. I found meditation practice an excellent way to learn how to maintain the more exalted states and, at such times, Alan would grow in importance to me. Furthermore, I became willing to put him ahead of Sasha because of his deep, spiritual commitment, which I came to realise was the most important thing in life.

But then the next time I would see Sasha, his mind always seemed to have improved in brilliance, in perspective. He was continually keeping up with important issues in society and the world, with an eagle eye directed toward preserving the individual freedom our American Constitution supposedly guarantees. I have given up the weighing now, as I

36

realise I find them both indispensable: personal spiritual fulfilment and the knowledge of how to best be of service to the world. Power to them both.

I thoroughly believe that any reasonably accurate assessment of the state of Western Civilisation will recognise that human understanding and functioning is, in many ways, going backwards. The great error, which is quite widespread, is the failure to see our true, fundamental nature. This largely results from putting a great deal of trust in our scientists, who do not discern the transpersonal aspect of human beings, and how important this dimension is to successful and fully satisfying living. I believe the appropriate use of psychedelics can rapidly and effectively reveal the spiritual aspect of our nature to the serious seeker – and Sasha Shulgin, through the development of some 200 compounds, has provided a wide range of vehicles to permit exploring the nature of one's personality, one's mind and the ultimate nature of reality.

It was the ingestion of 400mg of mescaline at the age of 34 that set the tone and direction of Sasha's life. At the time, he was a chemist working in the research labs of the Dow Chemical Corporation in Walnut Creek, California, where he had the opportunity to investigate some 2,000 analogs of mescaline. When Dow lost interest in this type of exploration, he decided to become independent and work in his own laboratory next to his home, on the 20 acres that he owned. His diligent work over a number of years resulted in his being able to publish complete information on 179 psychoactive compounds. These are described in his book *Pihkal*, co-authored with his wife Ann. All the compounds are described in detail including methods of synthesis, dose levels, duration and qualitative results. A number of these compounds, such as MDMA, 2C-B, 2CT-2, -4 and -7, to name but a few, have particularly important characteristics. All of these but MDMA are Sasha's own creations. Some have been investigated by other researchers and some have been manufactured in other countries. While the origin of MDMA dates back to 1912, Sasha began studying it further in the late Sixties and is largely responsible for initiating the widespread interest in the substance.

Sasha Shulgin is undoubtedly the foremost chemist in the compounding and exploration of psychoactive compounds, a love which he has been pursuing for over three decades. How does one go about making so many useful discoveries? With profound chemical knowledge, keen intuition, immense patience and, particularly, enormous courage. Put yourself in Sasha's shoes. You have just synthesised a brand new compound. You have no idea of its properties, appropriate dose level, what effects it might have on your body, whether or not it could be lethal. Many chemists work with laboratory animals but, when it comes to subjective effects, animals don't communicate very well. To Sasha, the most valuable information you can learn comes from ingesting the new compound yourself. So knowing that subjective experiences can vary all the way from heaven to hell, Sasha starts with extremely small doses that he is sure (hopes?!) are below the detection level. The dose is gradually increased on subsequent trials until an effect is noted.

Then it becomes interesting. Sasha's vast experience allows him to somewhat predict forthcoming events, as he continues to incrementally increase the dose of the compound. He carefully notes his reactions, determines whether the effects are useful and, if so, continues until the upper level of usefulness is established. If he is confident that its properties are significant and harmless, he will allow his wife Ann to replicate the process over the useful range to confirm the action of the new substance. If the compound looks truly promising, other experienced collaborators whose responses are well calibrated may be asked for their evaluation. Exploring the vast, formerly unknown areas of the mind is very akin to the early sailors who left familiar shores to dare into the unknown seas, without a clue as to what they may encounter.

The interval of time spent creating and evaluating these compounds represents a vast amount of experience, both in personal evaluation and observing and/or assessing the experiences of many others. The result is an enormous compilation of data on numerous aspects of psychedelic substances, the effects of various compounds and dose levels, the extent and nature of possible experiences and the factors which influence results. It is probably safe to say that Sasha and Ann Shulgin are among the most informed world authorities on psychedelics and the experiences they provide.

How do psychedelics effect the ageing process? Much information needs to be gathered on this subject. But if people were given the opportunity to spend some time with Sasha Shulgin personally, I have no doubt that psychedelic substances would be greatly in demand. Brain deterioration? Here is a person at the age of 74, who is alert, witty and full of fun, who is constantly expanding his understanding in a variety of fields. Take computers, for example. Understanding the capabilities and potential of computers, Sasha became thoroughly conversant with their functions and rapidly designed methods and procedures to best serve his needs. He is a master at exploring the internet to keep up with a variety of newsgroups and to obtain reference material from around the world. Upon writing *Pihkal*, he insisted on laying out the design and graphics of the book himself, and furnished the printer camera-ready copy.

Is it depressing to grow old? You could never prove this by Sasha. His quick mind, ready wit and outstanding sense of humour keep his companions entertained and in good spirits. While many of us are finding our memories deteriorating with the ageing process, Sasha is continually introducing new words that give subtle shifts in flavour to ordinary expressions. And because of his wisdom and experience, Sasha Shulgin is in demand as a teacher and/or lecturer on many aspects of the use of psychedelic chemicals. Because of his depth of knowledge and well-respected integrity, he is often called as an expert witness in drug trials, being hired by prosecutors and defenders alike.

As has happened many times in history, the established powers in society often fail to recognize creative innovators and the significance of their important contributions. The threat to the status quo is often met with repressive actions. In the case of psychedelics, official and public understanding are particularly distorted. Many were not surprised when the Drug Enforcement Administration took action against Sasha, which resulted in the recall of his license to work with Schedule I compounds, and a burdensome fine and legal expenses. Details of this traumatic episode are described in 'Invasion', the first chapter of Sasha and Ann's second book, *Tihkal*.

Despite the limitation of excluding Schedule I substances, there are numerous other areas where important discoveries remain to be made. I have no doubt that Sasha Shulgin will continue to pursue such interests and discoveries as long as he is breathing. While he shares the desire of many of us for a more conscious society, he is convinced that our major impact will be "one on one".

7

Ecstasy And The UK Press I

The drug in the news, 1985–1988

25 April 1985

Daily Express

'How The Evil Of Ecstasy Hit The Streets'

The first British newspaper story about ecstasy appears in the *Express*. With quotations from George Greer, Lester Grinspoon and Richard Ingrasci, much of the story is effectively a re-write of 'Getting High On "Ecstasy" ', an article which had been published by *Newsweek* magazine in the US a few days earlier.

1 May 1985

Daily Telegraph

'Ecstasy – The Latest Narcotic Menace'

The *Telegraph* follow the *Express* story with a report that an American DEA agent has briefed a conference of UK police and customs chiefs on ecstasy. The conference, which is held "behind closed doors" at a secret location in Preston, is also attended by Giles Shaw, a policy adviser to then Prime Minister Margaret Thatcher.

October 1985

The Face

'MDMA We're All Crazy Now'

Peter Nasmyth pens the first in-depth magazine article about ecstasy published in the UK: "There can be little doubt this drug is now with us here in the UK, arriving from across the Atlantic every week via 747, turning up in flats and nightclubs and parties as the latest product of American drug mythology."

17 March 1986

Daily Express

'Yard Stand-By As New Ecstasy Drug Arrives In Britain'

Officials at the US Embassy in London alert Scotland Yard to the imminent arrival of large quantities of ecstasy in the UK. The Embassy claim a Los Angeles drug syndicate is "known to be seeking a foothold in Britain".

14 April 1987
Sun
'Ecstasy For Sale!'
"An investigation" into "the jet-set danger drug ecstasy" takes in three London nightclubs – The Limelight, The Wag and Delerium at the Astoria. The newspaper's journalists reveal that the "weird love potion" is readily available in all three places. When one of the journalists visits the men's toilets at Delerium, he hears "the sound of a girl giggling coming from one of the cubicles". The girl emerges a few moments later, "with her blouse undone and skirt ruffled". She's followed by a man "who stumbled around and fell on to the floor where he lay laughing hysterically".

14 May 1987
Daily Mail
'Fashion Models In Ecstasy Drug Raids'
Around 500 pills are seized during police raids on a number of UK addresses. Three men and three women are taken into custody. One of the women is a former model who claims that she's worked for Jasper Conran and designed jewellery for David Bowie. The police say she is linked to "a ring of beautiful, top-class models" who are distributing E "to rich clients, including showbusiness stars", but she is later acquitted of all charges brought against her.

3 August 1987
Daily Telegraph
'Trading On The Ancient Appeal Of Ecstasy'.
The *Telegraph* tries the academic spin. Peter Davies looks at the word 'ecstasy' and its derivation from the Greek ekstasis – "a state of mystical exaltation in which the mind, or soul, seems to be outside the body". He says the ancient civilisations hadn't been averse to the odd mind-altering trip themselves, describing how the drug-influenced cult of Bacchanalia was suppressed by the Roman government in 186 BC with 7,000 executions. Davies calls the suppression "the biggest drug crackdown in history".

July 1988
Boy's Own
'Bermondsey Goes Baleric [sic]'
Paul Oakenfold, the host of the Spectrum acid night in London, writes

41

about ecstasy for the *Boy's Own* fanzine. "It takes you up and gives you a feeling of freedom," he declares. "You know what you're doing, you just feel more confident of love. People tend to take the drug and dance the night away (You hippie, Oakenfold – Ed)." The same issue of *Boy's Own*, which boasts the words "Drop Acid Not Bombs" on the cover, also quotes a "poncho-wearing clubber" outside Spectrum at 4am: "I don't mind telling you, matey, I'm right on one and I feel like I'm on holiday".

30 July 1988
NME
Letters
"In last week's *NME*, acid was mentioned on almost every page. Does this mean that the *NME* advocates the use of LSD? It would seem so."

August 1988
Soul Underground
News
A BBC television camera crew which arrived unannounced at Danny and Jenni Rampling's pioneering Shoom club – "arrogantly pushing their way to the front of the enormous queue" – weren't exactly welcomed with open arms. "Jenny [sic] showed them the direction of the door," crows the dance music fanzine. "A big round of applause goes out to Jenny Rampling."

20 August 1988
Melody Maker
'The Road To Utopia'
Melody Maker offers a self-styled "Consumer's Guide" to different types of pills, including "yellow capsules" ("a legendary bad batch") and "New York tablets" ("the most consistently reliable ecstasy . . . Highs come in peaks, the lasting sensation being one of unbruisability and general bliss, maan").

2 October 1988
Observer
'Off On An E'
Journalist Kate Ellerton describes her personal experience of ecstasy, which she took at a party at a friend's house, as "sensual, warm, appreciative, companionable". She says she found herself in a bedroom with three strangers. "We wanted to stay together forever," she writes. "We removed our clothes and formed human pyramids, turning orgiastically, stroking each other, admitting a hip bone here, the softness of a buttock there."

12 October 1988
Sun
'Bizarre' column
The tabloid's regular pop column calls the burgeoning acid house scene "groovy and cool" and famously offers acid house t-shirts to readers for "only £5.50, man".

19 October 1988
Sun
'Evil Of Ecstasy'
'The *Sun* Doctor', Vernon Coleman, warns of the dangers of E. "If you're young enough, there's a good chance you'll be sexually assaulted while under the influence," he says. He also talks about the possibility of flashbacks: "If you get one in the wrong place, you could kill yourself". The *Sun*'s acid house t-shirt offer is withdrawn. Smiley clobber is also banned from Top Shop, Chelsea Girl, Burton and C&A clothes shops across the UK.

November 1988
Soul Underground
News
"How long before soap operas on TV feature some matey who never gets up in the morning and gets into trouble for drinking all the lucosade [sic] in the fridge?"

2 November 1988
Daily Star
'Dicing With A Cocktail Of Death'
Scotland Yard believes that 60,000 ecstasy tablets are now being sold in London's West End every weekend, with "greedy gangsters" taking "a staggering £2 million a night".

2 November 1988
Soho News
'Jesus Saves!'
Photographed from behind in a London street is a guy in a hooded towelling bathrobe with a tatty vest cellotaped upside down to the back. Scrawled on the vest in felt-tip pen are the words: "Mr Rip Danger – Official Acid House Philosopher. I will solve any of your problems for 50p. Don't be afraid my children."

8

August 1988: What We're On Is Happiness

The following is an abridged version of 'The Road to Utopia' by Push, The Stud Brothers and Paul Mathur, an article which appeared in Melody Maker *on 20 August 1988 – one of the first articles published in the UK weekly music press about the acid house scene.*

"I was scared at the start – I thought I was going to fuck up and lose a club full of people," recalls DJ Paul Oakenfold. "The odd acid track or Balearic beat would clear the floor. The more I played, the more people complained. But I told them that, if they wanted rap, they should go someplace else, I wasn't interested anymore. Sometimes you've gotta say, 'I'm really into this, I believe in it and I've got the bottle to go through with it'."

One hour into Tuesday morning and Oakenfold can be found behind the decks at Heaven in London's West End. But this is no ordinary club night, this is Spectrum: Heaven On Earth – The Theatre Of Madness. To prove it, there might be a massive indoor fireworks display accompanied by 'The 1812 Overture'. Or a huge eye suspended at one end of the venue, lasers beaming into the centre, spinning out hundreds of green rays.

There's certain to be smoke, strobes, UVs, chasers and lasers. And everybody crammed on the floor, maintaining a trance dance or an ecstatic jack as they stretch up to touch the beams. There'll be people holding sparklers or lollipops . . . sweat and screaming and cheering and smiling faces all around. There's certain to be a queue outside a couple of hours after the doors have closed.

Together with Danny Rampling, Johnny Walker and Nicky Holloway, Oakenfold [forms] the 'Gang of Four', the quartet of London DJs who have spearheaded the rise of acid house and Balearic beat in the city's clubland since they returned from Ibiza at the end of last summer.

In an attempt to maintain Ibiza's holiday atmosphere, hedonism and freedom of expression, Oakenfold began throwing after-hours parties at his Project club in Streatham [in late 1987]. These were essentially re-unions, with Ibiza friends and associates making up the audience. The music ranged from U2 and The Woodentops, through Phuture and Farley 'Jackmaster' Funk, to Nitzer Ebb and Yello.

More and more people travelled to Streatham on Friday nights . . . Soon after, Oakenfield [sic] thought bigger, negotiated [the venue] Heaven on the only [available] and surely worst night of the week, Monday, and launched [the club] Spectrum.

[Oakenfold:] "At Spectrum, I keep [the music] up all the time. When I'm DJing, I work a crowd, make them shout and put their hands in the air. I'm trying to create a special atmosphere and I work closely with the lighting guy. I'll suddenly turn off a record, leave a gap and follow up with something completely different."

Danny Rampling is the man responsible for the consistently heard phrase 'get right on one matey'. His South London club, Shoom, which he ran with his wife Jenni, was the first club of its type to be opened to paying-in punters. It began at a small venue in Southwark Street shortly after The Project's biggest [Ibiza] reunion party. This spring, it moved to the West End in an attempt to cater to the massive crowds being attracted, but has now returned to its original venue and operates under the name Joy.

Today, Joy is where the smiley culture is at it's most obvious, with broad welcomes on badges, t-shirts and faces. The friendly, family atmos-phere cultivated by its hosts – [and] expounded in their own Shoom booklet – is of great importance. Presents are often given out to clubbers and all are treated as equals: there is no VIP lounge and no guest list. That doesn't stop Paul Rutherford [ex-Frankie Goes To Hollywood] from heading the queue at around 11pm. He comes to dance in the knowledge that he will not be hassled. Except, perhaps, by [Joy regular] John the Baptist, who's to be found in the gent's toilets, carefully splashing water over hot heads. Nobody cares: everybody's having a good time.

"We're touching hearts," say the Ramplings. "We wanted a place where you could go and dress up or down as you like, leave your egos at the door and have fun. That ethos has changed a lot of people's attitudes – they're more relaxed, more natural, friendlier. We're not about money. What we're on is happiness and that's got absolutely nothing to do with drugs. This scene is not drugs orientated. We wouldn't dream of taking [drugs]; we want to be in control of our minds. When kids of 15 or 16 think they have to take ecstasy to get into it there's something definitely wrong."

Paul Oakenfold notes that "if drugs are happening it's because they are a part of society's problems and it's something which we wish to combat, not encourage."

Another DJ, Steve Proctor, is noticeably angry at the way ecstasy has been portrayed as a significant part of the scene: "It's dismissive, the scene goes beyond that. There's a lot of hysteria being concocted by insecure, out-of-touch people desperately seeking a hook to hang on. They're wrong. They don't understand. We're talking about what is largely a group of highly responsible people.

"I guess [the acid scene is about] using music as a drug," he allows. "A night is a series of highs, the music undulates and a good DJ will lift it up a bit more as the evening progresses . . . every time you peak them, you peak them that little higher. The dancing is a real tribal thing: the rhythmic movements and the chanting, it's like a closely controlled hysteria. The beat pounds along, driving you – and you can't stop, you can't get off it. I've seen people dance for two or three hours: they're exhausted, and they can barely breathe, but they just can't stop. In the end, they almost go 'bang', mentally and physically. So they have a drink and 10 minutes later they're back, heads nodding, feet stamping, arms waving around."

London DJ Colin Faver agrees: "The whole point is to let yourself go – to sweat, not stand around at the bar, intent upon a cool pose. Once you're caught up in that groove, it's impossible to get out of it . . . suddenly all frustrations are lost, there are smiley t-shirts and smiling faces to match. The clothes are baggy – practical rather than making a statement. Mind you, it's now seen as fashion and a trend. But it's one which is going to continue."

Acid has given us a taste of freedom; an excuse to sweat, to alter attitudes and break down barriers, musical and social; the opportunity for a good time just about any night of the week. In many ways it's a reflection of the times. It's certainly a revolution for the London club scene and the reason it's all happening in such a dramatic way is that, deep down, there's the knowledge that, for once, there's a lot of catching up to do.

9

From Ibiza To The Summer Of Love:
A First-Person Account

The following is an oral history given by Nick Spiers, one-time Shoom regular and now a London-based record distributor.

"When I was a teenager, I got into the whole rare groove scene in London, the sound system thing, soul warehouse stuff like the Soul II Soul parties. It was all about dancing well and having the coolest records. It wasn't a very druggy scene. It had its roots in the reggae sound system culture, so it was all puff. And beer. Maybe the odd bit of speed for me every now and again. I'd never heard of ecstasy back then.

"I went to Ibiza for the first time in 1986, when I was 18 years old. In 1986, Ibiza was just a place to go. But when I went back there in 1987, things were different – you felt something was happening. I can't quite explain it, you just felt everything was opening up. Ecstasy was around in Ibiza then. It was around big-time. I didn't do E, though. I was scared. I was skint. I was also enjoying myself in Ibiza without it, although I later realised I'd probably have enjoyed myself more with it.

"Some clubs in Ibiza were outdoor clubs and it was wonderful! You were dancing under the stars! That was the main thing – you were free! From the dancefloor, you'd see the aeroplanes coming in to land and think, 'Ah! More party people! More people to meet!' It was so crazy in those clubs, loads of crazy women there, loads of, like, Brazilian-types up on the podiums going crazy. And at 2am, they'd turn on the foam machine and fill the dancefloor with bubbles.

"I know you'll think, 'Big deal', but it was. Living in Britain back then was shit for people like me, people who couldn't take part in the yuppie thing, people for whom the yuppie thing didn't register. The Conservatives were in power and it seemed like they always would be. There were a lot of underprivileged people, who the Conservatives didn't give a fuck about, and a lot of the working class youth were left hanging. In the

Seventies, we [the youth] had this view that we would always have soli-
darity. But Margaret Thatcher put an axe to that. I know my mindset
became, like, 'Fuck it, fuck politics. I won't bother with any of this
anymore. I just need to get out.' They were dark days: there was a reces-
sion and the weather was always grey, always shit, of course. I think many
people felt cramped, felt trapped. Dancing under the stars to amazing
music surrounded by foam and beautiful women in a club that looked like
the Playboy mansion? It *did* seem like paradise.

"You always heard a mish-mash of music in Ibizan clubs but, by 1987,
the mish-mash began to seem more cohesive. The sound people in
England started calling 'Balaeric' [after the fact that Ibiza is one of the
Balaeric islands] in 1988 was becoming more concrete: it was stuff you
would never normally think of listening to in a dance club – Thrashing
Doves, The Woodentops – along with house music and lots of Spanish-
sounding records, hot records like The Gipsy King's 'Bamboleo'. You
know DJs are talking about music being 'a state of mind'? Well, Balaeric
really was. It wasn't a genre, it was more a feeling. It was the feeling of
Ibiza.

"I guess the feeling was ecstasy, too. It was music which sounded good
on E. Of course, I didn't know that at the time. Strangely enough, I did
my first E in London, a year later, in 1988. It was when DJs like Danny
Rampling, who started the club Shoom, imported the Balaeric ideal to
London. It was then that loads of people started taking E and house music
became really big. The whole acid house thing . . . it started out of the
Balaeric thing.

"So my first E! I didn't actually take it at Shoom, I took it at this acid
house club [DJ] Mr C ran with some people who called themselves RIP.
Their club was in this dank, dark warehouse on Clink Street [south-east
London]. RIP was a very rough vibe, much more edgy than Shoom or
Spectrum [DJ Paul Oakenfold's acid club]. It wasn't a Balaeric club, it was
full-on acid house – house music with sirens, manic tunes, lots of repetitive, trance-inducing records.

"I had a lot of close contacts with people who were bringing E into the
UK. They were just regular blokes. In those days, it seemed like dealing
wasn't so criminal, not with E. My friends were bringing it in from
Amsterdam and, quite early on, from Ibiza. It was brilliant. This first one I
took, the guy who was with me was selling them for £25 – that was so
much money then – but the pills were strong, much better than the crap
Es around now. The pill I took was a capsule. You've probably heard this
a thousand times but, all of a sudden, the whole thing clicked. House
music, which I already enjoyed on a musical appreciation [level], suddenly
made complete sense. On E, it seemed like you became a cog in the big

wheel of the whole room you were in, this churning energy thing, and you became a part of it, you gave yourself over to the experience. That's what acid house was about.

"Things were so much fun in Britain in 1988. That summer – the 'Summer of Love' - you just didn't want to leave. I guess the most amazing of all the clubs around that year was Shoom. I always come back to talking about Shoom, but there is a reason for that: that club was simply life-changing. At Shoom, you really would see these rough people next to these gorgeous-looking pampered people on the dancefloor. The logo for Shoom was the smiley face and it was all a very communal, loving vibe. A lot of my older friends from the sound system days, black guys, they couldn't get into it, though. Even though they may have dropped E, Shoom was very alien to them. They didn't get all the peace and love hippie stuff, the tie-dye psychedelic happy stuff. I guess it was a very white aesthetic.

"A lot of people, naysayers, said Shoom was very cliquey. Jenni Rampling, who was the wife of the DJ, Danny Rampling, was on the door. She picked the crowd, she picked who got in, and many didn't get in. In a way, the Ramplings and the people who were regulars at Shoom were just being protective. The E at the club had bred this optimistic euphoria and it served as a gateway to what seemed like a whole new world. We all felt this thing, like, 'We are changing the times! This is it!' It's hard to share that, I guess. Hard to explain to people who aren't part of it. I mean, I'd had plenty of fun nights out before that, but they weren't fun in the way Shoom was. Shoom was playhouse fun! Brilliant fun! Nobody was *that* familiar with E yet, so I guess we forgot it was the effect of the drug. We just figured we had become kinder people. If you bumped into somebody, it was like, 'Oh, I'm so sorry. How are you?' Or if there was a bottle of amyl going around, it was like, 'Is it OK if I have some?' And it was like, 'Yeah, it's Shoom . . .'

"There is this myth that E erased elitism in the London club scene in the summer of 1988, when everyone tried it. It didn't. It just changed who was elitist about what. See, before acid house, the mid-Eighties London club scene people were extremely snobby, in a cocaine-snorting sort of way. Their scene was based on who was wearing Vivienne Westwood and Gaultier, on posing at the bar. There were all these 'club celebrities' and people spoke about the Eighties being 'the style decade'. If you look at magazines like *i-D* or *The Face* from that time, you get a pretty good idea of what it was like: obsessively bent on dressing up and being cool. Oh, it was awful. Anyway, with acid house, that mid-Eighties elite were suddenly dinosaurs! Overnight, that's how they seemed.

"I remember one face who used to run those sort of snobby style clubs

– Philip Salon, who ran The Mud Club. He was the king of that whole 'style decade' nightlife thing, the big face, and one night he came to Shoom. He looked so out of place. He was running around, asking all these people, like, really pestering them, 'Why don't you come to *my* club? It's much better at my club', and people at Shoom were like, 'Go away, I'm dancing! You are ruining my vibe!' He tried giving me a free ticket to his club. It was almost sad. His whole thing was so out-the-window – a few years before he would never have let someone like me into his club. But ecstasy – that INGREDIENT! – killed his whole trip and he was desperate. What Philip Salon and all those types wanted just didn't work anymore.

"After a while, though, acid housers became the new London club mafia and I suppose I was a part of that. Yes, we were very snobby, too, just in a slightly new way. We hated newcomers, for a start. In 1989, I remember meeting a girl I knew in a club, a girl I hadn't seen in a while. Bear in mind, the whole 'acid ted' thing had started by then – acid teds being all these horrible, cheesy ravers, these sheep from the suburbs cottoning on – and she seemed totally like that. I couldn't talk to her. She'd just found out about E and acid house. To me, that was sinful. I was like, 'You are wearing a smiley badge and t-shirt NOW? You are so late!' She was a sheep. And the sheep, as far as I was concerned, were beginning to ruin the whole thing.

"The sheep . . . there were many. So acid house became rave, so all the sheep could fit. I *hated* rave. I *hated* all that M25 orbital rave shite. It was too big, too impersonal! Raves were ripoffs! Run by gangsters! Filled with fools! By 1989, when rave had started, E had already become a bit of a cheesy thing for me and my friends to do. Actually, a lot of my friends were burned out from taking too much, so new people coming in and being all 'I LOVE YOU!' was pretty hard to take. A division started to happen. People like me, the old faces, went to what were called 'Balaeric' or just 'house' clubs in the city, and all the sheep went to big raves like Biology and Sunrise – navigating mud and thinking they were experiencing the real deal.

"My drug dealer friends, the blokes who dealt E, went to the raves because they could make loads more dosh there than anywhere else. One night, they asked me to go with them, so I forfeited a night of Balaeric heaven and went out to one of these Orbital raves. I was sitting in the back of this car, sandwiched between two guys, and I kept thinking, 'What the fuck am I doing?' It was just a total non-starter for me. I was in this car, going . . . I don't even know where we were going, really. Just rolling along on the M25. We get to a service station and some bloke there tells us, 'Oh, it's off! The rave's off.' So what do we do? We turn around. And

I was like, 'Never again! I am never going to go to a rave.' And I never did venture into that territory. As far as I was concerned, the new generation could have it.

"As with all new and old generations, I suppose I couldn't understand what they were doing. Even though now, in retrospect, I can see they were doing exactly the same thing I had done two years earlier. They were regular people discovering the extraordinary. Now I can see how that is the pattern of our E culture. But at the time, none of that was clear yet."

10

Busts, Raids And Clampdowns: A Policeman's Lot

The fireworks were really going off on Saturday 5 November 1988. There were no Guy Fawkes celebrations at the Essex home of Ted and Margaret Mayes, though. They'd built a bonfire, but it was to burn the smiley t-shirts and florescent jumpers which had belonged to their 21-year-old daughter Janet, who had died on 28 October as a result of taking ecstasy during an acid house party at The Jolly Boatman pub in Hampton Court, Surrey.

The death of Janet Mayes was the second in Britain linked to ecstasy. The first was that of Ian Larcombe, also 21 years old, who'd suffered a fatal heart attack after reportedly popping 18 pills in one go four months earlier. Janet's intake was small by comparison: she had taken just two tablets. Nevertheless, the coroner's report later revealed a massive overdose, the concentration of MDMA in her body registering higher than that found in Ian's.

Less than an hour before Janet Mayes collapsed on the dancefloor of The Jolly Boatman, the Hampton Court venue had been surrounded by almost 100 police officers awaiting orders to raid the party. The police had busted several acid parties in and around London during the previous few weeks, including one in Stepney on 5 September and another on the Isle of Dogs on 30 September. But the operation prepared against The Jolly Boatman was set to be on a far grander scale than any of these.

In the event, the news that someone inside had collapsed after taking ecstasy provoked a hasty re-think of police tactics. The all-out assault which had been planned was now deemed wholly inappropriate. Instead, a handful of officers were sent into the venue to launch an investigation which disclosed that Janet had bought the drugs from a friend, David Butler, who was initially charged with unlawful killing. This was later dropped when he admitted a charge of supplying.

Across the UK on the weekend of November 5, as the rockets rocketed and the bangers banged, thousands of party people freaky danced the hours away. As the events at semi-rural Hampton Court the previous week proved, acid house and the drug which fuelled it was rolling out from the city centres where the scene had held sway throughout the previous summer. Some of the parties took place in licensed venues, but an increasing number were in disused warehouses and factory units, the events advertised via garish flyers and by word-of-mouth.

The smiley people weren't the only ones frantically tuning into the party grapevine in the days running up to Guy Fawkes Night. So were the police, galvanised into taking tougher action by the media reaction to the death of Janet Mayes, which included a front page story in the *Sun* headlined 'Shoot These Evil Acid Barons'. The result was a string of busts and almost 60 arrests over the course of that weekend, with acid nights targeted all over the UK: from London and the Home Counties to Manchester and the West Country.

One of the most dramatic of these raids was Operation Seagull, which centred on a party on a Thames pleasure cruiser, the Viscountess, moored at Greenwich Pier in London. The boat was the sister ship of the Marchioness, which sank in the summer of 1989 with the loss of 51 lives. The waterborne party was infiltrated by several undercover detectives and, in the darkness, the Viscountess was surrounded by police launches armed with floodlights. Police frogmen circled in the waters, ready to react if anybody fell in. As the floodlights zapped on, officers from both the launches and the shore swarmed aboard the cruiser, arresting 18 people including two of the promoters of the party, Robert Darby and Leslie Thomas. Darby and Thomas were subsequently sent to prison for 10 and five years, respectively, for managing premises at which drugs were supplied. The commanding officer of Operation Seagull, Detective Chief Inspector Albert Patrick, was clearly delighted with his night's work. "The whole of the pier lit up as soon as I gave the order to attack," he told journalists. "It was just like Blackpool illuminations."

Another of the weekend's raids was on a party at a large derelict house in Sevenoaks, Kent, the walls of which were daubed with smileys. This one didn't go anything near as smoothly as Operation Seagull, though. As police officers entered the house, a section of the 250-strong crowd turned hostile, resulting in a pitched battle. The disturbance spilled out onto the street and took over 60 officers two hours to bring under control. A number of policemen and party-goers were injured in the affray, one officer receiving a serious head wound after being clubbed from behind. A total of 13 people were taken into custody, most of them on public disorder charges rather than for drug-related offences.

The Kent police force received assistance on the Sevenoaks raid from a Metropolitan Police back-up unit, a fact which *NME* journalist Steven

Wells wasn't slow to pick up on, voicing the popular belief among the acid house fraternity that the raids amounted to a well-organised clampdown. But the reverse was actually true. While Operation Seagull was part of a wider investigation, Operation Echo, which was being handled from Plaistow police station in east London and was connected to the September raids in Stepney and the Isle of Dogs, the rest of the authorities' action was unco-ordinated beyond a little ground-level help. Despite working alongside Metropolitan officers on the Sevenoaks raid, senior Kent officers knew nothing about Operation Seagull until they read about it in the newspapers. They didn't know anything about Operation Echo until months later.

The haphazard police response continued as winter turned to spring and spring turned to summer. By this point, undercover detectives were regular visitors to acid nights up and down the country. "They're easily recognised," one anonymous Brighton club promoter told the *NME*. "They're the ones getting into the police vans at the end of the night."

As well as keeping a tab on what was happening in the clubs, the authorities also started trying to hit at ecstasy supplies. In December 1988, after weeks of surveillance, a swoop on a car in north London netted 500 ecstasy pills and five men. The following month, several thousand pills were found during a raid on a house in Birmingham.

These and similar seizures did next to nothing to stem the increasingly widespread use of ecstasy, though, and the drug claimed its third British victim when 16-year-old Claire Leighton from Cannock, Staffordshire, collapsed at the Hacienda in Manchester on 14 July 1989. Claire had been given a tablet by her friend, Tim Charlesworth. He was later jailed for six weeks, despite Conservative MP Ivor Stanbrook calling for life imprisonment for anyone supplying E.

The Chief Constable of Staffordshire, Charles Kelly, was another who demanded tough action. He got it, too. And fast. No sooner had the news of Claire Leighton's death dropped onto the doormats of Middle England than a series of raids on private houses across Staffordshire uncovered a number of large consignments of ecstasy and led to 69 arrests. At around the same time but in a separate incident, police raided a house in Wembley, London, where they found what they believed to be Britain's first E factory.

The death of Claire Leighton was not, however, the first time ecstasy hit the headlines in the summer of 1989. Three weeks earlier, on 26 June, the *Sun* had published a front page report on an acid party called A Midsummer's Night Dream held by seasoned promoters Sunrise in an aircraft hangar at White Waltham, Berkshire. The main face behind Sunrise was Tony Colston-Hayter, a former professional gambler who had earlier been dubbed the "acid house king" by the *Daily Mirror*. The *Sun* story, which ran under the headline "Spaced Out!", claimed the event was attended by 11,000 "drug-crazed kids – some as young as 12" and that, when the party was over, reporters saw "thousands of empty ecstasy wrappers littering the floor". Beneath the *Sun*'s famous red logo were the words, "Thought: Curse of our kids".

The *Sun*'s account of the White Waltham rave was challenged not only by the party's organisers, but also by the police. They believed it was way over the top. The youth press were similarly unimpressed. "Tabloid reporters are known for keeping their brains in glasses of Steradent beside the bed overnight but this alone cannot explain the almost Python-esque inaccuracies in their copy," wrote the *NME*'s Barbara Ellen in a piece credited to 'Barbara E'. Yet almost every daily newspaper in the country repeated the story over the next couple of days. Television got in on the act, too, with the BBC News giving what amounted to a running commentary on the parties taking place the following Saturday. " 'Flavour of the week' is the expression, isn't it?" remarked Chief Inspector Laurie Fray of the Thames Valley Police. "Last week it was rottweilers."

There were countless large-scale gatherings like the White Waltham Sunrise rave during the second half of 1989, most of them pitched up within easy striking distance of the then newly opened M25 orbital around London. Colston-Hayter's Sunrise company now had many rivals: Jarvis Sandy's Biology and Jeremy Taylor's Energy, and a chorus of other outfits like World Dance, Genesis, Raindance and Phantasy. There were raves not just indoors, but in fields, chalk pits and forest clearings. There were euphoric sounds – Ce Ce Rogers' 'Someday', Kariya's 'Let Me Love You For Tonight', Lil Louis' 'French Kiss' – and eurhythmic lightshows. There were thick gushes of dry ice, firework displays, fairground rides and the odd bouncy castle. There was speed, acid, coke, cannabis and amyl. And there was always ecstasy. Of course. Never sold in "wrappers" as the *Sun* claimed, though.

For the police, the rash of orbital raves meant one giant-sized headache after another. Especially for Chief Superintendent Ken Tappenden, the divisional commander of north-west Kent, an area split in two by the M25. The southern side of the Dartford Crossing, the only way to get over the River Thames east of London, fell within his jurisdiction. So did Sevenoaks, the scene of the riot which followed the police raid on the smiley-daubed house in the early hours of 5 November 1988.

In the wake of the Sevenoaks bust, Ken Tappenden set up an incident room at Dartford police station to investigate the acid party phenomenon and it wasn't long before he was being flooded with calls from other stations. Not just from stations in Kent, but all over the UK. By the end of the summer of 1989, Tappenden's team had outgrown the Dartford office and transferred to Gravesend, acquiring an official name, the Pay Party Unit, along the way. From his original team of six, the Pay Party Unit now boasted a staff of around 250 officers, 200 of them on the ground, and incorporated satellite squads in 12 police forces across southern England and East Anglia.

Ken Tappenden was already an officer of considerable experience. He'd joined the Kent Constabulary in 1961 and worked as the senior investigator in over 30 murder cases. He'd had the unenviable task of taking charge of the bodies of British citizens recovered from the Zeebrugge ferry disaster in Belgium. He'd headed up Kent's fraud squad and drug squad, his stint with the latter including leading a £21 million LSD bust.

Tappenden says he first came across ecstasy long before anyone ever heard of acid house. He was initially wary of making too strong a link between E and the huge raves suddenly rocking the countryside, though. Like a lot of top policemen, Thames Valley's Chief Inspector Laurie Fray for one, Tappenden didn't believe the parties were propelled by drugs. They couldn't be. Not parties of this magnitude. Two raves in Kent in the space of two weeks during August 1989, one at Meopham and one at nearby Wrotham, changed his mind. After the Wrotham party, his men collected enough pills to fill six black dustbin bags.

"I really didn't know what was happening at first," admits Tappenden, who retired from the police force in 1992 with an MBE. "I didn't know for certain what the motivation was and I didn't know how to contain it, how to combat it. But after Meopham, our surveillance teams started filming the parties and we then knew we had a dreadful problem. We saw dealers bringing in drugs on barrows and security firms taking pills off people to recycle them, to sell them on again. We saw people collapsing and security men throwing them over the fence, so they were outside the perimeter of the party. There was no care for them. Then there was the aftermath. From lunchtime onwards on Sundays, youngsters would be taken to police stations or to village doctors by local residents who'd found them wandering around the countryside in a senseless state."

Ken Tappenden was astonished at what was going on. "The ravers were, by and large, nice people, but you could have lined them up against the wall and every one of them would have had a pill in their pocket," he says. But against his personal horror, he had to balance the logistical reality of the manpower at his disposal. A couple of hundred coppers into even just one party of 10,000 ravers simply didn't go. There was no way he could consider a direct hit on the large number of people taking E – a pragmatic abrogation of duty mistakenly perceived by many as police acceptance of individual use. Applying the same mathematics, to which he added his experience at Sevenoaks and an ill-fated attempt to bust the Meopham rave, he also recognised that trying to break up a party once it was in full swing risked sparking a riot.

Instead, Tappenden developed a policy of trying to stop the orbital raves happening in the first place. To this end, he did everything in his power. And sometimes a tad beyond. The Pay Party Unit monitored the pirate radio airwaves and the underground press, and undercover officers were sent into clubs and record shops to collect flyers. If Tappenden discovered somebody had agreed to hire out their land or property to a party organiser, he'd seek an injunction against them – although some of the smarter promoters got wise to that and arranged convenient holidays for landowners so they could not be served with the necessary paperwork required by law. From Wednesdays onwards, police helicopters would be on the lookout for fairground rides and steamrollers on the move, the latter often being used to flatten sites.

If a party got underway, roadblocks would be set up at strategic points. In the event of mass arrests, Tappenden had magistrates and solicitors on stand-by throughout every Friday and Saturday night, and made sure he knew precisely how many cell spaces were available at nearby police stations. Some of his other tactics were less coventional. He even set up pirate radio broadcasts from the Pay Party Unit's Gravesend office, with younger officers giving out false information on the airwaves.

"We'd pick up on whoever was pushing something that night, Sunrise for example, and we'd go out on the radio as Sunrise as well," laughs Tappenden. "We'd go out saying, 'the party's been moved to Ipswich'. We'd send them off in the opposite direction they were supposed to be going. The shit really hit the fan one Sunday morning after we'd sent them off towards Colchester. One bunch got so frustrated that they smashed up and looted two service stations on the way. Another time, a ravers' convoy of 160 cars totally blocked the M25 for something like eight hours. Everybody stopped their cars and threw their keys into the undergrowth beside the road. It was pitch black and we were snookered.

"We took liberties," he continues. "We overstepped the mark in relation to the law. I visited lots of firms who hired out heavy plant machinery and told them I'd do them for conspiracy if they hired to party organisers. I couldn't, but that's what I told them. I scanned the Public Order Act and pulled out stuff most lawyers had never even heard of. I claimed I could stop anybody I thought was going to cause a breach of the peace and the organisers' lawyers replied by saying I was making unlawful arrests. I'd already had that with the miner's strike. I'd stopped Kent miners going to picket in Nottinghamshire by blocking the Dartford Tunnel for several hours. I was hauled before the High Court for that."

The Pay Party Unit's biggest single success came in October 1989, when it stopped a Biology rave near Guildford, Surrey, at which a crowd of 40,000 was anticipated. Tappenden worked furiously to make sure the party didn't happen, co-ordinating an operation which involved not only several different police forces, but also the Tax Inspectorate, the VAT Inspectorate and UK Immigration. Biology boss Jarvis Sandy was put under surveillance for a week and, through one of his lieutenants, informed that he was looking at 10 years behind bars on a variety of criminal and tax charges if he tried to pull the party off. To ram the message home hard, Centreforce, one of the most important pirate radio stations, was closed down the night before the planned rave and Sandy's star attractions, American rap heroes Public Enemy, were held for four hours when they arrived at Heathrow Airport.

But despite going to such incredible lengths to cripple the party promoters, Tappenden had a grudging admiration for some of them. "You've run some bloody good gigs," he told Energy's Jeremy Taylor at a debate on raves hosted by *Melody Maker* in early 1990.

"All the promoters had was a bank of mobile phones, yet they could still move 10,000 people around on a Saturday night," says Tappenden. "And still get a fairground attraction in place without me knowing. And still start the music up before I got to them. And still run it for the next 20 hours. I had to admire that. We were used to planning big operations, but I don't think a top police or military team could have done what those lads did Saturday after Saturday. They were masters at it. They weren't real villains, either, they'd simply seen an opening, a way to fill their pockets. Jeremy Taylor's dad was a judge. Jeremy used to tell me what his dad said I could and couldn't do."

For some party promoters, the respect was mutual. One organisation, Raindance, even asked Tappenden to work for them when he retired from the police. But while Taylor, Sandy, Tony Colston-Hayter and the like weren't "real villains", others behind the scenes were precisely that, attracted by the opportunity to run drugs and protection rackets. In his book *Class Of 88: The True Acid House Experience*, Wayne Anthony of the Genesis organisation writes about how he was kidnapped twice, once by a gang of former soldiers - Falklands War veterans - who demanded half of all takings in return for security services. Bound, gagged and with a gun at his head, Anthony had little choice but to comply. Matthew Collin's *Altered State: The Story Of Ecstasy Culture And Acid House* book meanwhile notes the involvement in the party scene of the ICF, the Inter City Firm, the notorious football hooligan crew attached to West Ham United.

A lot of information of this nature came through to the Pay Party Unit by their use of HOLMES, a national computer database system first set up during the hunt for the Yorkshire Ripper back in the late Seventies. It was the first time HOLMES had been used to police drugs.

"The criminal element which infiltrated the raves was more sinister than anyone at government level ever wanted to know and more sinister than the public ever percieved," says Tappenden. "Using HOLMES, lots of the names which kept coming up were people we knew as robbery merchants and gangsters, people on the Criminal Intelligence list. They were thugs. They were heavy bastards. Across-the-pavement robberies were going down and drug-related crime was going up. Yes, we had kidnappings. Yes, the ICF got involved. Record shops in the East End of London were getting smashed up three or four times a month as a warning not to run parties without them. Some people got seriously hurt, seriously maimed. The message was, 'You don't want to look like him next month.'

"We also saw it in the fields with the security companies. It's hard for a policeman to admit to being frightened, but I got frightened lots of times. I got frightened for my officers. I got frightened for the youngsters at the parties. We recovered four sawn-off shotguns in one night at a rave at Ockenden in Essex. We filmed security men making rotweiller dogs attack people at Reigate in Surrey, putting 16 in hospital, and we saw them walking around with CS gas canisters. Oh, it was sinister. And it was never-ending. The moment we took one team of five villains off, another five would come in. I thought we would have mass slaughter with the gangs. I talked about the danger of a Hillsborough-type disaster if it suddenly went off at a crowded party. It didn't ever happen, but it's no exaggeration to say we were often on the brink of it."

By the end of 1989, Tappenden was exhausted. "The police weren't winning," he says. And on a personal note, Tappenden hadn't had a Saturday night at home for 15 months or more. He remembers how much he was looking forward to that Christmas, how he believed the holiday period would give him and his team a much-needed break. The promoters had been running raves non-stop through the winter months so far and they needed a bit of a break, too, didn't they?

As if. New Year's Eve fell on a Saturday. The number of illegal events logged by the Pay Party Unit in that one single night was 126.

Ken Tappenden woke on 1 January 1990 with a different sort of hangover to everybody else in the world. His headache was familiar to him, though. He'd had it for what seemed like forever.

Yet as if by magic, a mere six months later it had gone. During the first few weeks of 1990, there was a sharp decline in the number of illegal raves monitored by the Pay Party Unit in southern England – down from an average of 30 every week in November 1989 to under 10 by the following February. At the same time, more and more calls into the Gravesend office were coming from the Midlands and the north of the country. For a while, attention was particularly drawn to the scene based in the countless dilapidated cotton mills in the hills above the Lancashire town of Blackburn, a scene which had grown so big that it attracted ravers from as far away as Glasgow. This geographical shift became clearer as the year unrolled further and, in June, Tappenden's operation was closed to make way for similar units first in Warwickshire and then Liverpool. The HOLMES database, which by then boasted 55,000 files, went north.

What caused the sudden drop in rave activity in the south? Police pressure had something to do with it. If Tappenden thought he wasn't getting anywhere, he was wrong, especially after the controlling body of the Telephone Information Services were persuaded to stop British Telecom hiring out Voice Banks to rave organisers towards the end of 1989. These allowed for messages to be automatically relayed down several lines simultaneously and were crucial to the promotion of every party. The dip in the scene was also partly due to the progress through Parliament of the Entertainments (Increased Penalties) Bill, giving courts the power to levy fines of up to £20,000 and jail anyone organising an unlicensed party for six months. To further bolster this legislation, which was sponsored by Graham Bright, Conservative MP for Luton South and later Parliamentary Private Secretary to Prime Minister John Major, the police were granted additional powers of confiscation of equipment at raves by the then Home Secretary Douglas Hurd.

Ken Tappenden, however, believes that the spiral of gangster violence behind the scenes was a far more significant factor in the decline of the orbital raves than the actions of either the police or the politicians.

"The real heavy villainy and the guns had more effect than anything we ever did," he says. "Some of the organisers had been threatened so many times, they didn't know if they'd still be alive on Sunday morning. It got to the point where some of them were petrified to go into that field to take their money at the end of the night. They could cope with us nicking them, but they couldn't cope with what we got on film at Wrotham. Christ, they did beat them up."

Even so, there's no question that the passing of the Entertainments (Increased Penalties) Act gave the police extra muscle. They quickly flexed it, too. In the early hours of 22 July 1990, only one week after it became law, a party at a warehouse in the village of Gildersome on the outskirts of Leeds ended with a massive police bust. Many of the officers taking part in the raid wore riot gear and some were on horseback. Several thousand pounds worth of drugs were confiscated and a staggering 836 people were taken into police custody, the detainees being held overnight in 26 different police stations across West Yorkshire. It was the biggest mass arrest in the UK since 1819.

(P)

11

E Is For England: Ecstasy And Football

Italy, 1990. In the World Cup Quarter Finals, England's big-eared hero Gary Lineker nets a penalty against Cameroon to level the score at 2-2 with just eight minutes of normal playing time to go. Lineker's team-mate David Platt turns to the English fans on the terraces and dances as if he's in the middle of a rave: his feet stepping up and down, his upper body rocking from side to side, his arms extended in front of him as his hands tug at an invisible rope. The fans erupt into a bastardised chorus of New Order's 'World In Motion' – 'E is for England – En-ger-land!' – as the helmeted Italian police nervously finger their batons. There's nothing for the police to worry about, though. All those huge skinheads are doing is hugging other huge skinheads.

The Italian police couldn't believe the apparent friendliness of most of England's football fans at the 1990 World Cup. But for those watching the competition on their TVs back home in Blighty, the sight of smiley people on the terraces was rapidly becoming situation normal. The English domestic footie season which had just ended had seen a dramatic decrease in hooliganism – and it was all because the geezers who'd once spent their Saturday afternoons hurling ritual abuse and, on a good day, kicking seven shades of shit out of each other had started dropping ecstasy. They were too busy gurning to even think about scrapping. That's the widely told story, anyway.

"I think it's bollocks," says Bill Brewster, co-editor of football magazine *When Saturday Comes* from 1990 to 1993 and a writer for *Mixmag* for much of the Nineties. "I don't doubt all the stories of football crews going to acid house clubs like Spectrum, dropping Es and stroking their Millwall tattoos, but I don't believe there were any knock-on effects to the terraces."

Although it's true that the number of arrests at English football matches dipped by 22 per cent between the 1989–90 and 1992–93 seasons, it would certainly be incorrect to think that E was one of the main reasons for this. The setting up of the police's National Football Intelligence Unit, which identified potential troublemakers and removed them from the picture before they could cause a problem, was undoubtedly a more significant factor. As was the introduction of all-seater grounds, a move prompted by the 1989 Hillsborough disaster, in which 95 Liverpool fans were crushed to death. Hillsborough also marked a turning point in the way that newspapers portrayed football fans, the tragedy altering their media status from "scum" to "victims" overnight.

The year after the Hillsborough disaster, Paul Gascoigne's tears at Italia 90 after he'd picked up a disciplinary booking which banned him from possibly playing in the World Cup Final was front page news. The softer side of football was suddenly making the headlines. Which, in turn, influenced how fans saw themselves: they now had a different kind of reputation to live up to. It didn't stop them chanting "Eezer cunt, eezer cunt, the referee's a cunt" around the time of The Shamen's 'Ebeneezer Goode', though.

In some ways, the idea that ecstasy halted terrace violence was a misplaced logical conclusion of the rave-football link heralded by the *Boy's Own* club-cum-footie fanzine in the late Eighties. The reality was that, for the real hardcore thugs, the criminal element, E was merely a chance to make a bit of dosh by dealing. They took the stuff themselves, too, of course, but it didn't mellow them as a result – although the fact that so many people during the early Nineties believed that they did says much about the *perceived* wider cultural impact of the drug. According to a 1989 report in the *Daily Star*, hooligans were using ecstasy "to bring psychedelic terror to the terraces . . . to wind themselves up for violence". Far from being tabloid nonsense, in some cases, the *Star* was right.

"In around 1992 or 1993, I was in a cab on my way to Ministry Of Sound with a guy who was a serious Tottenham hooligan," recalls Bill Brewster. "At one point, this guy said to me, 'Have you ever had a fight while on E?' Then he said, 'It's fucking great. I love fighting on E.' I remember thinking, 'Hmm, he appears to have missed the whole peace and love point of it all . . .' But some people didn't get that side of it. Some people saw it as just another drug, just another way to get off their heads. That incident [in the cab] also shows how E doesn't radically change someone's personality, it simply magnifies what's already there. And if what's already there is dark, it makes it seem darker."

(P)

12

Manchester: Diary Of A Club Owner

This is an oral history given by Tony Wilson, former owner of The Hacienda nightclub in Manchester.

"How did E culture start in Manchester? Oh, that's easy. It was through Stella. Yes, the beer. Let me explain . . .

"In 1986, our club, The Hacienda, was half empty. There was the odd good night but, generally, the club was half empty. Two of our DJs – Mike Pickering and Graeme Park – had begun specialising in this obscure Chicago dance music called 'house'. House was a really cult thing, really minor. Nobody gave a shit about it, actually. So, as I said, our club . . . ? Half empty.

"Two things then happened. First, we got an offer on Stella, which meant that we could sell it for a quid a pint. At the time, Stella was the favourite drink of every scally and hooligan in Manchester. Stella was their drink. And the scallies and the hooligan clans were getting bored with being scallies and hooligans. They were looking for new things to do at night. We had cheap Stella. So, in they came.

"Now, at the same time as the hoolies started coming in for cheap Stella, something else was coming in. Ecstasy. I'm not sure how ecstasy – what I knew as being a cult American drug – got to the Hacienda, but I know it came in in 1987. And I know its arrival had something to do with [Factory Records artists] Happy Mondays and their shady friends. They'd discovered E in Amsterdam in 1986, then discovered it again in Ibiza. They were all selling it. So, suddenly, there were scallies on E instead of Stella. Listening to this black dance music called house. That's how it all began in Manchester. How terribly revolutionary!

"I didn't *really* know that we had something big on our hands until 1988. I remember walking into the club one night during that year and thinking, 'Ah, yes, I haven't felt this since watching The Beatles on TV as a child, or watching The Sex Pistols on stage as a journalist.' It was like, 'Oh my God, something *big* is going on.' I had the feeling of being in the middle of something huge but not yet defined. I became this crazy John The Baptist-like proselytiser, spreading the word to the media and so on. I had so much *faith* in all this ecstasy stuff. There was a new culture happening! As big as punk! And it was plain to me that the culture was growing around and out of the drug.

"I was enamoured with it all. Like, there were all these strange rituals popping up out of nowhere. For one thing, everyone at the Hacienda suddenly had their hands flung out all night long. That was the Manchester ecstasy dance. I believe it was initiated by [Happy Mondays frontman] Shaun Ryder. The way he used to describe it was: 'I got a great big fridge and a microwave.' Just imagine, his hands out in front: 'I've got a great big fridge and a microwave.' Kinda bending at the knees. Ha-ha, Shaun was the genius of his age. I've got a video of one of those 1988 nights and almost everyone is dancing like that.

"The dance was especially popular in front of an area of The Hacienda called 'acid corner'. I must tell you about this area. One night, I was looking for one of my colleagues and somebody told me I'd be best to look in acid corner. 'Where's that?' I asked. Well, it was the most wonderful part of the nightclub and I hadn't even known it existed – but then I never even got free drinks in my own nightclub either and everyone else did. Anyway . . . Acid corner was beneath one of the balconies. There were a couple of steps to get into the corner and there were always several rows of people dancing on those steps. But if you forced your way through, behind was a massive area with people sitting on stools and chairs and the benches that lined the walls, and they would all be rolling spliffs and digging into bags of E and dancing like complete loons . . . It was like going into Narnia, like going through the fucking wardrobe . . .

"The next year, 1989, I wouldn't have gone into that corner if you'd paid me. Because acid corner had become 'Salford corner'. Our fate in a nutshell, my dears. Salford is Manchester's twin. A lower working-class town, it's actually where I come from and it's where Happy Mondays come from, too. It's also a big gang town. So, as I'm sure you can guess, at The Hacienda, Salford corner was the gang corner. As E culture grew wealthier in Manchester, the gangs moved in more and more, and our problems at the club escalated tremendously.

"I have this theory that Manchester's [late Eighties] gang troubles were related to Manchester airport. It's a bit of an outlandish idea, but hear me out. In 1988, the armed guards in the freight division at Manchester airport had their guns upgraded to semi-automatic weaponry. That same year, the main armed robbery gang in town, Cheetham Hill, also upgraded their guns to semi-automatics. Coincidence? I doubt it. But what I know for sure is that, night after night, these Cheetham Hill boys would show up at The Hacienda *with their guns*. They'd show their guns to the doormen and say, 'We're going to come inside your club'. And in they would come.

"In that period, the power of Cheetham was skyrocketing and it was complicating everything. These guys were beginning to control the club. And we couldn't cope. We went to the police. We had a meeting with Manchester police for two-and-a-half hours. 'Listen, there is a problem!' we said. 'Yes, ecstasy!' they said. 'No, no, not E! Forget about that for a moment! There are guys wandering around with guns and, sooner or later, the other gangs are gonna realise they are out-weaponed. They're going to get guns, too, unless you *do* something.' 'Hmmm,' they said. 'Tell us. Who is Mike Pickering?! Is he connected to ecstasy dealing?' The police had just set up a section to monitor raves and all they could figure out was that Mike Pickering's name featured on three quarters of our flyers. I was like, 'We've got guys running around our clubs with guns! *Automatic weaponry!!* And you want to find out about Mike Pickering, a house music DJ!?'

"The police were just useless. All they could think about was the fact that The Hacienda was an acid house club – and that meant people did E there. They couldn't get past that. And we *needed* the police's help. There was this conversation we would have with the police, I'd say about once a month. It went:

" 'Hello again! We need your help! *Please* will you come on the door with us and help us?' 'No.' 'But in America they have policemen on the doors with people. *Please* can we do this?' 'No, no, no.' 'Why not? We'll pay the rates!' 'We don't do that.' 'But you do it at football matches.' 'Uh, that's different.' 'How is it different?' 'It's just different . . .'

"Of course, it wasn't different at all. It was almost illegal of the police not to help us. But they didn't. So things got worse and worse: I mean, in one 12-month period, The Hacienda spent £374,000 on 'protection'. Forget drug dealing, that's what the gangs were *really* doing. Running protection rackets, taxing us – which would have been fine if they actually *had* protected us, instead of using our club as a shooting gallery! There was bad shit going off every other month.

"In 1990, the police shut us down. We later reopened, but things were never really the same again. We put in a metal detector at the door and the metal detector never fucking worked. Also, since Claire Leighton [one of the first British E victims] died at The Hacienda in 1989, we had to try as hard as we could to keep drugs out of the club. It was so annoying: in 1990, every other club in Britain was loose and full of E, but The Hacienda had to be clean. Really clean. Ridiculously clean. We created the fucking culture in the club – and we then had to dismantle it. It was just a farce. We had to remove the drugs, and all we were left with were guns and violence and 500 gang members toasting each other. I remember standing in the club one night within that time period. I said to a friend of mine, 'Oh, look, isn't it a shame. The hands have come out of the air. I had rather liked it when everyone's hands were in the air.' To me, it seemed like the ultimate sign."

13

Scotland The Rave: Hanger 13 And Hardcore Excess

Jon Campbell grew up in what he calls "the worst neighbourhood in Scotland". The Gallowgate, in the east end of Glasgow. In the Gallowgate, football dictates who your childhood friends are and drugs dictate which of them are still around for adulthood. In the Gallowgate, pharmacists make sure people coming in with methadone prescriptions take their fix right on the spot. If they don't do this, the methadone would be resold to raise money for a bag of brown heroin. In the Gallowgate, public service machines, like payphones or soft drink vending machines, cannot be installed on the street – they get broken into for the change they hold within hours. Not long ago, Coca Cola came up with a machine designed to quench the thirst of those with a buck to spare in the worst part of New York's crack-addled Bronx ghetto. Their press release claimed the bullet-proof vending marvel was "impossible" to break into. They installed one in the heroin, methadone and temazepam-addled Gallowgate. Three hours later, the entire machine had been stolen.

The Gallowgate – so called because it was one of the last places in Britain where capital punishment by hanging took place, the area hedged by the Barrowlands concert hall at one end and Glasgow Celtic's football ground at the other – has the highest crime rate in Europe. Jon Campbell says you can't wear green ("Catholic colours") to some houses in the Gallowgate and you can't wear blue ("Protestant colours") to others. You can't be saving up to buy a new television set and tell too many people about it. The Gallowgate wasn't somewhere Campbell wanted to stay. He hoped, at least, to get to the end of his street, to the Barrowlands ("the venue with the biggest luminous sign in all Europe!"). He hoped, one day, to come back – not for a funeral of yet another friend who died young and not to participate in another football casual testosterone battle – but to "do a concert".

In 1990, Campbell was 21. He had a keyboard. He was interested in the "new dance culture" which was spreading across Scotland. He says he felt it was "the only way to escape the unescapable ghetto". He admits that his tale, what he calls his "hope-through-music story", is a bit maudlin, a story tailor-made for a Sunday papers human interest piece. "But I don't think anyone could really understand what it was like unless they were here, in a neighbourhood like mine in Scotland, when the rave thing really kicked off," he claims, in an accent painstakingly scraped of most Gallowgate-isms.

The story of Scottish rave is a bittersweet one. In the early Nineties, rave hit like a lightning bolt straight to the heart of Scotland's youth. Like many other places where life is tough, sometimes impossible to deal with, ecstasy culture eased its way into the housing schemes and inner cities and depressed towns and suburbs and – everyone involved will tell you this – made everything seem better for a time. Made, to an extent, everything *be* better.

Kids who had nothing to believe in before rave now had their bedroom walls covered with flyers from parties, clippings about DJs, and posters ripped off buildings and lovingly steamed back into pristine condition with mum's iron. Kids from places like Ayr and Saltcoats began boasting about their home towns, no longer backwaters but rave centrals to which people from Glasgow or Edinburgh happily travelled on weekends. Some who admit to having been petty criminals before rave say they stopped hustling. They were too busy promoting parties or playing at parties or making records. Rival casuals who hated each other started hating each other less. People who'd lost mates to heroin or other injected nasties suddenly weren't afraid of their own fates – because they wouldn't do H now they had E. And E wasn't a bad drug. It was a good drug, a nice drug. They had a friend who dealt and he wasn't shady, he was a sound fella.

It didn't last long, this halcyon era which popped up like a cardboard wonderland in an otherwise bleak and jagged environment. The bleakness eventually frayed the wonderland, first eating into its edges and then chomping right through. The drugs did get bad. Use did turn to abuse. Caring did sometimes turn to negligence. People did die. And through it all, Scotland's youth continued to rave – longer, stronger, harder and with more zeal, more unflinching hope, than almost anywhere else in the world.

Jon Campbell would become one of Scottish rave's top-notch stars. His group, TTF (The Time Frequency), would eventually play "the venue with the biggest luminous sign in all Europe". The Barrowlands audience would be chanting "TTF, TTF!" as the band got onstage. In 1990, though, Campbell was still an unknown DJ, without a single big gig to his name.

69

In West Scotland, rave culture was then taking off, mainly due to the efforts of two Motherwell football fans, Ricky McGowan and Jamsy McKay, who started promoting monthly nights called Street Rave at Ayr Pavilion. By bringing in the cream of UK DJs, especially those popular in northern England, like The Hacienda's Mike Pickering and Graeme Park, Street Rave attracted thousands from Ayrshire and outlying areas. They wouldn't give Jon Campbell a gig, though. "I asked and they said no, because I was an unknown, but also 'cause I was from Glasgow and they were Motherwell guys, you know, Motherwell casuals," he says. "They hired Motherwell people for their warm-up slots and stuff." Street Raves were the best nights in Scotland at the time and Campbell wouldn't be deterred. Especially not by Motherwell casuals.

"See, the Motherwell casuals, they were seen as wimps by people from Glasgow," says Campbell. "Like somebody from the Bronx seeing somebody from the Catskills – 'Aaw, Catskills wimp!' So I called my 'resources'. Most of my friends were Rangers casuals – Rangers are the biggest football team in Scotland – and one of them said to me, 'I know these Motherwell pricks from football matches! We used to slap them about! We'll get you a gig, Jon.' So they sorted it out. Got me a gig. Ricky and Jamsy ran away without paying me but, anyway, that's how it all started. Tensions were high, but ecstasy and rave were starting to have an effect on the casuals. Scotland's always been a pretty territorial place and, before E, football wars were a big problem here. A few years earlier, I may have been chasing these guys down the street! But there I was, playing records for them."

Ecstasy didn't erase football hooliganism in Scotland. Or the rest of the UK, for that matter. Police clampdowns and the yuppification of the game and boredom after too many years of running up and down other people's streets probably had more of an effect on the Nineties decrease in football-related crime. Ecstasy was just a good way not to have to admit defeat: it was the drug's fault. Which doesn't mean the mythical rave-age construct of the 'love thug' – the hoolie who changed his ways after discovering the joys of E – didn't exist. He did exist. He wasn't hugging his former enemies with daisies laced through his hair and 'Kumbaya' instead of 'You're gonna get a fuckin' kickin' ' running through his head, though, as legend had it. He wasn't knifing people for standing on the wrong terraces anymore, but he was still a thug. He was just a nicer thug. With a new career path.

"It felt great, I tell ya," recalls Boney Clark, Motherwell supporter and former Street Rave resident DJ. "It was nothing like the old days of kickin' people about and not being able to go to certain places in the country, 'cause you'd get a lickin'. I mean, we were runnin' a club! The old way wasn't the [right way] to operate anymore. At Street Rave, we had lots of people from rival groups come in and you'd just kinda talk to them. It was taking a liberty, but you'd talk to them. And if somebody got a kickin', you'd go see if they were all right, no matter where they were from. There was this guy, one of the top guys in Aberdeen, and he had the same idea as us at Street Rave – to do clubs. He booked us to DJ in Aberdeen and, after we'd finished playing, there were 50 guys waiting outside for us, ready to give us a kickin' because we were Motherwell. The guy who'd booked us walked into the crowd, punched someone and said, 'If anybody else has got anything to say, they can deal with ME!' And that felt really top, really good. He was defending us from his own guys. Aye, aye, things were changing."

The opening up of Scotland's subcultural map was a big deal to many of the 'old guys'. By 1991, DJs could DJ anywhere. Organisers could organise anywhere. But the kids – the real kids, the teenagers, the younguns – were never too bothered about territorial boundaries. That stuff belonged to the world of their big brothers. The kids had their own, new world. Saturday afternoons weren't terrace time for them. On Saturday afternoons, not to mention Sunday afternoons, they were creeping up to their flyer-drenched bedrooms, saucer-eyed, wobbly-jawed and exhausted from a night of full-on rave-o-rama, hoping a wink or two would come their way.

They had a reputation, these kids. People said they did a lot of E. Not just one or two pills a night, but maybe three, maybe four, five, six. English DJs and journalists who travelled north to Scottish raves remarked upon it: 'They're crazy up there, they're stacking like mad!' The DJs played music which was a bit faster, a bit harder, a bit more berserk, just to keep up. The journalists wrote about how Scottish ravers were more 'up for it' than they were down south. And it was true – they were more up for it. But were they really doing more E than ravers in England? It's difficult to know. Dealers don't keep sales records. How-many-did-you-take-last-weekend polls don't exist. In 1991, there were no glaring, rave-induced hospital reports to speak of yet in Scotland. In the early Nineties, though, it sure seemed like Scottish ravers were necking uncommonly high numbers of what they affectionately called 'ekkies'.

"There was an adrenaline-rush mentality to the Scottish kids," says Bethan Cole, an English journalist who moved to Edinburgh in 1991, and wrote about club culture for magazines like *The Face*, *i-D* and *Mixmag*. "Raving in Scotland very quickly became a working-class pursuit. And the working classes in Scotland haven't got it easy. I did one story where I spent a few days with some kids on a housing estate on the outskirts of

Edinburgh. Edinburgh is the most beautiful, gentrified city in Scotland, but drive just a few miles out and visit these structures which act almost like little autonomous towns, and you think to yourself, 'Edinburgh's a theme park'. The destitution on the estates was remarkable – you felt this terrible sense of oppression, of complete economic crisis. Much more so than on most estates in England. So when these kids went out and partied, they were looking for a place to UNCORK. They lived for raving and they spent everything they had on it. There was an incredible feeling of release at the parties. It was as if the kids were trying to cram all the pleasure which was missing from their lives into one single night."

Tom Wilson, a 13-year veteran DJ on Scotland's Radio Forth, agrees. "Had you been at some of the raves I played at around 1991 or 1992, the vibe would have blown your mind," he claims. "It was all or nothing and that affected everything from the drug habits to the music. Ravers in Scotland liked the most in-your-face music you could imagine. So, of course, when hardcore techno came along, that was the [genre] which most appealed to ravers here. Hardcore techno was hedonistic ecstasy music. It really struck a chord. It was a big sound in Scotland for longer than almost anywhere else I can think of."

Hardcore techno was, without question, the maddest music ever thrown onto the dancescape. It burned most brightly at suburban mega-raves throughout the UK between 1992 and 1994, and then stuck around, in one form or another, as a favourite style in Scotland well into 1997. Endlessly derided by the English house cognoscenti as the sound of the 'E-chomping proletariat', hardcore was blacked out or made into joke fodder by most of the UK music and style press, who concocted the all-in-one folk devil of the 'cheesy quaver' to describe the type of blockhead who might listen to this music.

On British hardcore productions, the sound was usually based around a speeded-up hip hop breakbeat, with helium-pitch vocals and a tooth-rattling sub-bass. Epileptic synth stabs, krazy-kartoon samples and successions of peaking peaks were also common devices. The result was so romper-stomper and extreme that it was incomprehensible to those outside the hardcore raveland. The bonkers E rituals – the dummy-sucking (to help with 'gurning' jaws), the waving of fluorescent lightsticks and the wearing of white gloves (to trip off the de rigueur lasers), the use of Vick's Vaporub (to heighten ecstasy tingles) – only reinforced this alienation. Running at an astounding average of 160 beats per minute, hardcore techno was the first complete genre of British dance music made by those who took ecstasy at raves for those who took ecstasy at raves. Or rather, people who took 'ecstasy'.

"By 1992, E was of a dubious quality in the UK," says Mike Cadger, project manager for Crew 2000, an Edinburgh-based drugs awareness organisation. "It contained very little MDMA, if any. By then, European ecstasy trade routes had solidified. The larger-scale manufacturers tended to be based in the Low Countries and they served northern European countries first. Countries like Germany. Large-scale manufacturers also opened up in Italy and they served the Mediterranean countries first. On both counts, Britain was at the end of the trade routes – and the drugs which came in were of a lesser quality. The bottom of the barrel, so to speak."

In the UK, pills sold as 'ecstasy' could contain an alphabet soup of synthetic chemicals (MDA, MDEA, 2-CB and so on). They often also contained amphetamine, which may explain why hardcore music was so fast. The hardcore-dodgy E connection becomes even stronger when looking at the established drugs trade routes within Britain itself: the places which got the worst Es, probably the speediest Es, were also the places where hardcore techno was most popular.

"The initial port of call for drugs in Britain is always London," explains Mike Cadger. "The drugs then slowly snake up through the country, with Edinburgh as the last major port of call. The quality of E is unbelievably degenerate by the time it gets to Scotland. The only places that get worse drugs are places on the periphery of urban centres – suburbs, lesser cities, places like that. They get the most horrid kind of rubbish."

So imagine what the E was like 33 miles from Glasgow, in the minute seaside port of Ayr. Imagine what kind of garbage was doing the rounds when Street Rave left Ayr Pavilion for new territories and the owner of the venue started up a Saturday event to fill the gap. They called the night Hanger 13. Hanger – where the sound was pure hardcore and the lightstick kids came not just from Ayrshire, but from all over Scotland's west and central belts. And took maybe six, maybe seven, eight, nine pills a night.

In early 1992, Jon Campbell's TTF were asked to play the opening night of Hanger 13. The club's competition was stiff and Hanger wanted to launch with a big name. By now, Scottish raves hosted by companies like Rezerection could suck in tens of thousands of patrons and smaller clubs, like FUBAR (Fucked Up Beyond All Repair) in Stirling, were also doing swift business. At the time, TTF were the toast of the Metro club in Saltcoats, a few miles up the coast from Ayr. A TTF single called 'Retribution', recorded live at the Metro, had reached Number Five in the Scottish pop charts in 1991. The following year, the group topped the charts for a couple of weeks with 'New Emotion'. "We were getting big," says Campbell. "But the Metro was still like our home. When we played the

Metro, there'd be 4,000 people in the place. The capacity was 2,000. They'd open the back doors and people would gush onto the streets."

Campbell was loath to go back to the Ayr Pavilion, the place where, two years earlier, Street Rave had booked him and not paid him. But the owner of the venue, Fraser MacIntyre, told Campbell that Hanger represented a new era for the venue. "I figured, 'What the hell, we'll play for the competition if they're gonna do things right'," says Campbell. "I mean, at the Metro they'd turn off the water taps, so people had to buy bottled water. I didn't think that was very good. So off to the competition we went . . ."

On Hanger's opening night, the kids came in droves. The boys wore track suits with no shirts underneath and Caesar cuts glued flat with hair gel. The girls wore lycra and trainers. Everybody brought whistles and lightsticks. Some wore surgical masks with the letter E painted on the outside and Vick's Vaporub slathered on the inside, so they could inhale the camphor balm all night and everyone would know why. Throughout the night, kids strolled onto the ocean-kissing boardwalk on which the Pavilion – a white edifice with twin Wembley-esque towers, originally built as a cinema in 1910 – sits. They watched the waves and bought soft drinks at one of the places open along the beach. When they wanted to re-enter the club, though, the bouncers made them take their shoes off.

"Security was tight at Hanger 13," says Fraser MacIntyre, whose family has owned The Pavilion since 1973. "Bouncers did shoe searches, because shoes are a popular place to hide drugs. We also had trouble with people hiding things inside the, ehm, the female form, places the bouncers couldn't search. But the bouncers were clever. They knew these girls would have to go to the toilets to retrieve their goods. So if a girl was under suspicion, a bouncer would wait to catch her on her way out of the toilets. Those were the kinds of silly lengths our bouncers had to go to."

Not that the bouncers were complaining. "The bouncers basically took over the Pavilion, like a hostile [takeover]," says Street Rave's Ricky, who emphasises that one of the main reasons his company left the venue was because of growing tensions with the security team. "They started running all the drugs in the club, bringing the stuff in, re-selling the stuff they confiscated. The bouncers basically realised there was a good market and moved in. It was a dirty scene. It wasn't Fraser MacIntyre's fault, though. He wasn't a bad guy. He just lost control of everything."

Except, maybe, the water. MacIntyre insists that he never turned off the water at Hanger, not like they are alleged to have done at the Metro: "With all those kids dancing!? They would have been thirsty!" He does admit, however, that there was one night where there was no water. The pipes had blown, he says. And, unfortunately, a journalist was in the club.

"That's how the rumour started," says MacIntyre – "the rumour" being that the taps at Hanger were always off. That it was as arid as a desert. Whatever the truth is, most of those who went to the club can easily remember the price of a bottle of water: one pound. "It was just another disgusting way for people to make money off kids who had none," says Campbell. "I suppose 'no water' was becoming a tradition at these clubs. Kids were dehydrating left and right on too many crap Es. The Pavilion was turning into a hellish pit."

Don't take more than you know you can handle. Drink plenty of water to avoid overheating, especially if you're dancing a lot. Don't mix ecstasy with other drugs.

The guidelines for a safe-side E trip can be boiled down to these three important pieces of advice and, by 1994, organisations like Edinburgh's Crew 2000 and the Bridge Project in Ayr were telling ravers so via drug information flyers left out on the bars and speakers of places like Hanger 13. Of course, they wanted to do more than give out bits of paper and host the odd seminar, but politics and money and the status quo (the "are you condoning?" issue) conspired against them. All they could do was leave the flyers and hope that Joe Raver, on nine Es ("or 10 or 12," states Jon Campbell), could adjust his pupils enough to read one.

E and the Sinai-like conditions under which many Scottish ravers did drugs wasn't the only problem, though. By now, polydrug usage had flourished. Some people had figured out that amphetamine was cheaper than ecstasy, so they'd buy perhaps half the usual amount of Es and take them with whizz. For others, who'd built up such an extreme tolerance to ecstasy that even double-digit dosing couldn't get them to where they wanted, E almost certainly served as a gateway to other drugs, like cocaine, heroin or street-procured methadone. Still others became so familiar with the E trip that they began tweaking it in ways only the seasoned user would know: taking supplemental drugs at the beginning of a trip to enhance the up, in the middle to prolong the peak, and at the end to soften the comedown and get some sleep.

Many ravers were looking worse for wear. "Masses of skeletons stripped to the waist, sweating, jogging on the spot, not even hearing the music," remembers Campbell. "In the old days, people would take their drugs and be like, 'Aaw, man, can you feel that beautiful rush!?' By 1994, it had changed to 'I'm really gouching', which meant 'I'm in a downbeat way'. It meant they couldn't lift themselves up from a kind of paralytic stupor. Just cabbaged. They were combining too much." One notable combo was mixing ecstasy with the very strong, very cheap Buckfast Tonic Wine early in the night, taking amphetamine in the E plateau phase, then smoking a bit of heroin or using the tranquilliser temazepam as a come-down device.

Temazepam was among the worst blights on Scotland's 'problematic' (as opposed to 'recreational') drug scene, the heroin scene rather than the E-fuelled rave scene, for most of the Nineties. The tranquilliser, which falls into the same medical class as Valium, was once one of the most pre-scribed anti-anxiety medications in the UK. Scottish heroin users would squeeze the liquid out of the temazepam liqui-caps (the pliable, transpar-ent capsules were soon given the street moniker 'jellies') and inject it along with H, to prolong and increase the zone-out aspect of their buzz. Because a temazepam capsule could cost as little as one pound on the street, the drug also offered a cheaper high.

In 1997, temazepam was made a Class C drug (it was previously just a controlled medicine) in Britain. The manufacturers of temazepam also changed the format of the drug, replacing the liquid inside the capsules with an almost solid gel in an attempt to stymie injectors. But users found ways around both the new legislation and the new capsules. Rather than diverting temazepam from other people's prescriptions, they began relying on dealers who would import the stuff from outside the UK. They then learned to heat the gel into a liquid. The drug was made even more dan-gerous through this method: after injection, the temazepam could resolidify in the veins, sometimes leading to gangrene, sometimes leading to an amputation, sometimes death.

Most of the people interviewed for this chapter mention that they knew people on the rave scene who swallowed jellies as a comedown. All say they never saw any ravers injecting the stuff. Some, however, add that they knew a friend who had a friend who injected. So were the problem-atic drug scene and the recreational scene, once relatively remote, collid-ing? "The two worlds did start touching each other," notes Mike Cadger. "In a small country with limited amounts of supply and lots of people using, that's bound to happen. At Crew 2000, we saw temazepam becoming a problem on the [rave] scene. We put out a leaflet called 'Jelly Time', targeted at clubbers and ravers. The message was: 'Temazepam is particularly dangerous when mixed with MDMA. Jellies are a sedative, E is a stimulant. And you don't know what's in your E to begin with, so you don't know how the drugs are going to interact.' Basically, we tried to tell people they were casting their fates to the gods."

On May 1 1994, eight people were taken to hospital after collapsing at Hanger 13. Two of the eight, John Nisbet, aged 18, and Andrew Dick, aged 19, died. The causes of death were "drug-related".

Fraser MacIntyre found out about the deaths the following day, in a phone call to his home. "I couldn't have expected anything like it in my worst nightmares," he says. "All those people shipped off to hospital. Two dead. We were completely unprepared for anything like that. I make no excuses: we weren't prepared. But then nobody was. We were the first club in Scotland where this happened and nobody knew what to do or what to provide, whether we should have chill-out rooms and drinking water or whatever. Nobody really had those kinds of facilities back then."

Hanger 13 closed for a brief time, reopening for the summer. Mac-Intyre turned the taps on high and put pitchers of free water on the bars. In August, though, 22-year-old Andrew Stoddart was rushed to hospital after collapsing at the club. He too died. Another "drug-related" death. The club closed again. It reopened on September 10. That very same night, five people collapsed at the Metro. One of them, James McCabe, aged 21, was dead on arrival at North Ayrshire Hospital.

"James had his own band, Reactive Bass, specialising in what one Glasgow magazine called 'the sound of full-throttle techno terror'," wrote journalist Andrew O'Hagan in an article in the *Observer*'s *Life* magazine in October 1994. "In an interview given to the [Glasgow] magazine, James, concerned at the deaths of three young ravers at the Hanger 13 club in Ayr earlier in the summer, advised his band's fans to 'take your time, life is for living'." On the night of his death, James is said to have snorted between three and four crushed tablets of what he believed to be ecstasy.

After the death of James McCabe, Scotland's nightworld became an oasis of free hydration. At FUBAR, the DJ would regularly slow down the music for a few minutes and punters were urged to go to the bar for some gratis water. Fraser MacIntyre had his staff freeze water on Fridays to provide dancers with ice pops during Hanger's peak Saturday hours. Shortly thereafter, in 1995, Ayr council forced his club to shut its doors for good. "When the kid died at the Metro, it wasn't 'the Metro death', it was 'another death like Hanger 13'," says MacIntyre. "Everything was back to Hanger." His family still owns the Pavilion, but the white building with the Wembley-esque towers remains boarded up. And although the Metro is still up and running, it now specialises in house, not hardcore.

"The hardcore scene petered out after the wave of deaths," explains Radio Forth's Tom Wilson. Rezerection went into liquidation in 1996. Street Rave changed their name to Colours and began specialising in imported American house DJs. TTF played the Barrowlands but, by 1996, the group had stopped charting. They took a break. "I was quite sad," says Jon Campbell. "I didn't want to play anything rave-connected anymore. I just kept thinking, 'What if my name on a flyer means some kid will come and that kid will risk dying?' " The diminishing hardcore rave scene didn't mean the deaths abated, though. In June 1997, at Monklands Hospital in

Airdrie, just north of Glasgow, 13-year-old Andrew Woodlock became the youngest ecstasy fatality in Britain. He'd been given three tablets by a friend, a boy of 14.

Jon Campbell, now working on music again ("commercial Euro-sound stuff – nice songs!"), believes every E death hurts Scotland's former ravers a bit more than most others. "Because it reminded us of what had happened to our dream, how it turned to a nightmare. Because we feel responsible. And with every death, it makes it harder to remember how good ecstasy felt at the beginning, harder to recall why we got into the whole thing to start with."

(MS)

14

Song Lyrics: Ebeneezer Goode

'Ebeneezer Goode', The Shamen's 15th single, was released at the end of August 1992. Described as "a parody on rave culture" by the group themselves and promoted with a video featuring madcap Scottish comedian Gerry Sadowitz, the record rocketed to Number One in the UK charts. It remained at the top slot for a total of four weeks, regardless of the fact that the chorus of the song was widely believed to be a reference to the benefits of MDMA. ('Eezer Goode' = 'Es are good'.)

'Ebeneezer Goode'
Words and Music by Colin Angus and Richard West
Copyright © 1992 Warner Chappell Music Ltd, London W6 8BS
Reproduced by permission of IMP Ltd

A great Philosopher once wrote . . .
Naughty Naughty

There's a guy in the place with a bittersweet face
And he goes by the name of Ebeneezer Goode
His friends call him 'Eezer and he is the Main Geezer
And he'll vibe up the place like no other man could
He's refined, sublime, he makes you feel fine
Though very much maligned and misunderstood
But if you know 'Eezer he's a real crowd pleaser
He's ever so good – he's Ebeneezer Goode
You can see that he's Mysterious, Mischievous and Devious
As he circulates amongst the people in the place
But once you know he's Fun, and something of a Genius
He gives a Grin that goes around from face to face to face
Backwards and then Forwards, forwards and then backwards
'Eezer is the geezer who loves to muscle in
That's about the time the crowd all shout the name of 'Eezer
As he's kotcheled in the corner, laughing by the bass bin

79

'Eezer Goode 'Eezer Goode
He's Ebeneezer Goode
'Eezer Goode 'Eezer Goode
He's Ebeneezer Goode
'Eezer Goode 'Eezer Goode
He's Ebeneezer Goode
'Eezer Goode 'Eezer Goode
He's Ebeneezer Goode
He's Ebeneezer Goode

"Has anyone got any Vera's ?"
Ya Ha Ha Ha . . . Lovely
A Great Philosopher once wrote . . .
Naughty Naughty, Very Naughty
Ha Ha Ha Ha

Ebeneezer Goode Leading Light of the Scene know what I mean ?
He created the Vibe –
He takes you for a Ride as if by Design
The Party ignites like it's comin' Alive
He takes you to the Top, shakes you all around
Then back down – you know as he gets mellow
Then as smooth as the groove that's making you move
He glides into your Mind with a sunny "Hello!"
A Gentleman of Leisure he's there for your Pleasure
But go easy on old 'Eezer he's the love you could lose
Extraordinary fellow, like Mr Punchinello
He's the kind of geezer who must never be abused
So when you're in Town and Ebeneezer is around
You can sense a presence in the sound of the crowd
He gets them all at it – the party starts rocking – the people get excited
It's time to shout LOUD!

'Eezer Goode 'Eezer Goode
He's Ebeneezer Goode
'Eezer Goode 'Eezer Goode
He's Ebeneezer Goode
'Eezer Goode 'Eezer Goode
He's Ebeneezer Goode
'Eezer Goode 'Eezer Goode
He's Ebeneezer Goode
He's Ebeneezer Goode
He's Ebeneezer Goode

Got any Salmon – sorted
Ya Ha Ha Ha
Ya Ha Ha Ha
Ya Ha Ha Ha

'Eezer Goode, 'Eezer Goode, 'Eezer Goode
Oh what a carry on
'Eezer Goode, 'Eezer Goode, 'Eezer Goode

Wicked
'Eezer Goode, 'Eezer Goode, 'Eezer Goode
He's Ebeneezer Goode
Oh what a carry on

Wicked

15

Ecstasy And The UK Press II

The drug in the news, 1989–1994

30 January 1989

Sun

'Ecstasy Wrecked My Life'

The *Sun* publishes an interview with former ecstasy user Guy Murray, the 21-year-old "son of wealthy west London parents". He tells how "my male friends all started screwing each other in a storage room" after taking E - even though "they were all totally straight, not gay at all". He also says he watched "someone he knows" have sex with "a 14-year-old virgin" who'd taken a pill. "It is the usual way to bonk a virgin on the acid house scene," he explains.

30 March 1989

The Times

'First Ecstasy Death'

An inquest into the death of Janet Mayes, who collapsed at an acid house party in Hampton Court, Surrey, in 1988 after taking two ecstasy pills, hears that the 21-year-old was found to have "20 times the drug's safe limit in her bloodstream". She is "the first person in Britain to die from an overdose of the drug".

26 June 1989

Sun

'Spaced Out!'

"Drug-crazed kids – some as young as 12 – boogied for eight hours yester-day" at an illegal acid party promoted by Tony Colston-Hayter's Sunrise organisation in an aircraft hangar at White Waltham in Berkshire, reports the *Sun*. "Evil dealers openly peddled drugs to the background of mind-bending music and lasers."

11 November 1989
Daily Telegraph
'10 Years In Jail For Acid House Party Organiser'
Robert Darby begins a 10-year prison sentence for "conspiracy to manage premises where he knew controlled drugs would be available". Darby had been the main organiser of three acid parties in London in late 1988, including an event on a Thames pleasure cruiser. "His party invitations offered youngsters 'a good trip' rather than a good time," comments then Home Office Minister David Mellor. "Most people will welcome the good long trip he has got in return." Darby's "assistant", Leslie Thomas, is later jailed for five years, his sentencing delayed because he bunked off to Tenerife while on bail.

10 March 1990
Melody Maker
'The Great Rave Debate'
Chief Superintendent Ken Tappenden, head of the police Pay Party Unit, and rave promoter Jeremy Taylor take part in a debate at the *Melody Maker* office. Tappenden: "What we're trying to do is control what's happening around you (pointing at Jeremy). We knew from the first few weeks of our operation – and I hope you won't mind me being as blunt as this, Jeremy – that any day you were going to get hurt or taken right out of the action . . ."

23 July 1990
Independent
'Police Criticised Over Acid House Raid'
A raid on a rave at Gildersome, near Leeds, leads to a staggering 836 arrests and is followed by complaints of police heavy-handedness. "I saw one lad on the floor being hit by truncheons," says one raver.

6 September 1990
Sun
'George's Hell On Ecstasy'
George Michael confesses to having taken ecstasy after Wham! split up in the mid-1980s. "They were perhaps my darkest days," he declares.

31 January 1991
Independent
'Gun Gangs Force Nightclub To Close'
The Hacienda in Manchester – "Britain's hippest nightclub" – announces it is to close after a gang threatens door staff with a handgun. It's the

second gun incident at the venue within a month. "We were forced into taking this drastic action to protect our employees, our members and all our clients," says owner Tony Wilson. "We are sick and tired of dealing with instances of personal violence." The club re-opens a few weeks later.

9 January 1992
London *Evening Standard*
'Killer Ecstasy Pills Flooding Into London'
Commander Roy Penrose, the head of Scotland Yard's Regional Crime Squad, reveals that 66,200 ecstasy pills were seized in the London area in 1991 – a 12-fold increase on the 5,500 seized in 1990.

17 February 1992
Daily Star
'Ecstasy Mega Bust'
Dutch police discover a staggering 2.5 million tablets in a raid on an ecstasy factory in a village near Rotterdam. The operation had been run from a garden shed, with tablets hidden in furniture and shipped to the UK. A total of 17 people are arrested, four of them in London. The Dutch authorities also recover £5 million in cash and "an arsenal of weapons, including sub-machine-guns and automatic pistols".

23 March 1992
Today
'TV Bob's Fury Over "E For Ecstasy" Shirt'
Bob Holness, the presenter of the teenage TV quiz show Blockbusters, threatens court action over a t-shirt featuring a picture of him holding a tablet below the words, 'Can I have an 'E' please, Bob?' The slogan picks up on the fact that, for months, contestants on the alphabet-based show have prompted sniggering from the studio audience when selecting the letter E.

10 August 1992
Woman
'Brian Had So Much . . . Ecstasy Ended It All'
The popular woman's magazine tells the story of 20-year-old Liverpool lad Brian Moss, who died after taking a single E in October 1991. His mother, Vera, found him in convulsions on his bedroom floor. "I put a peg in his mouth to stop him biting his tongue and tried to stop him choking," she says. "Foam started coming out of his mouth – white at first, then all mixed with blood." Brian subsequently died in the ambulance taking him to hospital.

3 September 1992
Sun
' "E" Kids Dog-Gone On Worm Tablets'
A welfare worker discovers that Bob Martin dog worming tablets are being passed off as ecstasy in the Manchester area. "We don't know whether to send in the drugs squad . . . or the dog wardens," says a police spokesperson.

2 October 1992
Daily Mirror
'Eee Orville! Are You On Ecstasy?'
Children's TV ventriloquist Keith Harris defends his appearances at raves with his puppet duck, Orville, in support of a dance mix of his 1982 hit, 'Orville's Song'. The track is based around the puppet's 'I wish I could fly' catchphrase. "I'm not promoting using drugs," insists Harris. "I just go out there and waggle my duck."

27 March 1993
Melody Maker
'We're Not Out To Shock People'
"Everything's so watered down now," complains King Duncan of industro-techno outfit Sheep On Drugs. "I mean, 'E's are good' – what sort of a thing is that to put in a song?"

3 June 1993
Daily Mirror
'Flake Girl Rachel Set For TV Comeback In Hair Gel Ad'
Rachel Brown, the model in the Cadbury's Flake chocolate bar TV advertisement, returns to work after spending three months in a psychiatric ward as a result of having her drink spiked with E at a party in Liverpool.

December 1993
The Face
'Wonderland UK'
"After 12 years of Conservative government our society has become disparate, cocooned and cold," writes Gavin Hills in an article sub-titled 'Why People Take Drugs And Go To Clubs'. He describes the clubs and drugs network as "one of the few communities that remains . . . one of the few support systems people have". Yet "while trying to live in a world of constant hedonism may be an admirable enough goal, you have to ask where it will all end up. When is it time to stop?"

3 May 1994
Daily Mail
'The Rave Of Death'
Two teenagers, John Nisbet and Andrew Dick, die in a single night after taking ecstasy at the Hanger 13 venue in Ayr, Scotland. "Six other youngsters who collapsed after taking the drug on Saturday night were treated in hospital and reports were still coming in yesterday of young men and women feeling unwell following the dance," says the *Mail,* whose story is published two days after the deaths.

July 1994
Mixmag
'Drugs And The Army'
A report on the use of drugs in the British Army. Among those interviewed is Kevin, who is stationed in Germany and belongs to the Lost It Posse. "I go fucking mental, me!" he declares. His "preferred mode of letting off steam" is "seven trips, four or five wraps (of speed) and a couple of Es, followed by 250bpm hardcore techno". He claims to know of 23 soldiers busted by the military police for possession of drugs in an 18-month period.

22 August 1994
Daily Mirror
'Close Disco Of Death Pleads Tragic Sister'
Andrew Stoddart, 22 years old, is the third E fatality at Hanger 13 in Ayr in less than four months. "I am numbed," says the venue's manager, Christine Ridha.

16

Ecstasy and Raving America I:
San Francisco, California

An oral history created using quotations from interviews conducted in San Francisco, California, in the autumn of 1997.

Scott Hardkiss (DJ/producer): You can't ask, 'When did the scene start in San Francisco?' You can't ask that. It started here the first time a buncha tramps got together with a buncha acid in their pockets. I mean, this is San Francisco, man! SAN FRAAANCISCO! We invented this shit. Not some fucking Brits who come in with American records, saying they're bringing a fucking psychedelic revolution . . .

Dianna Jacobs (promoter of Toon Town): There are a lot of Brits in San Fran. Things always happen the same way with them. They leave the UK thinking they're going on vacation. They arrive and are like, 'Oooh, this weather, this lifestyle!' Things are a zillion million billion times more laid-back here than in Britain. The economy's a lot nicer, too. So they end up staying. Poor dears, they all look so grey when they arrive.

Jenö (DJ with the Wicked Sound System): When we arrived, we were admired for being British. Imagine what it was like being white people arriving in Africa, when their whiteness meant they were received as gods. I mean, when I left London, I was just some guy involved in the squat scene. I used to find spaces in London for an acid sound system called Tonka. I DJ'd at some parties. I was just like some young, punk, animal-rights-north-London-squatter-DJ-person. But we were welcomed as gods.

Markie Mark (DJ with Wicked): We all left Britain in 1990, 1991, for the same reason – because we kept running into brick walls. I was a DJ with Tonka. But things in the UK were getting squashed. We were all kinda liberal, lefty, psychedelic, free party, you know, devotees.

But everything was becoming too difficult with the police or too commercial.

Jenö: Markie came with this friend of ours called Alan McQueen. Alan McQueen was this face who was promoting at The Brain club in London. He was involved in this whole weird scene in Britain, the zippie scene. They were all crazy, those zippies – theories about E bringing back prehistoric rituals and stuff. But Alan was a genius, he had great plans in his mind. He travelled to San Francisco with Markie in 1990. It was to hear Terrence McKenna speak at a psychedelic conference or something. They went with this other guy who was involved in all the zippie stuff, this journalist, Mark Heley. Mark Heley considered himself very intellectual.

Dianna Jacobs: Mark Heley had all this talk none of us had heard before. Zippies and schmippies and ecstasy taking us back to Eden. When I first met him I was like, 'Big words! A philosophy degree from Cambridge!' He scared me 'cause he took it all so seriously: ecstasy as a path and technology as your friend and all that. He had these big, owl-like glasses. So he was like a brain. So was Alan McQueen. Alan seemed to have a lot of history behind him.

Jenö: Before he left Britain, Alan McQueen said to me, 'If I don't come back, you've got to come and get me, OK?' He didn't come back. He sent me a postcard – one of those funky San Francisco cards with all sorts of colours and a VW Beetle on it. 'You gotta come out here!' he said. I wrote back, 'Love to come out, have no money.' So he wrote, 'Sell my car, buy a ticket.' So I sold the car. I came to San Francisco. With 50 dollars and a box of records.

Jason Walker (promoter of Come-Unity): They said they all came here with no agendas. But they had agendas. Ecstasy culture had seemingly failed in Britain in the early Nineties. Police. People too drugged out. Peace and love gone.

Dianna Jacobs: They saw San Fran as a second chance. A place where the rave dream could work. A Utopia. That's why everyone comes to San Francisco. To find their dreams . . .

DJ Garth (Wicked): I knew all these people – Markie, Alan, Jenö, Mark Heley – from Tonka parties back in Britain. I used to go to all the Tonka parties and dance. I'd moved to San Francisco a year before they all arrived, just to find myself. When they came, they were all sleeping on my kitchen floor. I was the only one with a flat and a green card. My apartment was like a little England.

Jenö: There wasn't much of a house scene here, no E scene. Just a kinda gay scene.

Dianna Jacobs: There was a really cool house scene going on here at the time the Brits were arriving – gays and straights mixing, lots of freaky club-kiddy kinda stuff. One DJ, Pete Avila, was doing this wild night called Osmosis. I was doing parties with my partner, Preston Lytton. We called them Stacey's Seafood Salad, Babar's Banana Boat and stuff like that. But the British weren't really into it. It was all American diva house and deep stuff, kinda New Yorky and not their acid business. So they made their own parties.

Jenö: My second night in San Francisco, we went to Baker Beach. We took a little sound system and set up the turntables. That was the first Full Moon rave. There were no flyers, we just called 50 people and they all came down. It was beautiful. It was my second night in San Francisco, and I was DJing, watching the sun come up, looking at the Golden Gate Bridge . . . I couldn't believe it.

DJ Garth: It was a beautiful morning, the fog rolling back over the Golden Gate Bridge and all that, and we were blown away that we'd actually done this. That we were in San Fran and we were having a proper acid house party. We gave ourselves a name – Wicked – and we did parties every month. Me, Jenö and Markie DJed, and Alan McQueen was the promoter.

Jenö: We took the acid house smiley face, we had whistles, strobe lights and stuff at the first parties – you know, things that had been new in Britain years before but had never arrived here: ecstasy house culture. Of course, in San Francisco, the end result was *nothing* like it had been in the UK. The attitude is too different.

Dianna Jacobs: The whole idea of rave and E was infiltrating in 1991, and supplanting the whole gay-straight club-kiddy glitter thing. The Brits were coming and saying, 'Oh, we've been doing this for years, we know about it and rave is the real deal, blah-blah-blah . . .'

Markie Mark: Within a year, a new culture had erupted. There were a lot of psychedelics, a lot of ecstasy. And everyone was looking for more. The Full Moon raves were huge.

Robbie Hardkiss (DJ/producer): In a way, San Francisco's a desperate place. It's full of drop-outs, psychos and runaways. Every kid who lands here comes looking for counterculture. And when they find a bit of what they think is counterculture, they go nuts with it.

Wade Hampton (record shop owner and manager of the Hardkiss Brothers): The Full Moon parties appealed to people here. Wicked had somehow tapered the British rave concept to appeal to a very San Francisco sensibility. Kids were getting pretty mental with, like hippy-shit naturalism and cosmic stuff. All kinds of freaky things started getting really popular. There was a kind of one-upmanship going on between the crowd: people hang-gliding, people nude, people on stilts, people on unicycles – every Northern-California-weirdo thing you could imagine, filling the sky and the beach for miles. They were ecstasy rituals, like creating a wonderland, but not with whistles and face masks. It was really back-to-Mother Earth California stuff.

Scott Hardkiss: Lots of people talked lots of bullshit at those parties. It would start raining and people would be like, 'It's a symbol! Maaaagic!'

Jason Walker: The day of a full moon is a very heavy day for energy. Like a Druid, pagan magic day, right? Celebrate the Mother. Lunar tides pulling and everything. I remember one Full Moon at Grey Whale Cove on Santa Cruz beach. As everyone started coming up on their ecstasy, a huge ring formed around the DJ. Thousands of people holding hands, running in a circle, spinning. To me, it was like going back to witchcraft, to pagan magic rituals. We were linking up with some pretty cosmic things. It wasn't like 'Yeah, now we're all going to hold hands'. Fuck, the music just made you do it. Well, the drugs, too.

Wade Hampton: I saw the same aliens as, like, 200 people at one Full Moon and I am not exactly a super-huge believer in that sort of thing. But I'm telling you right now, *that shit came in!* The parties and the drugs were, well, they were making magic.

Dianna Jacobs: It was like Wicked had some kinda higher power. They were like talented aliens from another planet. At one Full Moon rave, I went up to Jenö and was like, 'You are an alien, I've seen your space ship, you're from another planet. I know, I've seen your space ship!' We were all trippin' real hard with ecstasy. And I think we were all enamoured by the Brits. Their accents, their style of music, the fact that they had already had this really wonderful experience, which was part of what gave us our experience. We felt we owed something to them. Even though the whole Sixties thing was ours.

Malachy O'Brien (promoter of Come-Unity): I came to San Francisco from Ireland in 1991. And the second I arrived and saw what Wicked were doing, I thought, 'Yes, this could be something'. To me, what happened in Britain in the Eighties, with the Summer Of Love, is essentially what happened here with the Sixties Summer Of Love. In the Sixties, something happened to people on LSD and they wanted others to share it. It was the same with ecstasy in Britain. Something was trying to expand our consciousness. The same kind of movement. It was only natural for us to try to provoke an E movement in San Francisco. Like connecting the dots.

Ira Sandler (club owner): It was all very strange. These people coming from the UK and seeing San Francisco in these historical terms. You know, knowing about the great moments this city's had and wanting to recreate it. Kinda like coming to America and wearing cowboy boots.

Sunshine Jones (DJ/producer with the Dubtribe Sound System): But people here bought it whole hog. British DJs became 'shamen'. British promoters became 'spiritual leaders'. It was like British colonialism reinvented. With drugs to sedate people.

Ira Sandler: Ecstasy and rave culture did strange things to kids here. It made them want leaders. The British contingent became leaders.

Sunshine Jones: The people to tell our poor little confused American heads what it all meant.

Scott Hardkiss: All these people filling their heads up with lazy, neo-hippy British hippy *shit*!

Ira Sandler: Wicked were good party-makers, but I dunno if they really wanted all that social responsibility. But Mark Heley . . . He snuck in with Toon Town and became the Billy Graham of the rave scene here. He really took all the ecstasy spiritual leader schtick over the top. Everyone was hypnotised by him. He was a journalist, he had the talk. He was so British.

Dianna Jacobs: Mark Heley wanted to come in with Preston and I on our parties. Actually, I asked Mark to come in. Mark and I were dating

91

and it was a tragic love for me. He wrote for *i-D* and *The Face*, and he had all these great ideas and the ability to interface with the media. He had connections with this [Bay Area cyber/tech-culture] mag *Mondo 2000* and with people in Silicon Valley. It was a whole other world for me: technology and mind expansion and everything. Mark could really talk the talk. He built the hype around Toon Town, which is what we started calling our raves. He became the guru.

Jason Walker: There would be times at the Toon Town parties, this was around 1992, where groups of us would all just be lying around in heaps on E, you know, all touching each other and stuff. And Mark Heley would be there, observing us. It was like he was trying to be God. It was creepy. It was like we were research.

Dianna Jacobs: You know Douglas Rushkoff? The author. He wrote this book called *The Ecstasy Club* and he based the story on Toon Town, on me and Mark Heley. *The Ecstasy Club* is about a cult, but it's placed in a rave environment – it's like a rave cult with ecstasy and all that. There's this leader who brainwashes and hypnotises people, which is based on Mark, and I'm his girlfriend. From what Douglas said, he felt what he saw at Toon Town was very cult-like. Leaders and followers. Miramax bought the rights to that book and it worries me a bit, because I don't want my parents going to the movie and associating me with a cult.

Zach Levi, narrator of *The Ecstasy Club* (Harper Collins, 1997): "I guess the first thing people would want to know is how one decides to join a cult at all. Or, as in our case, to start one from scratch. I suppose for Moonies and Krishnas it's something one just falls into. You're bored or lonely or hungry – things basically suck in one way or another – and the cult can relieve the pain . . ."

Ira Sandler: Toon Town is where it started getting a bit weird. The way those kids talked! But all it was, was parties and ecstasy and false hope. I mean, 'Technology will lead you'? Where?

Dianna Jacobs: Mark Heley's master plan was to create a new interface between technology and rave. A tech-playground thing. A place where people could come and experience technology in a different setting. An example would be, if you took a computer and put it in a sauna room instead of on a desk in an office, and gave someone their first computer experience that way, they'd think very differently about what computers were meant for. And with that the person could perhaps devise new uses for it. So we had brain machines, lots of digital media like interactive TVs, a holographic exploratorium, things like that.

Sunshine Jones: The Toon Town crowd was very young. You know, second wave of rave, right? I think they really thought they were going to change the world with electronic music and E and fucking lasers and brain machines and smart drugs.

Dianna Jacobs: We always sold smart drugs to help people with their thinking processes. We pushed smart drugs really hard. Mark thought smart drugs were an important addition to our parties. Smart drugs are different nutrients and amino acids – you take them for enhancement of thinking and increased memory activity. Drugs to make your brain work better. The thing about them was that they were an alternative to dangerous drugs and alcohol. Like, 'Let's drink something healthy instead of taking something bad'. So it was a *positive* approach to partying.

Pete Avila (DJ): All the kids at the parties all took E. They only took smart drugs to make their E work better. But Heley and his little technology circle were experimenting with other, more hardcore drugs. Weird, psychedelic, unknown territory shit. Now, I've done my fair share of drugs, but DMT and all those rare psychedelics? No siree, keep that stuff *away*!

Dianna Jacobs: Things got really huge at the end of 1992. The parties went up to 7,000 people. Mark started going mental. He'd brought in all these heavy-duty investors and business types, and we were throwing these massive, successful parties . . . And there I was, living on some tiny salary, barely able to pay my share of the apartment rent. We broke up. I was sleeping in the Toon Town office for a while. I decided to take him to court, but I dropped charges because of emotional stress. You could say the San Francisco rave dream was falling apart – and fast. And not just with us. I felt bad. I kept thinking, 'What about the *kids*?' They relied on us!

Markie Mark: When the police began clamping down in 1993, they really demonised Alan McQueen. Alan was the official face of the Full Moons. And the chief of police's daughter got caught doing E and going to a Full Moon or something. So Alan became a devil. The police were on Alan's back all the time. Once they arrested him for carrying a hash pipe.

Jenö: The police forced us to move all raves outside the city limits. That's when things started going wrong, really. We were doing the Full Moons down in Santa Cruz. There was this really beautiful beach there called Bonnie Dune.

DJ Garth: Bonnie Dune was like a natural fortress, a beach protected by dunes and cliffs. You had to walk miles and down dunes before reaching the site.

Jenö: It was at Bonnie Dune that some guy fell off the cliff. Too many drugs. I'm playing records, right, and everyone is dancing, on E, la-de-da. I look down to change the record, look up, and nobody is dancing. I was like, 'Oh, what, bad track?' No! This guy had fallen off the cliff. You should see those cliffs, they are high, jagged, with very difficult waters underneath and rocks and stuff. He literally landed on his head. He stood up, wobbled about a bit and then he was fine, then he went off. The following month, this other guy – I guess he was having such a great time, he thought he was a dolphin or something – jumped off the cliffs into the water. Then another guy jumped in a fire nude a coupla times, all freaked out on drugs, and had to be dragged out. It didn't stop the party, but we were freaked. We were like, 'OK, we're getting to that point where things like this happen'. We had thousands of people on the beach and no control. It was a precursor, I can see it now, it was a build-up to what would happen. Malachy O'Brien's accident.

Markie Mark: To understand the magnitude of Malachy's accident, you have to understand the magnitude of Malachy.

DJ Garth: He had this weekly club night called Come-Unity which was very conscious – lots of information-giving and hugging and helping.

Martin O'Brien (rave promoter): He'd let homeless kids stay in his loft. He would give all his fuckin' money away to Greenpeace and shit. A real rare breed, y'know?

Markie Mark: Kids saw him not just as a promoter, but as a spiritual leader.

Jason Walker: Malachy wasn't like a Mark Heley-type. He didn't want glory or money or anything like that. Malachy was from Ireland, you know. Really into peace and love and intent on finding solutions to disillusionment. We did these weekly parties together called Come-Unity. Me and Malachy thought, 'Rave is changing consciousness as a generation, hopefully we can do something with it. Something positive'. We didn't want rave to be a drugs culture which got left in the dust. We wanted to show people how to translate those wonderful altered experiences into things that could work in their everyday lives.

Malachy O'Brien: It was like 'come, unity!' We were asking unity to be our friend. We wanted to teach people to live more holistically.

Markie Mark: Of all the people to be hurt. God! It was so unfair. I remember the night it happened. It was at the Full Moon in March 1993. Something about that party seemed different from the first minute. There was a real sense of community, which wasn't happening that often any more by then. But this feeling was really strong, almost eerie. Anyway, after the party, once the sound system had been packed into the Wicked van, Alan McQueen, his girlfriend Trish and Malachy went to drive home in it together.

Malachy O'Brien: We shared a joint and decided to go into Santa Cruz before going home. We wanted to get some coffee and donuts at this place called the Flying Saucer. Alan was driving the van, a rickety old thing. I was in the back with my dog and the speakers. Alan fell asleep and lost control of the vehicle around Candlestick Park, ironically, a location for one of the earlier Full Moons. There was a very amusing piece of art in Candlestick Park. It was called A Drum Set For Future Primitives and I loved it. It was all galvanized metal columns, sheared off, a big crude metal thing coming out of the earth . . .

Markie Mark: Alan fell asleep at the wheel and the van rolled into the Bay, just near Candlestick Park, the football stadium. Thankfully, the tide was out, so they just landed in mud.

Malachy O'Brien: My dog died in the accident. She got out of the van and got knocked down on the freeway. Her name was Una, which is Gaelic for unity.

Markie Mark: The van rolled over and the sound system rolled over Malachy. It crushed him, crushed his spine. He became paralysed from the neck down. It was a turning point for the scene. Everyone freaked out.

Malachy O'Brien: It was harsh after the accident. Alan and Trish came to visit me when I was in the hospital. I dunno if . . . I think they were getting into harder drugs then. Pressures, feeling guilty, you know. I don't know if I drove them to it or what.

95

Jason Walker: I went to visit Alan at his home, to talk to him, tell him not to fuck himself up, but he was so loony tunes. He kept pointing a flashlight out of the window and telling me people were watching him in the tree outside. He was pointing his light on the tree, looking for a government agent: 'Oh my God, there's someone there, there's someone there'. All this paranoid, schizoid stuff when I was trying to have a cup of tea with him and talk to him. It was horrible. After that, I saw that a lot of my dreams weren't materialising as I'd hoped. I'm sure a lot of people did. If you're really into ecstasy, a negative energy in an environment can be really damaging. For me, it became like psychic rape.

Markie Mark: There were a lot of people just lost. Like, the energy at the beginning of all this was wonderful. But people didn't feed it back into their lives. They gave up their lives and were, like, 'I want to live the rave, I want to live on E'. Eventually, many became full-time partyers, so they had no experience to feed back into the scene. They were looking for leadership in others when they couldn't find it in themselves. So when they lost their gurus – Alan, who had to leave, Malachy, who became wheelchair-bound, and Mark Heley, who went a bit mad and split town – they lost themselves.

Ira Sandler: It was like everyone suddenly had a dose of reality. Like, 'Embracing smart drugs and technology will lead you' . . . It didn't. 'Computers are going to lead you' . . . They didn't. 'Dancing outside is going to lead you' . . . It didn't. All these messages: 'We're at the golden age – nirvana!' . . . But it just wasn't. It wasn't.

Markie Mark: After the accident, people were searching for meanings wherever they could find them. People were trying to tack an almost religious significance on Malachy's misfortune, like, 'It's a sign'. All the Bay Area promoters got together to throw a benefit for Malachy. They called the party Unity. It started with this Buddhist guy blessing the party. There was also a big video screen of Malachy speaking from his hospital bed. And something about it made me feel very uneasy. People were painting Malachy as a saint, using his emotional and physical pain to give themselves something to believe in. I've never talked to Malachy about the party. But Malachy really had no time to be embarrassed. He had no medical insurance. He was an illegal here.

Malachy O'Brien: In the strangest way, the party was what I had always dreamed of. Like, the unity Come-Unity was calling for had finally arrived. I was glad, you see? The next day, my finger moved. It hadn't moved before. It hasn't moved since. But I really feel there is hope.

96

Nothing is ever in vain. You know, action, reaction. We may have screwed up, there may be no more Full Moons, but there will be another chance. There always is. In this city, there always is.

(MS)

17

Ecstasy And Raving America II: Orlando, Florida

An oral history created using quotations from interviews conducted in Orlando, Florida, in the summer of 1998.

DJ Icey (DJ/record producer): If you are tellin' the story of Orlando rave, you are tellin' the story of the rise and the fall. The fall? It was harsh, man. But the rise? Sweet as can be.

Kimball Collins (DJ): Everything started at a club I DJ'd at called Oz – Aaaz, people called it – in this beautiful, but run-down old theatre called the Beecham on Orange Avenue. The Beecham was like this big piece of faded Florida Art Deco in the middle of downtown Orlando. One of our oldest buildings. Oz started in 1988, the year acid house started in England. We were playing acid house, Chicago house, Depeche Mode. Me and this other DJ, Dave Canalte . . .

Dave Canalte (DJ): I had just moved from Milwaukee, where I was working for this cheesy Eighties club chain called Park Avenue. They sent me to DJ at the Park Avenue in Orlando. I played alternative music – The Cure, The Smiths. Kimball used to come see me. He was always like, 'Oh you gotta come downtown, you have to see this club I do at the Beecham.' Finally, one night I went and I thought, 'Wow, this is a great idea!' A big room, kinda dirty and all the music Kimball was playing and the ecstasy . . . I was like, 'What is this stuff?' It was magic. Kimball was like, 'I told you'.

Stace Bass (promoter of Oz): Oz was the first time in ages that people simply couldn't wait for Saturday night. I used to get on the mic in the middle of the night and say things, inspirational things, to all the people on E – 'We are one!' and stuff like that. It was beautiful, hon. This was no Orlando drinking scene.

Dave Canalte: By 1989, the scene was getting heavy. Other clubs in the area, like Andy Hughes' club, Brassy's in Coco Beach, started doing Oz kinda nights and staying packed 'til 7am. This rave club thing just grew and grew, and everyone became a DJ. I'm sure everyone you speak to here will tell you they are a DJ.

Andy Hughes (DJ): It was really clear that Orlando was going to be different from the rest of the US. That rave was going to be Orlando's biggest youth culture. And real quick. All the kids down in Coco Beach really dug it – they were all so laid-back, like beach-bummy surfer types. And in Orlando proper, 80 per cent of the kids work in the service industry, mostly at Disney World and the other theme parks. They all have easy, fun lives, they spend all day smiling at customers and saying, 'Have a nice day'. They're probably all pretty bored.

Stace Bass: Yeah, Orlando's a boring place. Kids just wanna rebel. Death metal is really big here. Hip hop is big with white kids 'cause their parents hate it. Florida is a Southern state, remember. There is a real right-wingy, Bible-thumping vibe about it. It can be pretty rednecky and straight. Kids here need release. Not from hardship, but from strict parents who are racist and go to church and stuff. From the status quo.

DJ Remark: Oz opened up a Pandora's box. The repression started flowing out. The club had a good run – it closed in 1991. That was the year Icey started playing at the Edge club and things started changing, getting younger, getting nastier. The first school of E users had dissipated and this was the next school. These kids – all under 21s, practically – were drawn to Icey. He had a tough-guy mystique.

DJ Icey: I got the name Icey way back. It's not a drug thing, not like 'ice'. It's 'cause I always kept my apartment so cold. I used to put the AC on 40 degrees and my roommate started calling me Icey.

DJ Sandy: I played at the Edge with Icey. He's a weirdo, like the kinda guy you never know what he's thinking. But the kids loved his mystery and his music, too. See, Icey played breaks – funky breaks – not straight house beats. What he played was like a hip hop-house hybrid, mainly influenced by Miami bass: the really heavy sub bass with a simple break running at 120 bpm and some electro on top. The Es here were always slow Es, not the speedy stuff, so the fast British hardcore shit never really kicked off here. Icey would play some hardcore records, but he would pitch 'em down to 120 bpm. I don't think people did that anywhere else. But in Orlando, people couldn't take anything faster.

AK 1200 (DJ): There was a real stigma surrounding the kids that went to the Edge, mostly made up by old school Oz people who were scared of the younger teens. People called the Edge kids 'trash gangster ravers'.

DJ Sandy: Gangster ravers. It was kind of a good description, except they were all pretty much middle-class. Not real gangsters.

AK 1200: They were just into the whole American cool-seedy-rave thing. They went so far out of their way – they'd have the bog chain wallet hangin' out and the super-big nasty jeans and the backpacks, and they'd try to act hard, walking by sideways, tippin' their hat at chicks and sayin' 'Yo'. They thought they were the shit, stayin' up until two the next afternoon and not taking a shower and havin' a big brown ring going round the bottoms of their jeans . . .

DJ Sandy: The Edge could fit 10,000 every Saturday. And it would get to capacity most weekends. It was like a big, crazy barn full of teenagers breakdancing to funky breaks. Now it's a country & western club. It's those wafers that killed Icey's club, man. Wafers were these large-sized Es that showed up a coupla years into the Edge. They were almost the size of a nickel.

Bevin O'Neil (promoter of the Firestone club): The people who brought the wafers in were out of town drug dealers, people from Texas. People called those pills Texas tallboys for a while. Then they started calling them wafers. They were shoddy shit and they came in because all the dealers in fuckin' America knew Orlando was a big scene, and that the kids would eat anything. I knew the main guy who brought them in. He was British. Got kicked out of England or something. Anyway . . . Nobody knew what the fuck was in those pills.

Chris Hand (Knight Life Records): They were synthetic! Wafers were synthetic! They were E but they were synthetic! It was in the newspaper, what was in them, and they said that they were melting fertiliser to keep the pill powder together. And fertiliser is poison.

Jeffrey Lee Alderson (DJ): I heard that they analysed one of those things and found some kinda bathroom cleaner in there. Or maybe it was Carbondo, that stuff you repair cars with.

'Danny' (high school student/raver): They were heroin, those pills. Kids getting hooked on heroin.

AK 1200: Heroin. That was such a big lie. Why would somebody want to cut an E pill with heroin, when H costs five times as much as E? Kids'd see the brown specks in the wafer pills and think, 'Oooh. Brown. Heroin.' They were these chocolate chip wafers, which were just loaded with brown dots, but I think the brown dots were crystal meth.

Chris Hand: Wafers would make you throw up. When you ate one, you threw up within 15 minutes – blowing the fuck up, puking like crazy. And you'd be high for 12 hours. I once ate four of them. I couldn't speak. I thought I was going to die. I ended the night crying in my car.

Jeffrey Lee Alderson: They might've been dirty, but they made you real high. You could take a half and blow the fuck up. They were that strong. People were sellin' halves for $30. And the half would get you out. You'd blow up on a half.

Chris Hand: Everyone at the Edge did 'em. 'Cause when there's one kinda E goin' round a city the size of Orlando, there's one kinda E. And for two years at the Edge, from 1994 to when it closed, there was a quality drought and wafers were all you could get. People starting dropping on 'em, but kids still did 'em.

Jeffrey Lee Alderson: I was at the Edge when one girl died. I was outside when it happened and saw them carryin' her. It was six or seven in the morning and they were runnin' with her, yellin' 'Get out of the way!', and she was already dead. I guess she just OD'd. She'd been sittin' in a corner of the courtyard. Her friends couldn't wake her up. So they got the security. I don't know how long they left her like that, but if she was already stiff when they were carryin' her . . . I thought this other guy was gonna drop on us that night, too, 'cause he had eaten three wafers at once. He was laying on the ground with two girls holdin' him, rubbin' him. His lips were blue and he was shakin'. I was like, 'Time to go home.' I'd had enough for one night.

Andy Hughes: It became some sort of twisted spectacle. 'Come! Watch them drop!' At points, it seemed like there was someone dying every two weeks. It got to the point where it was like, 'Oh, you know so-and-so? Yeah, he dropped last Saturday.' It wasn't any big scene people, like any of the important DJs, though. It was just kids. And people were becoming desensitised to it.

'Danny': I heard there were 52 deaths in Orlando in two years.

101

Chris Hand: That's what the papers wrote. Maybe not 52, but there were dozens of deaths. I'm sure lots were H, though. I think we have the number one death-rate in the US for heroin. Yeah, yeah, I think that's true. And there was some heroin gettin' onto the rave scene. But it's always hard to tell if there's H around. Like, one of my ex-girlfriends got hooked real bad, but I never knew. You just don't expect it in the rave scene. Maybe some kids took H 'cause they thought they'd already tried it in wafers.

'Danny': I was in the middle of the whole teen scene. All us kids, we used to take out rooms at the downtown Travelodge hotel on a big night. We called it 'Ravelodge'. This kid even blacked out the 'T' on the sign, so it read 'Ravelodge'. Anyway, this one night, a buncha kids took out a room. They were eatin' wafers and roofies [the sedative Rohypnol] and whatever, maybe H, and one of 'em was just sittin' there, like slumped over, and his friends were partyin' around him. He was dead – they were partying around a fuckin' corpse. They left him in the hotel room covered in drug [paraphernalia] and wrappers and went out raving. He was found later. That's a real story.

Eli Tobias (rave promoter): The media made it sound like a horror story – people partying around this dead kid all night – but it was just like he passed out. That's what his friends thought. People fall asleep. You've been to parties where people fall asleep. It wasn't that much of a tragedy. Not that much. Just another kid who died. Just another kid . . .

Bevin O'Neil: So too many people kicked the bucket and the Edge closed in 1996. And now Icey doesn't play Orlando because he's bitter. A lot of the reason is the kids OD'ing, a lot of it is also me. When I came into power at the Firestone club, Icey fucked one of my girlfriends. So I never hooked him up to play. He did a coupla shows against me and I won, 'cause people were sick of cheesy breaks and 14-year-old junkies. People wanted quality. So now Icey's some bitter DJ who makes little breakbeat records and . . . You know who Dave Beer is? I'm the Dave Beer of America! Except promoters like Dave Beer are adored in the UK. And me, I'm hated here. Everyone here hates a success story.

AK 1200: Bevin's a loud, proud little fucker. He came out of nowhere when the Firestone club opened, around 1996, and started doing all these big things, like bringing big-name DJs from New York and London. They wanted things classy at the Firestone. Him and the Firestone's owner, John Marsa, who was kinda like a father figure to Bevin, they were very anti the Edge scene. They banned breakdancing there, to keep the Edge-y kids out. They wouldn't let kids wearing backpacks in. The Firestone was all progressive house and shit. John Marsa had the money to bring DJs like Sasha in all the time. Sasha came to Orlando 12 times in two years.

Bevin O'Neil: The DJs, they all love it here. There is a lot of great pussy in Orlando. It's the best place to get laid in America and every DJ will tell you that. Here you've got all the big tittied, blonde hair, southern drawl, big ass sluts you could ever want. And she'll fuck ya and scream your name with her heels still on – it's great! And it kept the DJs happy.

AK 1200: There was a lot less E at the Firestone. Things started getting more sex [oriented]. You take the E out, other drugs come in and the sex comes back. People started taking more roofies and GHB. E became stigmatised. And so you had all these girls on these new sexy drugs, like, just wanting to fuck!

Stace Bass: You know why they call Rohypnol the 'date rape drug', right? Men were ploppin' the stuff in girls' drinks when the girls weren't looking.

Eli Tobias: Rohypnol is odourless and tasteless and dissolves super-fast in a drink. You can't see it in a fruity or mixed drink. People were slippin' that shit in everyone's drinks. Even mine! I went to the Firestone once and I ordered a Cap[tain Morgan rum] 'n' Coke. I always order that. I was sippin' on my Cap 'n' Coke and, half an hour later, I was out! Something was really wrong. I couldn't focus, I couldn't keep my head up. It was the worst experience I ever had. You slip a roof in someone's drink and they're completely fucked up, they don't know what the hell they are doing, especially a little 90 pound girl. Like, a quarter of a roofie knocks me out. A quarter in a little bitty girl's drink and . . . Think about it. You're takin' home a sack of potatoes.

AK 1200: People would buy strips of roofs. A strip of 10 for 25 dollars. They make you pass out, but first they make you feel reeeaaal drunk. All of a sudden you get really turned on, you just really want to have sex. It's not something you want to do with somebody you just met. Especially 'cause roofies have an [amnesiac] effect and you can't remember a thing the next day. There was one guy that got sentenced to 20 years because he would slip roofies in girls' drinks, then take the girls home and take videos of himself doing the chicks, with the chicks passed out. The girls couldn't remember it, but it was all on tape . . . Him fucking all these girls all passed out, like, dead lookin'.

Eli Tobias: So there was that, the roofie problem, all over CNN, all over the newspapers. But the biggest problem was people mixing GHB with alcohol.

AK 1200: GHB was supposed to be, like, the next level of drugs. It's really sexy, kinda like E but a bit more of a downer.

Eli Tobias: Muscle men use it, 'cause it also builds muscle mass.

AK 1200: It's cheap, too. You just buy a little vial for 10 bucks, put it in water and drink it. But GHB became major trouble. It's no trouble on its own. But you can't mix that shit. Mix it with alcohol and it can put you in a coma! Mix that shit with booze and plop!

Eli Tobias: You could always tell who the GHB dealers were, because GHB is like a steroid, like a muscle-builder, and so all the body-builders would come into the clubs and deal it. Medium-shirt jock guys, I called 'em, 'cause they wore their t-shirts tight, like, size medium not large. GHB and alcohol mixing, that became the big problem at the Firestone. You saw people fallin' out on it all night. Respiratory arrest! Send them off in an ambulance!

AK 1200: Drug dealers don't give you instructions. None of the kids knew that you can't mix it.

John Marsa (owner of the Firestone): If we had given out safe drug-taking flyers in the club, we would have been shut down in a minute. It would have been admission. That's what it's like here.

Bevin O'Neil: Drug education?! In a club?! That would've been an invitation for the authorities: 'OK, yeah, we got drugs, now come in and revoke our license'. No way, man. No drug education in Florida clubs. Not allowed. It's so fucked up, man.

Stace Bass: In 1997, there were ambulances parked outside the Firestone every Sunday morning. And there are, like, 20 churches in downtown Orlando. The one the mayor goes to every Sunday morning is right across from the Firestone, where every Sunday morning there'd be hundreds of kids outside, in the middle of Orange Avenue, either doing cartwheels or fainting.

DJ Remark: All the strung-out people outside the Firestone, walking the streets, tweaking at 9am? Ambulances? Girls floppin' around on roofies? When all the churchgoers were going to church? Bad news. Our scene was going to get shut down. We knew it.

John Marsa: There was this vile senator who was looking to make a name for himself. He felt like this drug situation was going to be his ticket. So the state was pressuring the city and the city put together a volunteer task force called the Rave Review Task Force – even though their efforts were mostly aimed at clubs. The Rave Review Task Force was made up of community leaders. I think there was four or five members of the church in that group. They did a good job. They spent months on the issue. The local drug enforcement division had an ongoing and in-depth undercover investigation of all the clubs. Especially my club.

Bevin O'Neil: Why was the city so eager to shut everything down? Disney! Disney! It's all about money. Orlando's gotta be a family town! So they get what they call 'an independent task force' together – teachers and reverends. A reverend doesn't want anybody out past 11. And how is he able to relate to an atheist who is a waiter and gay and gets the same kind of spiritual reckoning at a club at five o'clock in the morning as the puritan bastard in church at fucking nine o'clock in the morning? When the Rave Review thing happened, it was really a wake-up call for me as an individual. Like, how grotesque the system really is. How civil liberties mean garbage around here. They raided my house! Like, it's four in the morning, I'm eating cereal with my cat. And six SWAT team motherfuckers with black hoods on, with grenades and shit, come to my house, look through everything, raid everything! A neighbour who knew I was connected to the Firestone had said there was a lot of traffic coming through my house. So they were trying to pin me as a dealer.

John Marsa: Both the local and state governments were trying to put new bills in place in really heavy-handed ways. And before you knew it, we had all these new, draconian bills to deal with. All clubs close at 2am, curfews for kids under 18, police at every street corner. I tried to get amendments before it all came crashing down. I mean, I don't like politics, I'm just a club owner, but I suddenly found myself speaking before senate sub-committees in Tallahassee [the state capital] every weekend. I hammered at them continually. But they did what they wanted to do. Just another notch in America's tradition of late, piss-poor, misguided responses to our society's problems, all pushed by political ambition.

105

Bevin O'Neil: It's like the Thirties Prohibition all over again.

John Marsa: It's like the Prohibition age. And what's ironic with Prohibition, is that Prohibition drew more criminals into the club business. Nobody stopped drinking, though.

Bevin O'Neil: John Marsa took on the city and lost. Our city is dead and everyone hates John Marsa because they say he caused all the problems. He became the scapegoat. And why? Because he's the only fucker around who believes in civil liberties! The only motherfucker in town who believed enough in Ben Franklin and George Washington to get off his ass and fight! But nobody in the club scene supported him. They just bitched that things aren't as good as they used to be.

Eli Tobias: Now there's no scene in Orlando. The city squashed it. Kids go to Disney to party now. Or outside city limits or in people's houses.

AK 1200: There's still just as many drugs. Now there's crystal meth and shit going around. The only difference is people do it in places where you can't see 'em. Places where there ain't no John Marsa callin' ambulances for them. It's all under the covers now.

Bevin O'Neil: The history books will say this is where the problem went away. The President's State of the Union Address will say how America is winning the War on Drugs. Bullshit! A coupla politicians now have fatter pay cheques. Kids are still OD'ing. That's the real State of the Union. Now kids die in little houses off the sides of the road. And all our Disneyland government cares about is that it's out of view. They figure, 'the club scene's dead. The problem's gone.' Gives a whole new meaning to 'Just Say No.'

(MS)

18

The Rise And Fall Of The Chill-Out Ideal

The quick rise of rave and club culture in Britain at the break of the Nineties brought with it a sudden increase in health risks. Of course: more people than ever were taking drugs. Unmonitored. In some pretty kooky, outlaw environments, too. There wasn't much talk of 'ecstasy health' those days. Dancefloors could be broiling, boiling, downright tropical. Of course: the general houseland wisdom of the time was the more yellow splotches your t-shirt amassed from dripping condensation, the better. And if the paint on the walls was softening and bubbling from the heat? And if someone passed out on the dancefloor? Well, then you knew you were in the right place. Locked in, waving an empty Evian bottle in a personal space equivalent to one floor tile, dancing like a loon on increasing numbers of ecstasy tablets.

In 1990, 'safe E' pamphlets in hand, drug information services like Release and Lifeline began knocking at the doors of club owners and rave promoters. The services noted that most clubs and events had nowhere for people to rest and cool down, and saw this as a major problem in terms of keeping the drug damage-load low. They said that a place to chill out, to get away from the blitz of beats and strobes, from the heat and barm-cakes boogie, was essential for reducing the risks being taken by E users. Many E users agreed.

"I remember going to one party somewhere around Manchester in 1991," says former raver Daniel Boulanger. "It was in a non-ventilated warehouse. One big, packed room. I was on quite a few Es and I needed space. I felt like my brain was closing in on me. I tried going out the front entrance but a bouncer informed me that, if I went out, there was no coming back in. I tried an obscure exit at the arse-end of the warehouse but was thrown back into the place by a security man who had been planted outside.

"I thought I was going to go crazy. I was sweating like mad and shivering all at once. I ended up curling myself into a ball in the corner of the warehouse, surrounded by rubbish. I was wearing a woolly hat and I pulled it down over my eyes and ears. I just needed some peace. I was too high. I couldn't go home – I couldn't have found my home. A chill-out room? Yes, I needed that. Anyone taking E that night needed that."

The concept of chill-out backrooms fanned out across UK raves and clubs in 1991 and 1992, greatly helped by the period's vogue for ambient house – the tranquil, 'horizontal dance music' of artists like The Orb and Mixmaster Morris. One of the major templates for these areas was created in 1989, at Paul Oakenfold's Land of Oz acid night at the gargantuan Heaven club in London. Land of Oz featured a couch-full back-of-the-club salon called The White Room. In this room, DJ Dr Alex Patterson of The Orb played ambient music, from Eno to Mike Oldfield to Pink Floyd, surrounded by video screens projecting soothing, aquatic images. The music was gentle, the lighting was soft, and people used it to escape the woopi-woopi acid sirens and lasers of the main dancefloor.

As the Nineties progressed, the chill-out room became more and more ingrained in the blueprint of rave and club design. But the changing tides of fashion often made the vibe of such spaces less and less conducive to actually chilling out. By mid-decade, ambient music had cleaved itself from the ecstasy massive: the 'head music' pretensions always inherent in the genre lead it out of the nightlife and returned it to the realm of the at-home listener. Back in 'avin-it clubland, some chill-out spaces began featuring DJs playing other sorts of music – often sounds as beat heavy as those in the main club. Some chill-out rooms offered live PAs. Some even boasted dancefloors. The couches remained, but the idea of creating an ideal space for E burn became muddied.

Almost ironically, First Aid areas were becoming more common in the same period. In many cases, these quiet medical spots became the only place available for ecstasy overloaders to escape the barrage of beats and dancers.

(MS)

19

Nicholas Saunders: A Personal Perspective

The following is an essay on 'ecstasy guru' Nicholas Saunders, British author of E
For Ecstasy, Ecstasy And The Dance Culture *and* Ecstasy Reconsidered,
*written by Dr Karl Jansen. Dr Jansen is a psychiatrist with the South London &
Maudsley NHS Trust and the author of* K: Ketamine, Dreams And Realities.

Nicholas Saunders (1938-1998) was a warm, big-hearted, high-energy
man. He was one of those great facilitators and generous assisters who tend
to look for good in others, rather than bad, and he was enormously toler-
ant of many different approaches to life. He has been described as a 'social
inventor', as he built a range of bizarre Professor Branestawm creations to
amuse his friends in the Sixties and Seventies, including an indoor duck-
pond, a vertical garden, a cockerel alarm clock and a fish maze. As a child,
he always wanted to know how everything worked. His respect for the
truth – and the importance of standing up for it without hypocrisy –
remained with him throughout his life.

Thirty years ago, there was an item on the London TV news about
bubbles which were coming out of a hole in the side of a building in Earls
Court. Passers-by were asked what they thought it was. One suggested it
was a Chinese laundry. Another said that he didn't know but "it was obviously dangerous and there ought to be a law against it". The inventor of
this bubble-making machine was Nicholas Saunders.

Nicholas first became known to a much wider audience with the publication of *Alternative London* and later *Alternative England & Wales*, which
came out in many editions and sold in massive quantities. This was initially
a how-to-do-it book for squatters. Around that time, a girl who was
staying with him (many girls stayed with Nicholas over the decades)
knocked over a meditation candle in his papier-mâché igloo. She didn't
know the number of the fire brigade and his place in Chelsea burned
down. No more ducks would wander in and out of the living room. A
Danish hitchhiker had a lasting impact in another way, returning home to
Scandinavia where she gave birth to Nicholas' son. Opportunities to be

fatherly were very limited, but Kristoffer came to visit when he was 15. I recall Nicholas describing the paternal affection he felt, holding his son's hand while the latter had his nipples pierced.

Nicholas moved from Chelsea to the then derelict Neal's Yard in Covent Garden. He started a wholefood shop and other now famous businesses in the area. He was an alternative entrepreneur and, at the time of his death, he was leading the fight against the local council's plan to turn the Yard into yet another treeless, table-choked tourist trap. Nicholas had a great sense of humour, too. He only owned one tie, a bright red leather monstrosity created when the Sex Pistols were in the charts. I remember inviting him to give a lecture at the London Institute of Psychiatry and telling him that he should wear a tie. Had I seen it first, I would have told him the opposite! It was a remarkable lecture, Nicholas speaking to a theatre filled with the UK's most conservative psychiatrists (it was really packed – there wasn't even standing room) about a fun afternoon on E in 1988, walking with his friend Claudia in Kew Gardens.

Needless to say, many of those present immediately decided he was mad. In many important ways, though, Nicholas was probably one of the sanest and most level-headed people in that theatre. He knew how to grasp life with both hands and avoided pettiness whenever he could. He may have looked like a vicar, but he had a wide mind and was a delightfully unpredictable eccentric. I was astounded to come to dinner at his loft, to dine with the originator of Neal's Yard Natural Foods and the owner of a vegetarian restaurant, only to be fed fatty barbecued chops! He did have a notoriously bad memory – probably the reason why he failed his engineering exams. The next time I went to dinner at his loft was with my girlfriend and we had naturally assumed he would remember that she was a vegetarian. As we sat around before the meal, the topic turned to food and I recall saying how disgusting sheep meat was. And what were we having for dinner? Barbecued lamb, of course!

Nicholas and I went to a Psychedelic Drugs conference in Hiedelberg in 1995. It was winter, snowy and frozen, but the town was beautiful. As he was a millionaire, I presumed that he had booked himself into a major hotel, but he had arranged the smallest hotel room I have ever seen in my life – almost like one of those Tokyo coffins. He decided against buying a can of Coke at the airport as he felt that it was over-priced. His genes were showing. His father was Sir Alexander Carr-Saunders, Director of the London School of Economics. Nicholas did a lot of good with the money he saved, though, and was known to make generous and substantial gestures. He spent much of his own money – and huge amounts of time – running the ecstasy.org internet website and assisting the Institute of Social Inventions run by his friend Nicholas Alberry.

That afternoon on E at Kew in 1988 became a minor legend – like Albert Hofmann's bike ride – and led to the book (now a collectors' item) called *E For Ecstasy*. Nicholas was one of the first to use mirripaper for a book cover, an innovation which has been widely copied since. He piled the books into his van and set off for the Glastonbury Festival to squat a stall. The book soon sold out, and he next produced *Ecstasy And The Dance Culture* and his final work, *Ecstasy Reconsidered*, which is by far the best of the three and a 'must read' for anyone interested in this drug.

Nicholas spent a large part of the year travelling to many different countries, in later years on the trail of psychedelic plant ceremonies in Europe, South America and Africa, collecting information for a new book he was writing about drugs and spirituality. While in South Africa in February 1998, shortly after his 60th birthday, a car driven by a young friend of his left the road and Nicholas was killed instantly. His 'green funeral', conducted by Nicholas Alberry, took place on some woodland he owned in the Sussex countryside. It was like the burial of a great tribal chieftain.

A few weeks later, some of his friends held a small, private farewell for him with some skyrockets from the top of Primrose Hill, shouting "Goodbye Nicholas, Goodbye!" up into the darkened heavens, just before his Bardo Body (which is said to circulate the Earth for 56 days) took off into the Great White Light for good. After he died, I donated a copy of *Ecstasy Reconsidered* to the Institute of Psychiatry Library and, in the future, I am hoping to send copies to all the major libraries in the UK and in other countries.

20

Script I: Snowball

Snowball was a seven-minute film made in 1994 by London clubbers Stephen Ashurst and Jake Seaman working under the name of Gonzo Productions. Taking its title from the super-strong, MDA-based pills widely available in the UK in the early Nineties, *Snowball* won the Institute of Contemporary Arts' prestigious Dick Award the year of its release. The film knits together grainy, jittery, black-and-white footage of a crop-headed guy in a dimly lit flat – watching telly, taking a leak, smoking dope, trying to kip – with a manic voice-over. The script was written by Ashurst, who also played the film's one and only character.

Snowball
Written by Stephen Ashurst
Gonzo Productions, 1994
Reproduced by kind permission

Three of us this evening, Markie, Alex and me. In the queue outside Club D there are maybe thousands of people and the waiting to get inside takes a fuck of a long time. I watch the girls out there, in between cigarettes to keep warm, looking principally at their faces and asses and admiring the fact that there's a lot of pretty, fat-assed birds just hanging around smoking, chewing gum, waiting and giving it a lot of loud-mouthed gas. A lot of gassing. And there's me and Markie and Alex hanging around silently, like not saying very much, smoking, waiting. Alex and me are also trying to pick out Steve and anticipating his wicked snowballs, fucking dancing magic balls. He's a nice geezer and his middle name's quality, QUALIT-E. This adds a certain nervous tension to the proceedings. A certain pleasure in waiting for it, ha-ha. I present to myself the now inescapable conclusion that I have a well serious addiction to fat birds, birds with extra. I fucked 12 birds this year and the only one with serious potential had this fucking beautiful plump body and brown skin all over my face shoved her pussy on my mouth give me wet fucking honey bliss. Fucking magic it was.

We get inside EVENTUALLY and find Steve chatting to his happy silent mates and after a bit of prowling around and standing and I managing to find some coins to fit the fucking cigarette machine and we wait upstairs, watching this blinding bird DJ control the fucking chaos below this toaster screaming in the mike. I want to ask Markie but he's concentrating on something so I don't. A couple of Evians and a bit of chat later and there's this fucking kick and it's this fucking beast with no name for me sneaking and snaking, ducking and diving in the central nervous system fast but its only cruising half-power yet it's only playing around so far finding its own special route to the pleasure-pain fucking synapse fucking central control centre then the fucker FUCKSHIT bends up your back and some fucking E-NORMOUS voltage has overloaded it and fuckshit here it is fuckshitfuckshit.

There's Alex and Markie dancing around in front of me, Alex fucking glasseyeballed and holding his head with some mean motherfucking hair-cut done by himself in the mirror. Me I'm worried about Markie quite worried and Alex comes over and shouts why don't you fucking SMILE you CUNT in my earhole so I smile a little ha-ha. Fucking birds every-where it seems then this girl I've noticed a little with leather jeans on and I'm contemplating the effect on her of trying to find out her name so I make this little plan and Alex fucking leans over to her smiling and she's asking him a question I cannot HEAR and he says PARANOID and grins, the cunt. She dances a little closer in this fucking strobe she's not MOVING then she fucks off after a little while I don't see her go but she does. Then these two birds Kelly and Carol appear Kelly's got on these littlehotpants and a velvet leotard piece and they look like they're flying along and they've got these OUT OF IT IT'S NOT MY PARTY boy-friends one big fucker who's Kelly's slave or love slave or cigarette porter or some shit it turns out and Carol's got this dickhead in a baseball hat with his hands down her jeans they all seem to be tolerating each other, we all suck some lollies.

Alex passes me the Vix and I can hear the toaster rapping on like a preacher, fucking insane rapping (this from Alex earlier upstairs when some birds were pointing at me) (when my knees were fucking moving around a little out of control) (this upstairs I thought my fucking heart was going to give out and I was wondering about my heart and was I going to die this time) (this time? What about last time Alex: you lost it mate, you fucking lost control – a maniac on the loose in the cloakroom queue talk about funny looks ha-ha).

So anyway I go and get a cigarette from some poor bastard who's just staring at me like he's been faced with a giant psycho and as if I'm going to rip his head off even if he thinks he might not want to and anyway I get one and go to the GENTS. It turns out to be a long way, way too long feels like half an hour to get there and I get my dick out and piss and it looks like a fucking cocktail sausage but it's chiller in here, chiller than downstairs but I'm worried about Markie so I make the trek downstairs. On the way there's this bird, this bird in lycra, a white lycra holster top, she's in the corridor just dancing by herself fucking dancing like she's coming, alone in the corridor so I have this little sit down and watch her and she just dances on anyway I can't handle it so I walk on downstairs. Markie's sitting down on the dancefloor and I ask him if he's alright but he just smiles back and looks at me and says yeah, man, yeah. So Alex comes over and says what are you doing there being so fucking BORING and I don't know. I'm getting a little edgy there's this guy dancing behind me like Michael fucking Jackson and I'm keeping a very clever eye out for steamers and knives in the fucking gut and I realise I have to sit down and chill a little. So then there's these three birds sitting next to me, all in black jeans and VELVET-E fucking tops with belt bags and fucking Stussy hats maybe tourists? And they're talking a lot and snorting big fucking gulps of amyl so they share some with me and their eyes are rolling right round their skulls and I want to take one of them home and give it some really good fucking violent action and then stroke her under a pile of duvets, as many as she's got and so I make a plan to say something but I don't know how but anyway I start dancing and walking around again and I see Steve in his favourite corner and we have a little chat and he talks a lot and then I buy some fucking water I love that particular ripoff.

The lads appreciate this little gesture but I'm a little tired now and I'm worried about Markie and anyway we all look like vampires and the Evian's gone and the toaster announces another hour of hardcore fucking uproar so then Alex has got these three cigarettes and we get up and go and get our cloaks from the room which takes a few minutes ha-ha.

So Alex I can't figure out if he's pissed off or not or wants to stay or what but he says no man, what the FUCKING HELL and I chat with him about Corinne last week the fucking sixteen-year-old who squeezed her well-overdeveloped body into a one-piece lycra skinnyribs suit all sweaty with these perfect tits who danced with me behind her my fingers on her ass touching her hot little snatch from between and I ask Markie if he's alright OK yes he is I just keep checking and we go for the exit along this corridor with people staring at each other and outside FUCKSHIT it's freezing and pissing rain allover but it's not too bad when the animal electric eel in my back twitches hard. This slippery little buzz. We dodge the decidedly dodgy traffic and then Alex and Markie head off for the Bermondsey bus and Alex rapping on about fucking Brixton so I just get on the fucking 26 and head for home. I climb upstairs and attempt ha-ha to sit at the back normally and I do. I'm not as cold as I think I should be so a series of really heavy body checks is commenced and with a bit of talking and twitching there's all the bus staring at me like I'm some crazed crackhead who's gonna hurt them maybe I will but I attempt to sit still a little longer so I can get home and sweat some more ha-ha.

21

Script II: Coronation Street

In 1995, *Coronation Street*, Britain's longest-running television soap opera, featured a storyline about ecstasy involving the character of Tracy Barlow, the then 18-year-old daughter of Ken Barlow and Deirdre Rachid. In the narrative, Tracy collapses after taking an E at a club and was rushed to hospital, where she suffers kidney damage. She subsequently undergoes a kidney transplant, the organ taken from her stepfather, Samir Rachid, who is killed in an accident a few weeks after Tracy is first hospitalised.

The following script excerpt is set in the intensive care unit of the hospital, just as Tracy is coming round.

Excerpt from *Coronation Street*
Written by Peter Whalley, Barry Hill and Sally Wainwright
Granada Television, broadcast 31 March 1995
Reproduced by kind permission

Scene 9 – Hospital (Intensive Care)

Deirdre Rachid – Anne Kirkbridge
Tracy Barlow – Dawn Acton
Lorraine Baker – Katie Bancroft
Cathy Power – Theresa Brindley
Nurse – Tracy Booth

(Deirdre sitting by the bedside. Tracy is now breathing without the aid of the machine. Tracy stirs, opens her eyes. All her dialogue is mumbled)

Deirdre: Nurse! (Delighted, to the nurse) She's awake . . .
Nurse: Calm down Tracy.
Tracy: Mum.
Deirdre: Oh love. Thank God.
Nurse: How are you feeling, Tracy?
(She takes Tracy's temperature, checks the various bits of equipment during the following)

116

Tracy: Hurts . . .

Deirdre: I know it does, sweetheart . . .

Tracy: DJ's rubbish. Can't dance to this. Too hot . . .

Deirdre: Tracy love, you're in hospital. And you've been very ill.

Tracy: Where's Eddie gone with them drinks?

Deirdre: Who's Eddie?

(But Tracy had drifted off to sleep again)

Nurse: (Sympathetically) She won't make much sense for a while yet.

Deirdre: I must phone her dad, let him know she's come round . . .

(Cathy Power enters)

Cathy: There's a friend of Tracy's here. She can see her for a few minutes, if that's all right with you?

(Lorraine enters. She's Tracy's age, but streetsmart and slightly tougher looking than Tracy. Deirdre instantly takes against her, she needs a scapegoat)

Deirdre: (Cool) Hello.

Lorraine: Lorraine. You must be her mum. How is she?

Deirdre: (Not inclined to make things easy for her) Well she won't be going dancing for quite a while. Weren't you here the other day when her dad was here?

Lorraine: (Nods) I brought her some flowers.

Deirdre: You do realise she could have died taking that muck?

Lorraine: (Indignantly) Wasn't my fault! (Then) She's never done it before, she doesn't do that sort of thing.

Deirdre: Then why did she that night then?

Lorraine: She'd been at work since early, she was knackered. This lad gives her this tab, yeah? Says it'll give her a high. Energy, like.

Deirdre: Eddie?

Lorraine: (Evasively) I don't remember his name. (Then, clearly feeling some responsibility in spite of her denial) They said she was better. She will be all right, won't she?

(And they both look at Tracy and all the equipment still around her. Cut to Scene 10 – Hospital Waiting Area)

117

22

Interview: Paul And Janet Betts

Leah Betts died in 1995 after taking a single ecstasy tablet at her 18th birthday party. Her death was the most publicised E death in the history of the drug. Leah was the only daughter of Paul and Dot Betts, who divorced in 1982, when Leah was four years old. Leah initially lived with her mother, a school teacher, but Dot died in 1992. Leah then went to live with her father, a police officer, and his second wife, Janet. Paul and Janet, a nurse, had married soon after Paul's divorce and lived in the tiny village of Latchingdon, Essex. They have since moved to Scotland. Paul and Janet have three other daughters – Wendy, Emily and Cindy, all from Janet's first marriage and all older than Leah – and a son, William, who was 11 at the time of Leah's death.

Janet Betts: She was a very happy person, very fun-loving. She loved fashion, loved pop music, loved going out with her mates. She wasn't what I'd call a regular clubber, though - not as in every weekend. She loved swimming. She could swim like a fish. She was trustworthy. Careful with her cash. Always stuck up for the underdog. She was doing well at college. She did her homework religiously. She took a lot of interest in her projects. She wanted to be a teacher, following in her mum's footsteps.

Paul: She wouldn't stand out in a crowd. She was an ordinary 18-year-old who enjoyed fun, enjoyed going out and socialising, but wouldn't mind having an evening in watching the telly, either. A normal person. I think initially some people thought she was a clubber and that she was out every night, flexing her right elbow or popping pills. But she wasn't. She was just an ordinary teenager who'd have a bit of fun when she could but study when she had to.

Janet: She went to Basildon College. It's not easy to get there from here by public transport, so she would often stay with her friend Sarah [Cargill] during the week. Sarah lived in Basildon and they'd known each other a long time. They'd been at school together.

Paul: We nicknamed Sarah 'The Shadow'. They were always together. They were totally different girls – chalk and cheese – but it was incredible the way that they got on. We're still in touch with Sarah now, though we haven't seen her for a while.

Janet: They did all the things most teenage girls like to do. Just normal things. If someone had asked me which of my children was the one most likely to take drugs, it wouldn't have been Leah.

Paul: Leah's birthday was 1 November and the party was set for Saturday 11.

Janet: The weekend straight after her birthday was Bonfire Night. She wanted to go to a party over at her college that weekend.

Paul: At the start of that year, I'd been medically retired from the police. Not then having a wage and with Jan working only part-time, we couldn't afford to pay for both a big present and a party. So we gave Leah the choice and she decided on the party.

Janet: We had it at the house. Leah had this thing about tuna at the time and she wanted to have tuna sandwiches, tuna vol-au-vents, tuna everything. I'll always remember that. I can even remember the route I took around Tescos to buy the food.

Paul: Leah went off to her Saturday job as normal, which was at Allders department store in Basildon, and I went to pick her and Sarah up to bring them back here at 4pm. We set the food out in the kitchen and cleared all the furniture from this room, the lounge, so people could dance and it wouldn't matter if anybody spewed. In my mind, I went back to when I was young and, at that time, you got rat-arsed. I never once thought any of my kids would use illegal drugs.

Janet: We hardly knew the drug scene existed. Not this kind of drug scene. We'd see the odd newspaper headline about ecstasy, but we were your typical head-up-your-bum parents. Our kids wouldn't do that sort of thing. We didn't need to know about it. I was working as a school nurse at the time and we'd been given no formal training about anything to do with drugs, no information other than, 'Oh, this is the local advisory agency if you should need them'. As a hospital nurse, I'd seen a few heroin overdoses and alcohol poisonings in Accident & Emergency, but that was about it. It was the same for Paul.

Paul: I'd formed the good old stereotypical attitude. Being a copper and picking them up off the streets to take them to Accident & Emergency or to the morgue, to me, people who took drugs were all drop-outs. Either

119

that or they were filthy rich and could afford to buy coke and so on, but that was a totally different scene anyway.

Janet: We just didn't know what was going on. We had no reason to talk to our kids about drugs and they didn't talk to us about it. You don't, do you? Well, you didn't then.

Paul: Leah and Sarah had bought four Es. Apples. They'd collected them on the Saturday morning and brought them back here with them that afternoon. I know it's stupid, but I now carry a little word in my head: 'If'. If I had educated myself about drugs and I'd spoken to Leah, might she be alive today? Nobody can answer that and it is so painful for me. Unless you've been in that kind of situation, you can't know how guilty you feel, how responsible you feel, and how much it hurts.

Janet: Leah and Sarah spent what seemed an eternity upstairs getting themselves ready for the party.

Paul: When Leah finally came down, I remember thinking, 'She's a young woman now.' She was wearing a brushed velvet maroon top and a long black pencil skirt. She looked gorgeous. As she walked along the hallway, she did a little spin, put her arms up and said, 'Will I do?' Oh, she was gorgeous. Then she came and sat on my knee and gave me a cuddle.

Janet: She was worried nobody would come, but almost everyone did. About 25 of them, I think.

Paul: They started arriving around 8.30. Some of her friends we had met before and others we hadn't, but they were all ever so nice. The hi-fi was on, there was a bit of dancing, some of them were sitting on the stairs talking. Jan and I were in the kitchen, looking after the food and watching *The Bodyguard* film on TV. People would come in, sit down, have a bit of food, have a chat, watch a bit of TV. I even came into the lounge on a couple of occasions to have a dance with Leah. At midnight, we brought in the birthday cake, which was in the shape of the figure 18. A bit later, at about quarter to one on the Sunday morning, Leah's little brother William ran into the kitchen and said, 'Can you go upstairs, Leah's not feeling well.' Jan and I sort of looked at each other and smiled. I thought, 'Silly girl's got pissed.' Jan disappeared upstairs, but within about 30 seconds William came in again and said, 'Mum wants you upstairs with Leah now.'

Janet: She was in the bathroom with her back to me, leaning over the washbasin. When she turned round, her eyes were black, like eyes in a horror film. Her pupils were totally dilated and there were no irises. I asked her what she'd been up to and she told me she'd taken an ecstasy tablet.

Paul: By the time I got upstairs, Leah had sort of collapsed around the toilet. She wasn't having convulsions exactly, but she was going rigid, then relaxed. Jan told me Leah had taken ecstasy and I remember stuff going through my head about water and so on. By now, Leah was getting very scared, so Jan and I decided to get her out of the bathroom and into our bedroom. I don't know if you've ever tried to lift somebody who has collapsed, but every bit is wobbly. The body just sags. Even though Leah was only a lightweight, it was a hell of a job to get her out. It's a small room and the door opens inwards. When I got her into our bedroom, I laid her on the floor and I automatically reverted to a police officer. It was one-word questions – what, when, where, how. She told us she'd done E four or five times before, that she'd used speed, that she'd lit someone's joint. She gave us the names of the people she'd bought the E from. Then she started to scream from a terrible pain in her head. I went to put her into the recovery position and she just stopped breathing. Jan and I looked at each other. We couldn't believe it. I gave her a shake – 'Come on, come on' – but she didn't start breathing again. I gave her mouth-to-mouth resuscitation and she started to regurgitate. We didn't know it then, but that was when Leah became brain dead. From the time she first felt ill, it took just 10 minutes for her to die in my arms on the bedroom floor.

Janet: I called the emergency services and told them Leah had taken E. Once her friends downstairs found out what was going on, the lads went into 999 mode and opened the gates ready for the ambulance.

Paul: She was taken to Broomfield [Hospital] in Chelmsford and put on a life support machine. I thought she was in a coma, as most people did at the time. But Jan, being a nurse, thought it was more than that.

Janet: Paul didn't understand what the doctors were talking about, but I did. Even so, I refused to believe it. It was as if the medical facts didn't apply. Not to Leah. I was hoping for a miracle, I suppose. The only time I dared come out with the truth was with my friend Peggy, who's also a nurse. At one point, we went for a walk outside and I said to her, 'She's not going to get through this, is she?' And Peggy said, 'I think you're right.'

Paul: Leah was in hospital for four days. On the fourth day, they carried out two sets of brain tests which proved that she was brain dead. We then had to discuss Leah's wish to donate her organs. It was one of the hardest things I've ever had to agree to. To look at her, she was perfect. There wasn't a mark on her, her chest was still going up and down, she was still warm, still cuddly . . . To then turn round to six different teams of transplant doctors and say, 'Go on, you can take your spare bits' . . . It really was hard.

121

Janet: The hospital arranged the transplant teams to come in the middle of the night to avoid the media. It was a big story by this stage, and there were reporters and TV crews everywhere. I remember being in the corridor and hearing the doctor who was in charge of the Intensive Treatment Unit, Dr Alasdair Short, on the phone to the Home Office pathologist, who was whingeing about getting more samples because of the nature of Leah's death. Dr Short was yelling into the phone, 'You can't expect the family to go through another night of this.' And I'm standing there thinking, 'That's not my daughter he's talking about.'

Paul: We didn't want her to die alone, but I couldn't bear to go down to the theatre. So Jan said she would go. I just sat in a chair. At three minutes past six in the morning, I shot upright. It was as if I'd been electrocuted. That was apparently the exact time they clamped the heart and . . .

Janet: Andy was with you, wasn't he? Your friend Andy.

Paul: Erm . . . I can't remember. Was he there at the time?

Janet: Yes. Yes, he was. Those four days . . . It was like being on another planet, wasn't it?

Paul: I was holding onto hope. I didn't know.

Janet: It was hard in the theatre. I didn't expect to be let in there, but I put it to the transplant teams that I was used to the sights and sounds in a theatre, I wouldn't be shocked by the equipment because I had seen it before, and they agreed to it. They put a screen up so I could only see Leah's head and the monitor, so I knew the point at which it went to a straight line. When they clamped her heart, she suddenly went cold and clammy. At the same time, blood poured down a tube into a bucket by my feet. I had nightmares about that for a long time afterwards.

Paul: The inquest into Leah's death was held a month to the day after she died.

Janet: I thought it was two months.

Paul: When was she buried?

Janet: 1 December.

Paul: Wasn't the inquest before the funeral?

Janet: No, it was after the funeral.

Paul: Erm . . . I don't know then. When Leah died, there were rumours that it had been a bad tablet, that she'd drunk too much water . . .

Janet: That it was the first time she'd done ecstasy. That was another one.

Paul: But the death certificate shows she died of ecstasy poisoning. There was no other drug in the tablet, it was pure E, and she'd had no alcohol. She suffered from a condition known as coning. The top of the spine is shaped like the base of an ice-cream cone and her brain swelled so much that it was forced into the spine. It cut off the blood supply, killing the brain stem. Her respiratory system collapsed, but her heart and her other organs were still alive and working on automatic pilot. That's why the organs could be donated to other people.

Janet: Eight people were helped that way. One had the heart and lungs, two had a kidney each, two had a cornea each, someone had the liver, someone else had the pancreas and a baby had part of the trachea from the throat. They also took bone grafts, which they froze and kept.

Paul: I know it's silly, but when you're thinking about them making cuts and taking bits, you think, 'Are they hurting her?' I believe the body is only the mortal part and the soul leaves, but at what point does that happen? When the heart stops beating? I suppose it's just that feeling of guilt you can't get rid of.

Janet: Leah and Sarah got the ecstasy from a club in Basildon called Raquel's. They didn't want to go in and buy the drugs themselves, though, so they asked another friend, Louise Yexley, who asked her boy-friend, Steve Smith. He was the person that Leah named as she was dying. Steve then allegedly asked one of his mates, Steve Packman, to buy the Es, which were apparently passed along the line to Sarah, then Leah. Louise and Sarah both got referred cautions. Steve Smith got two year's conditional discharge.

Paul: Steve Packman denied Steve Smith's story and went to trial twice, but there was a hung jury both times so he was found not guilty. The people at the top of the chain, though, were supposedly Tony Tucker and Patrick Tate, who were said to have controlled the drug supply in the clubs around Basildon and Romford. Just a few weeks after Leah died, they were found dead in a Range Rover in the woods at Rettenden, about five miles from here. Their driver, Craig Rolfe, was also found dead. All three of them had been blasted with a shotgun.

Janet: Allegedly over a cannabis deal which went wrong. Two guys are now in prison for the killings.

Paul: The day after these three guys were topped, we had a visit from the police. Well, more than a visit really. We were taken off to the police

123

station, our clothes were seized, the guns that we used for clay pigeon shooting were seized . . .

Janet: We were separated and questioned, once here at the house and once at the station. The police said that they knew we hadn't done it, but they had to be seen to be covering all options. It was still a very frightening experience. On the night of the shootings, we were here, being interviewed by Timothy Evans, a presenter on Anglia TV. The next day, when the police asked me where I was at whatever time it was and could anybody corroborate that, I suddenly saw Timothy Evans come up on the TV, which was on mute. I said to this copper, 'See that man? Well, he was sitting right where you are now at the time.' The next time Timothy came here, he told us the police had gone to Anglia TV and asked him about it.

Paul: Leah's death has affected us in lots of different ways. For me, I had to have some good come from it. There was the 'Sorted' poster and video, then Jan and I set up Action for Drug Awareness – ADA – and we give presentations to schools, colleges and so on. It's easy for kids to see the pleasurable side of drugs and dispel the other side. We talk about all aspects, the pleasurable side and the other side.

Janet: With regard to Leah's sisters, it was very awkward for Wendy, the eldest. She's a mental health nurse and many of the people on her unit are there because of drugs. She still has bad days over Leah. She told me that the other day. Emily, the next one, was still a student when Leah died. She came straight home and couldn't go back [to university] for a long time. She kept packing her bag but then she'd say, 'It's no good, I can't go.' That went on for several weeks. Cindy, our third daughter, was also at university at the time and, unbeknown to us, she knew Leah had been experimenting with drugs. She won't talk about Leah or about drugs now. Not at all. I think she feels guilty that she didn't say anything.

Paul: William was 11 when Leah died. After that, we had six months of hell with him at school. He was a little so-and-so. He was bullied, he had kids making up rhymes about his sister, then he did the bullying. His schoolwork went downhill and nobody could do anything with him.

Janet: We had letter after letter from his school, phone call after phone call, until one night Paul really lost his rag. He's not proud of it, but he felt like panning him. I said something to William and he collapsed in a flood of tears. It turned out that, on the night of the party, he'd been upstairs talking to the girls while they were getting ready, making a pest of himself as 11-year-old boys do, and he'd seen Leah take the pill. He thought it was a headache pill or something, but it didn't take long for him to put two and two together, to realise what he'd seen. I think he felt he should have protected his sister, he should have warned her. He didn't tell anyone he'd seen her take this pill, he thought he'd get into trouble. After that, we got the problems at school sorted out. I don't think William's ever really got over it, though. He was good friends with Leah.

Paul: Jan and I still have bad days. When I give a presentation, there's no guarantee I'm not going to end up in tears. It's something you never get over. You just learn to live with it, you learn to cope with it. And some days you can't cope very well.

Janet: There's no textbook way of managing it. You take each day as it comes. You get days when you want the whole world to go away. You get days when you want to jump in the car, drive up the nearest motorway and just keep going. But you don't. Not usually.

(P)

23

"I Done 12 One Night, Y'know What I Mean?"

"I know, 'cos I've done pills myself. I done 12 one night, y'know what I mean? Loads of them, I've been off it on them, y'know what I mean? And the thing is, if you bang one, you go out, you have a good night and, if it brings out the better in someone, then really, in the long run, it's a safe pill and it ain't doing you no harm. I don't see the problem. It just brings something out in you. That's why people do it. They like it."

Oops. Brian Harvey's remarks about ecstasy, made in a radio interview on 15 January 1997, caused outrage. But the media hullabaloo which followed wasn't just because Harvey said that ecstasy "brings out the better in someone" and described the drug as "a safe pill". Nor because he claimed to have once popped 12 pills in a single night. Nor because, elsewhere in the interview, he said he'd driven a car while on E. No, the real outrage was because all this came from the lips of one of the most pinned-up pop pin-ups of the Nineties – the lead singer of East 17, the band which fuelled a thousand teenage girls' dreams. Oops and then some.

The day after the interview, conducted by a journalist for Independent Radio News during East 17's rehearsals for an appearance on *Top Of The Pops*, Brian Harvey's comments were plastered across the front page of every newspaper in Britain. For Eugene Manzi, the senior press officer at London Records, East 17's record company, it was the biggest headache of an illustrious career in music PR which stretched back to the early Eighties. The first that Manzi heard about Harvey's remarks was three or four hours after East 17 had left the *Top Of The Pops* studio, when a tabloid journalist called him up and asked him what he thought of the outburst. Manzi's initial reaction was disbelief. For a start, he didn't know the interview had even taken place.

"It hadn't been arranged through London Records and, to this day, I've never found out how it came about," says Manzi. "It was all a bit strange, really. I mean, getting collared by a freelance journalist working for independent radio at the *Top Of The Pops* studio . . . ? I've never had that with any other artist. Radio interviews simply don't happen at *Top Of The Pops*.

"There were other odd things about it, too. Why did the interviewer suddenly start asking Brian about ecstasy? How did he get hold of Brian rather than Tony Mortimer [the group's principal songwriter]? Tony normally did the interviews, not Brian. And how did the tabloids get hold of the story so quickly? I also think it was strange that, only a few weeks previous to this, Tony had talked about ecstasy in an interview with the *Guardian*, but the tabloids hadn't picked up on it. It wasn't as outlandish as anything Brian said, but I remember thinking at the time, 'Oh no, fancy Tony saying that'. Nobody picked up on it, though."

Then 22 years old, Brian Harvey was the youngest member of East 17. A former plumber and sweet shop assistant who first tasted pop stardom within days of his 18th birthday, he had a reputation for being a bit cheeky, a bit arrogant, a bit of a lad. To the band's fans, it was all part of his charm. That he was naive, too, almost goes without saying.

As soon as Eugene Manzi heard about the radio interview, he telephoned Harvey at home. By now it was late in the afternoon of 15 January and Manzi says the singer was "completely taken aback" by the press reaction. Harvey told Manzi that reporters were camped outside his front door and that his phone hadn't stopped ringing. "He said one of his local newspapers had called him up and he'd gone down to their offices to see them," recalls Manzi. "I told him, 'Brian, don't go anywhere, don't answer the door, don't answer the phone. Stay put and don't speak to anyone.'"

Switching into what Manzi calls "damage limitation mode", the London Records press team didn't get much sleep that night. The strategy they came up with centred on a personal apology from Harvey. "I realise I was completely out of order and am horrified at the thought that anything I have said could influence anyone," it read. "All I'd like to say now is never take ecstasy – it can kill you."

It was too late, though. By the time the apology was issued on the morning of 16 January, the ramifications of the story were being felt, with a dozen radio stations announcing a total ban on East 17 records. Although that night's *Top Of The Pops* appearance went ahead as scheduled, Central Television pulled an interview with the band which had been set to be screened a few days later. Even then Prime Minister John Major got involved. "I regard any comments of that sort as wholly wrong," Major told the House of Commons on the afternoon of 16 January. "Drug taking, whatever the drug may be, tends to lead to hard drugs. We have seen often enough the tragedy that then occurs."

The following day, 17 January, the newspapers were again full of the Brian Harvey story and its spin-offs. The most dramatic response came from the *Mirror*, which devoted its cover to a full-page picture of a white pill embossed with a gigantic 'E' and overlaid with the words "Ecstasy Shock Issue". Below the pill it read: "A million young people take E every weekend. East 17 pop star Brian Harvey caused outrage yesterday by claiming the drug 'makes you a better person'. It can also make you a dead person."

"The tabloids went well over the top," says Manzi. "Their argument was that people could be influenced by Brian's comments but, if that really was the case, why did they report the story in so much detail? I thought the papers were just as irresponsible as Brian. One of the tabloids even wanted him to pose with a picture of Leah Betts – a picture or a poster or something like that – and the mere fact that they actually thought of that was far more outrageous than anything Brian had done. It just shows how cynical some of them are."

Cynical or not, it was now clear that Manzi was powerless to save Brian Harvey's skin. London Records might have been prepared to stand by their man, but Harvey's fellow East 17ers – Tony Mortimer, John Hendy and Terry Coldwell – and the band's manager, Tom Watkins, a flamboyant character who had previously steered the careers of Bros and The Pet Shop Boys, were not. As a result, on the afternoon of 17 January, they issued Harvey with a writ sacking him from the band. A few days later, Mortimer visited the House of Commons, where he met Home Office Minister Tom Sackville and other MPs to "receive a pat on the back", as *Melody Maker* put it.

The sacking didn't kill the story off, though. Ten days later, on 28 January, Brian Harvey was back in the news after Oasis' Noel Gallagher spoke out in support of the former East 17 singer at the *NME* Brat Awards. Gallagher's description of taking drugs as "like getting up and having a cup of tea in the morning" appalled a lot of people, including Leah Betts' parents, to whom the Oasis man swiftly apologised. His assertion that "there's people in the Houses of Parliament, man, who are bigger heroin addicts and cocaine addicts than anyone in this room right now" didn't go down unanimously well, either, with several MPs demanding that he be prosecuted for inciting drug abuse. Gallagher's main point, though, was that Brian Harvey had a right to talk openly and honestly about his personal experiences: "If he did do 12 Es in one night, and he's saying that he did, if he's being honest, then fair enough."

Most of the next day's newspaper headlines played on the "cup of tea" quotation. Now it was Noel Gallagher's turn to be shocked at the media reaction. That afternoon, believing he'd been badly represented, he issued a more considered statement which read: "I've never condoned the use of drugs, I just slam as hypocrites those politicians who simply condemn drug abuse as a criminal activity and think they've done something positive! The criminalisation of drug users simply isn't working."

The following day, 30 January, the bulk of the press performed a remarkable volte-face. The *Mirror*, for example, two weeks after their "Ecstasy Shock Issue", ran a front-page story headlined "Why Noel's RIGHT On Drugs" and, in a subsequent phone-in poll, 87 per cent of *Mirror* readers said they supported Gallagher. Brian Harvey must have been gobsmacked.

Throughout the Brian Harvey episode, the rumour mill churned at full steam. There were stories about the East 17 singer suffering intense stress in the weeks running up to his outburst. There were stories about him being targeted by tabloid journalists who thought that he needed taking down several pegs. The conspiracy theorists even talked of a government set-up, pointing out that the incident happened at precisely the same time that anti-ecstasy legislation was going through Parliament: the *Mirror*'s "Ecstasy Shock Issue" was published on the morning that the legislation was debated in the House of Commons. Another rumour centred on unsubstantiated reports of a rift in the East 17 camp which went back months before Harvey was ousted.

"I don't know anything about that, but I must say that I was shocked when the band themselves sacked Brian," says Eugene Manzi. "I felt the punishment was too severe. Yes, he made a big mistake, but he was young, he was naive, a lot of it was just bravado . . . and he did apologise. It was a sincere apology, at that. He was horrified by the press reaction. To be honest, I felt sorry for him. He was an ordinary lad from the East End and all he did was tell the truth as he saw it."

Harvey's sacking from East 17 might have knocked his music career off-course, but it didn't halt it altogether. By mid-1998, with Tony Mortimer having embarked upon a solo career, he was back working with his old friends John Hendy and Terry Coldwell under the truncated and not a little ironic name of E-17. The new-look group were snapped up by Telstar Records in a deal said to have been worth £1 million.

(P)

24

Agitation And Legislation: The CJA And Beyond

Graham Bright, the Conservative MP responsible for the 1990 Entertainments (Increased Penalties) Act, the legislation designed to crush the first
wave of outdoor raves, knew his stuff. He impressed his Right Honourable
Friends with his knowledge of where the term 'acid house' came from. He
held his own in *Melody Maker*'s 'Great Rave Debate', at which he appeared
alongside Chief Superintendent Ken Tappenden from the police Pay Party
Unit, Energy promoter Jeremy Taylor, Coldcut's Jonathan More and
rave-o-rama pop star Adamski. Bright attended a couple of acid parties, too,
albeit in one of Tappenden's police cars rather than in a smiley t-shirt. He
drew on his personal experiences when speaking in the final parliamentary
debate on his legislation, even offering his thanks to his wife Valerie and son
Rupert "for allowing me out all night one Saturday".

Graham Bright's Entertainments (Increased Penalties) Act promised jail
sentences of up to six months and fines of up to £20,000 for anybody
found guilty of organising an unlicensed party. Yet in spite of Bright's
labours, the efficacy of the legislation is open to question. Sure, it gave the
magistrates greater power. Sure, it gave the police fresh impetus. Sure, it
had an effect on the first generation of outdoor rave promoters, forcing
some to withdraw from the scene and others such as Energy and Raindance to switch to legal operations. The outlawed parties didn't stop,
though. Not by any means.

During the first few years of the Nineties, countering the spread of clubs
swollen with people turned on to dance music by chart-toppers like Snap's
'The Power' and The KLF's '3am Eternal', an altogether different strain of
rave promoters took to the highways and byways of Britain. Spiral Tribe,
DiY, Bedlam, Techno Travellers, Circus Warp and their ilk shunned the
increasingly mainstream thrust of club culture. Joe Bloggs flares off the
rails of Top Man? Forget it. Friday and Saturday nights on the razz, then
back in the office on Monday morning? You're fucking joking, mate. Half
an E to see how you get on? Bollocks – have some ketamine.

The crusty ravers, as they were dubbed by the music press, were full-time and full-on. Shaven-headed or dreadlocked, tie-dyed or camou-flaged, they were self-sufficient units, running their own sound systems and retaining their own DJs. They embraced anarcho-punk principles, New Age mysticism, green issues and millennial conspiracy theories. And they cared nothing about the threat of six months in jail or a £20,000 fine. Rather than being any kind of deterrent, it merely served to spur them on. Graham Bright's legislation gave them a political *raison d'être*. This really was a fight for the right to party.

Many crusty rave crews hooked into the long-standing free festival scene, turning what had previously been low-key hippy gatherings into banging techno parties. The hippy-raver alliance was a natural one: both groups shared a political ethos and had a common enemy in the amorphous shape of the authorities. There was plenty of talk about oppression around the camp fires. The so-called Battle Of The Beanfield, when the police launched a brutal attack on a large convoy of hippies travelling to the Stonehenge Free Festival in 1985, was still fresh in the minds of the hippies. And the ravers believed it was only a matter of time before something similar happened to them.

The hippy-raver alliance snowballed throughout the summer of 1991 – pulling in a substantial part of the disenchanted underground urban dance crowd – and culminated in a party at the Avon Free Festival at Castle-morton Common, Worcestershire, in May 1992. The Avon Free Festival had always been a fairly insignificant date on the hippy calendar. But through the labours of Spiral Tribe, DiY, Bedlam and half a dozen other crews, the 1992 instalment turned into the biggest illegal gathering ever in the UK. The crowd at Castlemorton was estimated at upwards of 30,000 people. Some said as many as 50,000. For the hardcore of the hardcore, the partying went on for a week and, much to the chagrin of local residents and national newspaper columnists, it went on with very little interference from the West Mercia police. It was only after the rave that the authorities made their move, arresting a total of 23 people, most of them members of Spiral Tribe. No convictions followed, though, despite a two-year legal battle which reportedly landed taxpayers with a bill of £4 million.

Back at Westminster, the Castlemorton rave horrified politicians of every hue. New and far tougher legislation was clearly needed to prevent anything like it happening again. It took a while to come and when it did it was encompassed in the 1994 Criminal Justice & Public Order Act (better known as the CJA). One of the most confusing pieces of legislation ever passed in the UK, the CJA lumped together 172 often seemingly unconnected articles. The anti-rave measures sat alongside laws to crack down on child pornography and terrorism, a reduction in the age of consent for homosexuals from 21 to 18 and a clampdown on the publication of racist material. Calling the CJA hodgepodge doesn't come close to describing it.

Most pertinent to the party people was Part Five of the CJA. This section of the Act sought to control the mass movement of people around the country and threatened custodial sentences for ravers. It gave the police powers of dispersal and confiscation if they "reasonably" believed that 10 or more people were organising an outdoor rave for 100 or more people. Anybody they "reasonably" believed to be heading for such an event could be turned back up to five miles away. The CJA even offered a description of rave music: "Sounds wholly or predominantly defined by the emission of a succession of repetitive beats". Maybe Graham Bright – later Sir Graham Bright – helped out with that line.

Both Graham Bright's Entertainments (Increased Penalties) Act and Part Five of the CJA were designed to put a stop to raves, or other large and illegal gatherings of people. While they undoubtedly embodied an unwritten hope that they would also help fight the spread of dance drugs, they were essentially public order enactments, the latter being directed at the traditional enemies of the state – people in funny clothes with funny hairstyles whose lifestyles didn't conform to the norm.

The third and final piece of legislation associated with UK club culture during the Nineties was quite a different story. It was targeted directly at drugs and specifically at ecstasy. It was there in the name: the Public Entertainments Licences (Drugs Misuse) Act.

The legislation was originally proposed as a private member's bill in 1996 by Barry Legg, Conservative MP for Milton Keynes South West since 1992. The Public Entertainments Licences (Drugs Misuse) Bill was essentially an amendment of the 1982 Local Government (Miscellaneous Provisions) Act, which set down the conditions under which nightclubs held entertainments licences from local authorities. Barry Legg's legislation proposed to give local authorities the power to immediately revoke a club's licence if informed of "a serious problem relating to the supply or use of controlled drugs at or near the licensed premises" by the police. In the event of this, a club owner would have three weeks in which to lodge an appeal, with the premises being closed pending the appeal process.

The main impetus behind Barry Legg's Bill was the ongoing situation at Club UK in Wandsworth, south London. According to the MP, the owners of Club UK were "exploiting the law". The saga began in December 1994, when a police raid on the club resulted in two arrests for drugs offences. The following autumn, believing that drug dealing was still taking place, undercover police attended a variety of different Club UK nights over a number of weeks and a second raid was staged in October 1995 under the codename Operation Blade. Around 150 officers were involved in Operation Blade, some of them with dogs and others on horseback. Ten arrests were made. A couple of months later, 19-year-old Andreas Bouzis collapsed and died at the club after taking a single ecstasy tablet. Perhaps not surprisingly after all of this, Wandsworth Council decided to withdraw Club UK's licence. In response, the owners lodged an appeal and the case dragged on for the whole of 1996, with the venue remaining open throughout this period. It was finally shut for good on 6 January 1997, over two years after the police had first identified a problem at the club.

Beyond the events at Club UK, though, was a wider worry. By the mid-Nineties, ecstasy use in the United Kingdom was on a scale unimaginable only a couple of years earlier. The number of people taking E at any given point in time has always been nigh on impossible to gauge, but a series of drug and crime surveys conducted between 1993 and 1996 indicate that these were the peak years. A 1996 study by Release, the drugs advice service, found that a whopping 85 per cent of people who described themselves as clubbers had tried E. Two years earlier, the 1994 British Crime Survey estimated that 43 per cent of all 16- to 29-year-olds had tried an illegal drug of some description. The figure was particularly high among 16 to 19-year-old males, of whom 50 per cent claimed to have tried drugs. What's more, the rise in ecstasy use brought a rise in ecstasy deaths. According to the Office of National Statistics, an average of 17 deaths a year in the UK between 1993 and 1996 involved the ingestion of E – one victim roughly every three weeks.

It wasn't only the popularity of ecstasy which spiralled during the mid-Nineties, either. Prior to E, most users' entry point into the world of illegal drugs had been cannabis, a Class B substance, a 'soft' substance. But by 1993, the entry point was as likely to be ecstasy – a Class A. The result was often catalytic, making a lot of people more open to the idea of trying other 'hard' chemical substances. This idea is born out by Home Office statistics for drug convictions and cautions in the UK. In 1987, the year before acid house, 26,278 people were convicted or cautioned for a drug offence. By 1991, this figure had reached 47,616. By 1995, it had rocketed to 93,631. In particular, there were two gigantic leaps in 1993 and 1994 – from 48,927 convictions and cautions in 1992 up to 68,480 in 1993 and up again to 85,693 in 1994.

Perhaps an even more significant factor in the backdrop to the Barry Legg Bill was Westminster's slowly dawning realisation that the typical E user wasn't that dreadlocked crusty raver, after all. The average E user was actually the average young person. They weren't the type to listen to the advice of LSD guru Timothy Leary – "turn on, tune in, drop out". Most of them didn't even know who the fuck Timothy Leary was. Most of them had turned on to E, tuned in to Radio One and carried on carrying out from McDonalds twice a week. Aside from popping the odd pill, they weren't indulging in any other criminal activity. They certainly weren't robbing old ladies to pay for their next hit. They didn't need to. By and large, they had decent jobs, decent prospects. They paid their taxes, they shopped at Our Price and WH Smith and Boots. They weren't just a part of mainstream society. They were at the very heart of it.

The all-important House Of Commons Second Reading of Barry Legg's Public Entertainments Licences (Drugs Misuse) Bill took place on 17 January 1997, 10 days after Wandsworth Council had finally closed down Club UK. Several worlds away from the kaleidoscopic hullabaloo of clubland, the historic leather benches of the Westminster chamber were packed for a debate which lasted a mammoth four hours.

Although a private member's bill, Barry Legg's proposed legislation had the full support of the then ruling Conservative government. There was no formal opposition from the Labour benches, either. Nobody was surprised when the Bill was unanimously passed, although there was anger that the Second Reading part of the process should take so long. The last two hours of the debate were littered with complaints from Labour MPs that Conservative members were deliberately prolonging the discussion in order to leave no time for the next item on the agenda: a Bill to give extra money to pensioners during severe winter weather proposed by Audrey Wise (the Labour MP for Preston). But as well as illustrating the sometimes dubious workings of the British parliamentary process, the Barry Legg debate stands as an intriguing insight into British politicians' understanding of not only the issue at hand, but of youth culture in general. For some, this understanding was clearly limited: David Evans (Conservative, Welwyn Hatfield), for example, who asked Barry Legg, "When my Honourable Friend refers to nightclubs, does he include discos?"

The first round of speeches concentrated on the key wording of the Bill: "a serious problem relating to the supply or use of controlled drugs at or near the licensed premises". Several MPs asked for clarification on what constituted "a serious problem". That should ultimately be left to the discretion of the police, said Legg. "I think that the word 'serious' implies that dealing is taking place or that many people are consuming drugs," he added, which merely invited the question of what might be considered "many people". The phrase "at or near" the premises also needed careful consideration, argued several MPs. As Andrew Hunter (Conservative, Basingstoke) noted, it would be "entirely wrong" to hold clubs responsible for activities carried out in public places over which they had little control. Not only that, but it opened the legislation up to inconsistent interpretation by the police and the local authorities.

During the weeks leading up to the parliamentary debate, several MPs had been contacted by the British Entertainment & Discotheque Association and the Association of Metropolitan Authorities. Both organisations were concerned that the Legg Bill would deter promoters from undertaking harm reduction schemes – training staff to deal with E casualties and handing out drug information leaflets, for example – as these might be perceived as evidence of a problem at their club. The importance of such safety measures was expressed to the chamber most potently by Tim Rathbone (Conservative, Lewes), the founder and chairman of the All Party Committee on Drug Misuse. Although an old-style Tory, Rathbone was one of the few MPs prepared to listen to young people. Nine months earlier, he'd met a club promoter, a DJ and four E users at a forum organised by *Muzik* magazine. No wonder, then, that his parliamentary speeches came with a hefty dollop of realism.

Paul Flynn (Labour, Newport West), a long-time critic of 'Just Say No'-type messages, was another enthusiastic participant in the Legg debate. Although he'd never advocated the legalisation of recreational drugs – "and the next newspaper that says that I have will pay my election expenses," he warned – he recognised the need for a fresh approach: "Every year we hold a drugs debate. Every year, hanging over the chamber in that debate, is a statistic that mocks our efforts. Every year more people use drugs than before." Flynn also talked about the hypocrisy of introducing tougher legislation on illegal drugs while largely ignoring the dangers of alcohol and tobacco. It was no surprise, he noted, "that young people with a different drug of choice turn to us and say, 'There you are in your Parliament with its 15 bars telling us not to do drugs – you standing there with a glass of whisky in one hand and a cigarette in the other, and a couple of paracetamols in your pocket for your headache tomorrow morning.'"

Sir Michael Neubert (Conservative, Romford) countered that Paul Flynn's "rational considerations" merely served to confuse the issue. But then Neubert was already confused. For a start, he hadn't cottoned on to the radical changes in drug culture which E had initiated. "Those of us who are fortunate to lead ordinary working lives cannot imagine the life of the drug taker who lives by the day or by the hour, robbing in order to obtain easy money to pay for a quick fix," he declared. Balanced against this inaccurate stereotype perception of most Nineties drug users, though, was Neubert's belief that it was important not to deprive young people of their Saturday night clubbing fun. Especially as his Romford constituency "has some claim to be the night spot of the south," he said. He told

Parliament how, five years earlier, he'd spent an evening at one of Romford's clubs and had been impressed with the door policy. "Anybody wearing dirty jeans was rejected," he said, presumably thinking this somehow helped to prevent possible drug use.

Elsewhere, there were speeches about the role of security staff at clubs, with references to a Home Affairs Select Committee report revealing that 279 of 476 doormen interviewed in the Merseyside area had criminal records, 28 of them for drug offences. The then recent pro-E comments by East 17's Brian Harvey was another subject for discussion, with the singer coming in for heavy criticism from every quarter. The music business itself was also censured. David Shaw (Conservative, Dover) spoke about the economic importance of the industry – "a net earner to this country of approximately £1,000 million a year" – but said that Parliament "must send a clear message to the industry that we do not want its success to be based on a drug culture". No Elvis, Beatles or The Rolling Stones, then?

Some of those participating in the Barry Legg debate resorted to unhelpful, tabloid-style clichés: "the drugs scourge", "a menace to society" and "pushers poisoning our children" all came up. But the most disturbing speech of the day came from David Evans, the MP who couldn't work out if 'nightclubs' included 'discos'. "All minor offences must be punished," he solemnly declared. "I propose a system of zero tolerance for drug abusers, which would mean that those found in possession of an illegal substance would be given an automatic jail sentence." A spell in jail wasn't David Evans' ideal solution, though. "If I thought that it was remotely possible," he concluded. "I would advocate the death penalty for those in possession of drugs."

(P)

25

Editorial I: "Press The Panic Button"

The following editorial first appeared in New Scientist *magazine, 25 January 1997 issue. Reproduced by kind permission.*

Panic reigns. Fear overwhelms logical thought. Pointless activity replaces reason, and sensible advice is no longer heard.

Sometimes whole nations are affected. A threat appears – a religious cult, a rare disease, aliens who take you up into their saucers – and rationality flies out of the window. Parents lock up their children lest they be abducted. No one eats beef, or eggs, or whatever is causing the latest panic. Previously sensible people see flashbacks of the aliens' green eyes.

In the middle of a panic, what's needed is for everyone to calm down. And that's just the treatment Britain requires for the current panic over the drug ecstasy. Following the heart-rending deaths of several teenagers who were apparently trying ecstasy for the first time, it has become impossible to express any sensible opinion on the drug. Either you condemn ecstasy use out of hand, or you risk being seen as in favour of killing children.

Amid the hysteria, confused new legislation is being hurried through Parliament. The idea is to allow clubs to be closed down immediately if there is a suspicion that ecstasy is being sold in them. As the drug is easily concealed, the law can do no more than punish clubs for failing to achieve the impossible. Unjust and ineffective legislation is a classic symptom of national panic.

The real problem in dealing with ecstasy is the huge gap in the perception of the drug between those who take it and those who do not. And the real scandal is our lack of understanding of its long-term risks.

Ecstasy (or MDMA, as it is known chemically) inhibits the uptake of the brain transmitter serotonin, and so amplifies the signals it transmits between nerve cells. The result is a raised heartbeat, an emotional 'high' and increased energy levels.

In Britain, it is estimated that at least half a million people have taken ecstasy and that around a million tablets are consumed each week. The benefits are seen by users as a state of euphoria, closeness to fellow humans, and the ability to dance all night. Users consider the short-term risks to be small, a perception that available statistics tend to bear out. Over the past 10 years, six people a year are thought to have died as a result of taking ecstasy in Britain. This number appears small compared to the hundreds of thousands who die each year from long-term alcohol and tobacco abuse. It is dwarfed by the 1,000 people who die each year in traffic accidents caused by drivers under 21 years of age, and the 600 or so who are killed each year in Britain by drunk drivers. Even pursuits such as mountain climbing, skiing and horse riding kill more people.

Six deaths a year from ecstasy are six too many, but it seems pretty clear that the short-term dangers are not as great as the media and many public figures portray them. Ecstasy takers know this, and become understandably cynical about warnings issued by those in authority. Trust disappears – another victim of panic. It would be far better to present an honest assessment of the risks and benefits of illegal drugs and maintain the trust without which any influence over young people is impossible.

The search for truth is also at risk in times of panic. Little has been done to investigate the long-term dangers of ecstasy use, not least because in Europe it has been more difficult than it should be to get funding to carry out research.

The information is badly needed so that a full and honest picture of the effects and dangers can be presented to users and would-be users. The evidence so far suggests that, at very high doses, ecstasy can damage the brain cells that produce serotonin, and they never fully recover. Unfortunately, we don't know if the same is true at the doses taken by ordinary users, and we don't know what the effect of such damage might be. Alcohol also damages brain cells. The worst prognosis is that irreversible injury will show up as today's ecstasy users get older.

These are questions that need to be settled. Recreational drug taking is an emotional issue, but we have to accept that ecstasy use is widespread and deal with it rationally. Attempts to curtail the supply of the drug have failed. So we must learn as much as we can about its effects, and present that information honestly.

26

Editorial II: "Ecstasy – Editorial Comment"

The following editorial first appeared in Muzik *magazine, March 1997 issue. Reproduced by kind permission.*

Whatever you think of Brian Harvey's comments on ecstasy, he should at least be thanked for putting the subject back on the agenda. The ex-East 17 man's words made the front page of every national newspaper, with one printing a full-page picture of a tablet under the banner 'Ecstasy Special', and there were TV debates on everything from *Newsnight* to *Kilroy*.

So what new information did we get from all this media coverage? What fresh opinions? What have we learned in the year or so since the death of Leah Betts, the last time ecstasy was such a major point of public conversation? Very little, it seems. So little, in fact, it's increasingly hard to believe that E users and those opposed to the drug are even talking about the same thing. As *New Scientist* pointed out in an editorial column (one of the few voices of reason to rise above the hysteria), "the real problem in dealing with ecstasy is the huge gap in the perception of the drug between those who take it and those who do not".

Spot on. However often and however hard the authorities warn people about the dangers of ecstasy, about how it could do you serious harm, how it could kill you, their words will continue to fall on deaf ears until they acknowledge this does not correlate with the experiences of most of those who have taken and are taking the drug. Regardless of whether they're right or wrong, nobody who pops a pill believes it's going to do them any harm. If they did, we wouldn't be talking about an estimated million pills consumed every week.

But we're not going to begin bridging the gap in the way E is perceived with people like Barry Legg around. If you don't already know, Mr Legg is the MP responsible for a bill currently going through Parliament which will give local authorities the power to immediately shut down a club if the police suspect drugs are being taken on or near the premises. The club will then have to stay closed until an appeal hearing. Which could, of course, be months.

New Scientist called the proposed legislation (the Public Entertainments Licences (Drug Misuse) Bill) "unjust and ineffective". Spot on again. It makes you wonder what Mr Legg thinks people will do if their club is shut. Go home for a cup of Horlicks? Make arrangements to go bowling the following weekend? Get real, Mr Legg. We're talking about a dedicated and highly mobile section of society, many of whom frequently travel across the country for a good night out. And the more clubs which are closed down, the more likely it is that the dance scene will be driven back underground, which brings a whole bunch of other problems regarding hazardous buildings and poor medical facilities, to say nothing of presenting the criminal element with a golden opportunity.

Another possible danger is that penalising clubs will make owners and promoters nervous about some of the harm reduction policies which they currently have in place. Most of them are well aware of the situation and are acting responsibly by providing chill-out areas and free drinking water, and by giving out drugs information leaflets. Some of the big clubs even have trained medical staff on duty. Under Mr Legg's Bill, though, isn't the presence of medical staff tantamount to an admission of guilt? Taking E may well be illegal, but undermining the safety measures doesn't help. You don't take away somebody's seat belt because they sometimes drive at more than 70mph on the motorway, do you?

In short, Barry Legg's Bill does nothing to move the debate forward. We're just going round in ever-decreasing circles of sense. Instead of attacking club owners, how about giving them more support for the work many are doing to try to make their venues as safe as they can? How about spending more money on drug education based on an honest assessment of the situation? How about more research into the long-term effects of E, about which we still know very little? How about looking more seriously at the possibility of testing E in UK clubs, as they do in Amsterdam? Although this brings yet another set of problems and might not be the answer, we won't know until somebody poses the question.

None of this is going to occur overnight. Especially not with a general election on the horizon. A considered approach to drugs is not exactly a Middle England vote-winner, is it? On the other hand, if you feel strongly about the subject, now's as good a time as any to make your voice heard. Contact your local MP and the candidates standing against him or her in the election. Find out their views on ecstasy and tell them yours. Write to a newspaper or a magazine. Talk about it with your friends. Yes, you may be putting yourself on the line, but an open discussion is the only way to bridge the gap.

In the meantime, it's vital that you know as much as possible about the effects of E. Know what it does to your heart rate and your body temperature. Know that you need to replace the fluids you lose as your body heats up. As a rough guide, you should drink about a pint of water every hour. Sip it regularly rather than drinking large amounts in one go. Know that you should try to eat something salty and drink fruit juice, fizzy drinks or sports drinks to give you minerals. Know that you should take plenty of breaks in the chill-out area. Know that alcohol and E is an extremely dangerous combination.

You should also know that over the last 10 years around 60 people are believed to have died as a result of taking E and that, according to the latest statistics, at some point during the next couple of months one clubber is going to die as a result of necking an ecstasy tablet.

If you are thinking of taking an E at any point in the future, whether it's your first time or your 100th, make your decision an informed one. And don't think you're so special that the 'one clubber' in those statistics couldn't be you. You never know.

27

Harm Reduction And Safer Dancing

Rewind to 1967. It wasn't all peace and love, though, man. Che Guevara, the Cuban revolutionary leader turned hippy hero, was hunted down and killed in Bolivia. The Middle East exploded as Israel launched sudden attacks upon its Arab neighbours. The Vietnam War, by now three years old, raged on and on and on some more, with relentless American bombing raids on North Vietnam causing widespread civilian casualties and triggering violent protests in Washington, London and other Western capitals.

For many of the people who took part in the London anti-Vietnam protests, drugs were also on the agenda. British campaigners for the legalisation of cannabis organised a public rally in Hyde Park during the summer of 1967 and placed an advertisement in *The Times* headed 'The Law Against Marijuana Is Immoral In Principle And Unworkable In Practice'. The signatories included all four Beatles, as well as Brian Epstein, David Dimbleby, Dr Jonathan Miller, David Hockney and David Bailey. The drug debate was further fuelled by the arrest of Rolling Stones' Mick Jagger and Keith Richard, Jagger for possession of four amphetamine tablets and Richard for allowing cannabis to be smoked in his home. They were subsequently sentenced to three and 12 months in jail, respectively, although both were released after just one night of porridge.

Jagger's sentence was subsequently overturned, partly as a result of *The Times*' instantly famous 'Who Breaks A Butterfly On A Wheel' editorial. Written by *The Times*' editor himself, William Rees-Mogg, the piece centred on the question, "Has Mr Jagger received the same treatment as he would have received if he had not been a famous figure?" According to Rees-Mogg, the answer was no. But he was wrong: the answer was actually yes. Since the passing of the Dangerous Drugs Act in 1965, the authorities had adopted an ultra-tough stance on illicit drug use. In this particular instance, the main difference between Mick Jagger and Joe Public was that Joe couldn't call upon a national newspaper editor to deal him a 'Get Outta Jail Free' card.

Joe could, however, call Release, a drugs advice service founded in 1967 by London art students Caroline Coon and Rufus Harris, who had launched the world's first 24-hour drugs advice telephone line, which initially operated from Coon's bedsit. Over the next few years, as their resources gradually grew, Release offered drug users assistance and information whenever and wherever needed, often in 'trip rooms' at psychedelic all-nighters like Middle Earth and clubs like the UFO, the place where Pink Floyd first made their mark.

"We were fired up by the legal injustices we saw," says Caroline Coon, who quit Release in 1971 to work as a music journalist and briefly managed The Clash before embarking on her current career as a painter. "The police were using the drug laws to harass the hippy movement – they were kicking people's doors in at four o'clock in the morning and dragging them off. People would disappear and you wouldn't hear from them for two weeks. It was outrageous. And it made no sense. I had a friend who was sentenced to six months in prison for illegal possession of a gun and three-and-a-half years for having a few grains of marijuana."

Although Caroline Coon's original aim was to protect civil liberties, an increasing number of people also came to Release for health advice, partly as a result of the dramatic rise in the illicit use of barbiturates (downers) in the early Seventies. Dealing with the problems associated with barbiturates, the pills which sent both Jimi Hendrix and Marilyn Monroe to their graves, was the initial impetus behind Lifeline, a similar service to Release which was set up in Manchester by psychiatrist Eugenie Cheesemond in 1971.

By the middle of the Seventies, much of Release and Lifeline's attention had been drawn to LSD. The original hippy hit of choice, the resurgence of LSD in the mid-Seventies sparked Operation Julie, the biggest police drugs investigation in the UK prior to acid house. Operation Julie was launched following the Watchfield Free Festival, which took place in 1975 at a disused airfield owned by the government in Oxfordshire. Unknown to the crowd, the site was stuffed with undercover police officers. A few years later, Release and Lifeline found themselves tackling a spiral in injected heroin use, a problem compounded by the onset of AIDS in the early Eighties. The focus of their work at this time fell on harm reduction measures, in particular free needle exchanges, by which they hoped to arrest the spread of HIV through shared works.

The sudden popularity of ecstasy in Britain in the late Eighties caught the two drug services unprepared. For a while, they struggled to formulate their response to E: they had never come across a substance like this before. The limited literature on MDMA available at that point was

143

almost entirely American and much of it was positive. The drug had been widely used in therapy for nearly 10 years, often with reportedly amazing results, and the DEA's own law judge had declared it should be available on prescription. There was also the fact that, as Harry Shapiro from the Institute for the Study of Drug Dependence in London concurs, users might become psychologically dependent on ecstasy but the substance is not physically addictive in the way that heroin or even alcohol are. Traditional detoxification and rehabilitation-type treatments were consequently inappropriate. What's more, the majority of people taking E seemed to suffer no lasting ill effects. Of those who did, though, some ended up on a mortuary slab.

All in all, it was quite a conundrum. But for Mike Linnell, Lifeline's Director of Communications, the need to develop some sort of policy on ecstasy hit home when the organisation moved their Manchester HQ to Oldham Street, a few steps from Dry, the bar where the city's club cognoscenti convened before a night on the razz. It was 1990 and the E-fuelled Madchester phenomenon was in full baggy flow, with Happy Mondays and The Stone Roses on the cover of every other magazine in the land.

"The street would be packed with people dressed in trumpet flares, most of them out of their boxes," says Linnell. "But they weren't going to drug services like Lifeline, partly because they didn't have problems and partly because they didn't think what we did was relevant to them. And they were right. Nearly all the people we saw in the early days of E came to us because they'd been busted rather than because they had a health problem. It was then we started to identify two different types of users – Group A and Group B. Group A are, for want of a better word, junkies. Their drug of choice would be heroin and 97 per cent of them would inject. They're basically fucked-up people. Group B, on the other hand, which includes E users, have far more in common with people who don't take any kind of drugs than they have with people who inject heroin on a daily basis."

There's no question that typical ecstasy users and typical heroin users are very different animals. Yet since the early Nineties, Release, Lifeline and more recently established drug services like Hit in Liverpool and Crew 2000 in Scotland have based their approach to the former group on the harm reduction ethos advanced in relation to the latter.

Pioneered in 1940 by American sociologist Alfred Lindesmith, the basic premise of harm reduction is that, whatever the preventative education and combative legislation, some people will still take illegal drugs and it is important to minimalise the risks they are consequently taking. Opponents of the concept argue that it's fatalistic and effectively puts a section of society above the law, thereby encouraging illegal drug taking. Against this, supporters say it's pragmatic rather than fatalistic and that meeting health needs should take precedence over meeting the demands of a piece of paper.

The socio-political justification for heroin harm reduction measures is largely centred on the link between shared injecting equipment and the spread of HIV, a link which has made heroin use a wider public health issue. Free needle exchanges aren't viewed as just protecting heroin users. They're for protecting non-users, too. And although clean needles might help arrest the spread of HIV, it's clear that they will do nothing to stop users dying as a result of their drug habit: however clean a user's needle might be, it's still dirty. In other words, the measures don't undermine the accepted wisdom that heroin is a dangerous drug, that there can be no distinction between use and abuse.

It's a radically different story with ecstasy harm reduction measures. While the message to heroin users remains 'there is no safe way to do what you do', the message to E heads is 'there is a safer way to do what you do'. In other words, the ecstasy harm reduction ethos draws a line, albeit often a shaky one, between use and abuse, between use and misuse. In this sense, then, ecstasy harm reduction policies run on a totally different track to the 'Just Say No' train.

"The last thing I'm doing in a club is telling people not to take drugs," says Ciaran O'Hagan, Release's Dance Events Outreach Co-ordinator. "I've got some guy or girl who's having a good time on ecstasy or whatever and I am supposed to tell them to stop? It just doesn't work. It doesn't do drug services any good for the future, either. Because if that person has a problem at some point later on, they'd say, 'Well, I know what those guys are about and I'm keeping away from them.' It's important to approach people the right way and I sometimes find it easier to engage in conversations regarding the law than the health issue. Most people will say, 'I'm alright, man, I haven't got a problem.' But then you can say, 'Okay, fine, but do you know about the drug laws?' Then you're in. Then they're listening to you."

Beginning in the early Nineties, drug workers with an interest in ecstasy focused their attention on clubs, on the places most closely associated with the drug. Knowing the effect of E on the body temperature, there was concern that the hot, sweaty environments were contributing to the potentially fatal risk of heatstroke. With the help of localised Safer Dancing campaigns, first in Manchester and later in London, Scotland and elsewhere, the services tried to raise club promoters' awareness of the dangers of overcrowding and the importance of providing chill-out areas and free drinking water. Some were immediately responsive, but it remains very much an ongoing struggle with others. And as Mike Cadger from Crew 2000 points out, it's also sometimes a battle persuading local licensing authorities to devote resources to ensuring clubs maintain such safety measures.

As well as targeting clubs, the drug services have targeted users. Since the early Nineties, this has primarily been with self-help harm reduction information about drinking sufficient water, taking breaks from dancing and so on. "Our aim has been to tell people how to take their drugs properly," says Ciaran O'Hagan. "And the way this information is conveyed is crucial."

To quote Jock Young's 1972 social textbook, *The Drugtakers*, material aimed at drug users "must be phrased in terms of the values of the subculture, not in terms of the values of the outside world." Realising the importance of flyers in club culture, the services produced countless different ecstasy harm reduction leaflets throughout the 1990s, the designs mirroring the ever-changing graphics of clubland – tripped out early in the decade, stripped down by the end – and the explanations of the risks involved in taking drugs and how they might be reduced delivered without moral judgment. The leaflets were then distributed not just at clubs but also via record shops, cafes and bars.

One of the very first ecstasy info shots was Lifeline's *E By Gum!*, which appeared in 1990 and adopted a similar tone to a magazine the Manchester service had been producing for heroin users called *Smack In The Eye*. *E By Gum!* featured a cartoon character known as Peanut Pete, whose ragtag appearance and buzzed-up antics kept clubbers amused while the advice he gave attempted to keep them out of casualty wards. His popularity led to Pete taking a starring role in numerous other Lifeline leaflets throughout the Nineties. The cartoon character was invented by Mike Linnell, who has degrees in both Health Education and Fine Art.

"Peanut Pete was actually based on one of our early clients and a lot of the situations in the first leaflets were based on ethnographic research – real situations which happened to real people," says Linnell. "We took the side of the users, we tried to understand the world as it was to them and to reflect that world in the language and humour we used. It was the same with *Smack In The Eye*, which had characters like Grandpa Smackhead Jones. It was very naughty, very rude, and our funding was threatened for producing it. We were even interviewed by the Director of Public Prosecutions."

The often controversial nature of harm reduction tactics is something to which Pat O'Hare can bear witness. In the early Nineties, O'Hare was the head of the Mersey Drug Training & Information Centre (MDTIC), the Liverpool drug service which now operates under the name of Hit. Set up in 1985, the MDTIC had pioneered needle exchanges for British heroin users, but the flak they initially inevitably took for this was nothing compared to the response which greeted their *Chill Out − A Raver's Guide* leaflet, which was first circulated in clubs towards the end of 1991. Commissioned by the Mersey Health Authority, written by the MDTIC's Alan Matthews, edited by O'Hare and with an original print run of 20,000, *Chill Out* offered advice on three drugs − E, acid and speed − and also talked of the importance of maintaining a healthy diet and getting enough sleep.

Chill Out was an instant success with Liverpool clubbers. Not with the *Liverpool Echo*, though. On 28 January 1992, the local newspaper ran a cover story entitled 'Raving Mad' which described the leaflet as "a youngster's guide to taking drugs that looks and reads like part of a sales brochure". The article also included comments from two local Conservative MPs, Linda Chalker and Ken Hind, the latter declaring the leaflet "a disgraceful waste of public money".

The following day, the story was picked up by the *Daily Star* and the *Sun*, who both devoted their front pages to the subject. Under the splash 'What A Dope!', The Star dubbed O'Hare a "daft do-gooder" and his MDTIC team "crackpot crusaders". The paper advised local parents to "dump all 20,000 copies of this pernicious pamphlet into the Mersey, followed by Mr O'Hare". The *Sun* meanwhile honed in on one line in the leaflet which was aimed at raising AIDS awareness among clubbers − "If you are going to have sex, while on E or at any time, use a condom" − to carry an absurd report headlined 'Fury At Sex Guide To E'.

"I was on my way to do an interview at Radio Merseyside on the morning after the *Echo* story and I tuned into the programme to hear the presenter say something like, 'Pat O'Hare is coming in − have you seen him on the front of the *Star*?'," recalls O'Hare, who now works as a drug adviser in Italy and is also the editor of the *International Journal Of Drug Policy*. "I nearly died. Then the presenter read out the headline of the *Star* and I thought, 'Fucking hell . . .' And when I saw the *Sun* . . . Oh dear . . . I can't begin to tell you how I felt. Terrible. Horrendous. I couldn't believe the sheer *stupidity* of it all."

Back in Liverpool, the *Echo* continued to hammer O'Hare and his team for the next couple of days. During this period, though, it became clear that the newspaper was severely out of tune with plain Scouse nous, as dozens of Liverpudlians gave their backing to *Chill Out* in local radio phone-ins and television vox pops.

"I was dead famous in Liverpool for a while," laughs O'Hare. "I'd walk into restaurants or pubs and people would come up and say, 'Fantastic, keep going.' I can only remember one negative reaction from the general public. I was in a pub when an interview with me came on the news on the pub's telly and a bloke turned to me and said, 'Listen to that stupid bastard.' Even after he'd spoken to me, he didn't realise I was 'that stupid bastard' on the telly."

The *Liverpool Echo's* rival newpapers in the north-west of England, including the *Liverpool Daily Post* and *Manchester Evening News*, also weighed in with positive articles about the MDTIC campaign. The following week, on 4 February, the *Echo* realised it had misinterpreted public opinion and gave its letters page over to the subject. Of the 15 letters published, only two condemned the leaflet. "I am writing as the concerned parent of a 19-year-old son to comment on your front page report, 'Raving Mad'," said one of the correspondents. "The most accurate part of the story is the headline . . . but only if applied to you."

There are more than 500 drug services currently operating in the UK. Release, Lifeline, Hit and Crew 2000 are quite small compared to many of the others, even though Lifeline, the biggest of the four, employs around 100 full-time staff and has five offices across the north of England. Moreover, although almost all of the services receive statutory funding, Release, Lifeline *et al* rely more heavily than most on charitable donations and private trusts. This is especially true of Release, 80 per cent of whose annual funding in any given year comes from private or charitable sources.

Part of the way in which statutory money is distributed to the 500 plus services is through Drug Action Teams (DATs). These were first set up in 1995 by John Major's Conservative government to co-ordinate the efforts of local authorities, health authorities, police forces, probation officers and local drug experts, and formed the practical backbone of the Tories' national drugs policy, 'Tackling Drugs Together'. There are some 100 DATs across the country, mostly co-ordinated by staff with on-the-ground experience of dealing with drugs but invariably chaired by chief executives of local authorities or health authorities. In the words of one DAT co-ordinator: "These are enormously senior people who have staffs of thousands and budgets of millions but whose whole knowledge of drugs is based on what they saw on *The Bill* last night, what they read in the newspapers this morning."

A tricky business, then. Especially when it comes to ecstasy. While the drug services which rely on substantial independent funding run Safer Dancing-type campaigns and produce harm reduction leaflets, very few of those more closely linked to statutory money offer programmes aimed specifically at ecstasy users. Although the London Dance Safety campaign of 1996 was largely funded by government money, this type of situation is a real rarity. Part of the reason for the apparent lack of support for ecstasy harm reduction measures from the statutory-backed services is because they were, by and large, set up to treat heroin addiction through detoxification and rehabilitation. In contrast, Crew 2000 are the only service with its origins in dance drugs, having been set up in 1992 in response to the huge numbers of Scottish clubbers experiencing problems as a result of using Temazepam as a post-E comedown at that time.

But there is also the fact that, a decade on from their introduction, ecstasy harm reduction measures have remained a political hot potato. Especially in the light of the increasingly politically popular concept of zero tolerance, by which those committing even the most minor criminal offence can expect to feel the full weight of the law. As Lifeline's Mike Linnell puts it: "It's not acceptable to say, 'Well, more than half the young people in Manchester have chosen this chemical fire escape as a way of passing their Saturday nights and there's bugger all we can do about it.' Even though, in reality, that's about it." Ecstasy harm reduction is such a hot potato that Lifeline make a point of ensuring that Peanut Pete leaflets are not financed by statutory money. "It would make us vulnerable if they were," says Linnell.

In terms of ecstasy, consecutive British governments have directed the bulk of their health and welfare resources to preventative education programmes in schools and colleges - into stopping people popping pills in the first place. Which is all well and good, but what about those who are already committed to taking E, whether it be a couple of times a year or every weekend? Are there really so few statutory provisions made for these huge numbers of people?

"There are limited resources available for tackling drugs and, to be truthful, no DAT with any sense is going to invest lots of money in recreational drug use," says one DAT co-ordinator. "Political rhetoric has never supported harm reduction, but public policy has also shifted in recent years, with the links between drugs and crime taking centre-stage on the agenda. We don't offer treatment to drug users because we have an ethical duty to provide health services to people, but because it might reduce levels of crime. And in that sense, ecstasy isn't a problem. You're not getting kids robbing grannies to buy pills at the weekend. It just doesn't happen. It's not part of the big crime loop."

No amount of harm reduction measures can guarantee complete safety. Moreover, such measures only deal with the immediate physical effects of a drug. They have no impact on the psychological effects which may accrue over a period of time. And the list of psychological effects associated with ecstasy is long and varied: anxiety, panic attacks depression, insomnia, grandiose delusions, persistent perceptual changes, paranoia and mania, to name just a few.

"What you have to look at is whether psychiatrists are seeing increasing numbers of people with ecstasy-related difficulties," says Harry Shapiro from the Institute for the Study of Drug Dependence. "While it's true that you don't get loads of people going to the drug services with ecstasy problems, it could be that some of them are going to the psychiatric services. It's a tough one, though, because they might not necessarily be revealing that they've been using drugs."

The Royal College of Psychiatrists is unaware of any studies which suggest a growing number of people are seeking help for E-related psychological difficulties. Dr Karl Jansen, a psychiatrist with the South London & Maudsley NHS Trust who has written extensively about ecstasy, believes that the incidence of such problems might actually be over-estimated. Other medical experts, however, believe the opposite is true and, because of the uncertainty over the long-term effects of ecstasy on the brain, warn there could be a dramatic increase in the number of psychological cases associated with the drug in the years to come. In which case, the drug services might well find themselves landed with additional responsibilities.

In the meantime, the harm reduction work goes on. Lifeline now produce between 50 and 70 different leaflets every year – a total print run of around one million – and Peanut Pete still pops up from time to time. Taking up where the MDTIC left off, Hit continue to churn out *Chill Out*, updated every couple of years and now subtitled *A Clubber's Guide*. John Derricott, Hit's Training Manager, says he "couldn't possibly even begin to guess" how many copies the Liverpool service has produced since 1992. Release are meanwhile working with Damon Taylor, a lecturer at the renowned Buckinghamshire Art & Design College, to come up with fresh ways of grabbing the attention of Britain's notoriously fickle youth. One idea is projecting images onto the walls of clubs, the images designed to be both visually entertaining and make people think a bit deeper about their drug use.

"If somebody isn't into drugs, they would probably have a problem understanding the images," says Ciaran O'Hagan. "But we're not interested in those people. Not in the context of a club. Prevention is to take place elsewhere. While you'll always get people in clubs who don't take drugs, you are far more likely to get those who do or who are contemplating doing so. The difficulty is getting their attention. If drug services want to be taken seriously in the youth market, we have to recognise that we're competing with the likes of Coca Cola and Playstation, companies which change their advertising campaigns all the time. Nothing lasts more than six months. We have to realise that our campaigns need to change all the time, too.

"The beauty of Peanut Pete was the first time ecstasy users had something tailor-made for them and it's important to maintain that exclusivity. Too often, information targeted at dance culture ends up filtering through to other groups of people and then it loses its impact. We need to make it so tight that, if you miss something the first time, fuck it, it's gone. It's like it's deleted, like a record. In the club scene, everyone wants something exclusive, they want that limited edition vinyl, that new remix, that white label. You have to be sharper than the rest and that goes for the drug services, too. If we're not as sharp as every other fucker, nobody will listen to us, however valuable our information is. There's always that bit extra everyone is pushing for and I don't think that's something any government will ever grasp."

(P)

28

Leaflet: Chill Out

Chill Out – A Raver's Guide was one of the first harm reduction leaflets produced in the UK. Designed to mimic a club flyer and with a picture of the crowd at an Adamski gig on the front, it gave the lowdown on the effects of ecstasy, acid and speed. It also included information on what to do if a friend felt ill after taking drugs. The tabloid press claimed the leaflet encouraged drug-taking and variously described it as "crackpot", "pernicious" and "sick".

Excerpt from *Chill Out – A Raver's Guide*
Written by Alan Matthews
Published by Mersey Drug Training & Information Centre, 1991
Reproduced by kind permission

If you have taken drugs and start to feel ill, tell someone and ask them to help. If you are going to help someone in this situation or someone gets panicky, take them to a quiet place where you can be on your own (e.g. a chill out, another room, or go for a walk out of the club) and calm them down by explaining that they are experiencing the effects of a drug which will wear off within a short while and by reassuring them that they are quite safe.

Do not give them tea, coffee or alcohol to drink, or any other drugs to take (if they smoke, a cigarette may help to calm them) and don't let them have anything to eat. Sips of fruit juice or water can be given if needed.

If someone is breathing rapidly, help them to breathe slowly and deeply by counting each breath slowly in and out with them. Quite soon they will begin to calm down. However, if they get more panicky and you cannot cope, phone an ambulance or take them to a hospital casualty department. When you get there, don't mess about, explain to a nurse and/or doctor what your friend has taken and how long ago.

If someone faints, it may be because of heat, exhaustion or drugs – or a combination of all three. Make sure they are getting enough air, give them space, and check they aren't hurt if they fell. When they come round and are OK, take them somewhere cool, sit them down with their head between their knees. They'll soon feel better, but don't let them get up too soon, give it 10–15 minutes.

If someone collapses (eyes rolled back, erratic breathing, skin cold and clammy), CALL AN AMBULANCE IMMEDIATELY – if anyone has first aid experience, get them to help. Lie the person on their side with head turned to one side (the recovery position), and keep an eye on their breathing and pulse. When the ambulance arrives, tell the medics what the person has taken and how much – don't be afraid, this could save their life.

29

E Testing

Amsterdam takes its reputation as the pleasure capital of Europe seriously. The city's prostitutes, of which there are an estimated 5,000, have a well-organised trade union. And despite the fact that, contrary to popular belief, prostitution is not technically legal in Amsterdam, the government has no qualms about making the girls who flash flesh in the windows of the red light district pay tax on their earnings. They're a pragmatic lot, the Dutch – sometimes confusingly so.

The Dutch authorities' attitude to drug use can be similarly puzzling to the outsider. In Holland, drugs are controlled under the Opium Act, which was originally passed in 1919 and has been tweaked numerous times in the years since, but the national legislation allows for different cities to develop different drugs policies within a set of given parameters. The policies are consequently determined by varying local conditions and issues. Amsterdam takes a much more relaxed view than elsewhere in the country, particularly towards cannabis, with the spiky leaf often employed as an alternative-lifestyle coat-of-arms. But while it is not considered a criminal offence to possess a small quantity of cannabis for personal use, anyone found carrying more than 30g (a few crumbs over an ounce) could face legal action. The city's famous coffee shops can sell the drug only under tightly controlled permits and are not allowed to make individual transactions of over five grams. They are also not allowed to have more than 500g of cannabis on the premises. Any coffee shop breaking these rules runs the risk of being closed down.

The authorities' distinction between possession for personal use and possession with intent to supply others isn't made only in relation to cannabis, but to all drugs scheduled under the Opium Act. When it comes to ecstasy, which was declared a Schedule I drug in Holland in 1988, carrying a single pill (or up to half a gram of ecstasy powder) is officially treated as a misdemeanour rather than a criminal offence. The police will confiscate the tablet, but no further action will generally be taken. In practice, many police officers will allow the possession of up to four or five tablets before taking action beyond confiscation. Handling a large amount of ecstasy or any other Schedule I drug is quite another matter, though. Dealing in Schedule I drugs is punishable by up to eight years in prison and cross-border trafficking by up to 12 years. If it is a repeated offence, the sentence can be increased by up to one third of this eight- or 12-year maximum.

Treading lightly on the consumer end of the drugs world while directing the weight of the law towards the upper links of the chain, the Dutch approach has frequently been criticised by politicians in other countries as encouraging drug use. Yet the perception of Holland as some kind of drug haven is a long way from the truth – at least as far as the harder stuff goes. During the mid-Nineties, 20 years on from the initiation of the Dutch model, 1.6 persons in every thousand members of the population were estimated to be addicted to hard drugs (principally heroin) compared to 2.6 persons in every thousand in the UK.

As everywhere in the world that the boom-boom beat prevails, ecstasy use in Holland is closely associated with the dance scene. Since the start of the Nineties, vast parts of the Dutch scene have been dominated by hardcore techno and gabba – ultra hard and ultra fast sounds (the bpm rammed up as high as 300) deliberately designed to act as a direct counter to warm and soulful house music. The title of LA Style's 'James Brown Is Dead', one of the earliest big records of the Lowlands hardcore genre, says it all. If the energy levels at gabba parties could be harnessed, the Dutch wouldn't need power stations. The crowds are totally nuts.

A common sight both at gabba raves and at other, tamer dance events in Holland is the Adviesburo Drugs stall. Set up in 1986 by drugs advice worker August de Loor and operating under the banner of the Safe House campaign, Adviesburo Drugs have long promoted the same kind of harm reduction policies as the likes of Release and Lifeline in the UK. But the Dutch organisation takes the concept of harm reduction several steps further by offering ecstasy users a tablet testing service, not only at their rave stalls but also outside of normal party hours at their Amsterdam office.

Testing a tablet is a complex process. The starting point for the Adviesburo Drugs staff is to perform an indicator test using a colourless chemical reagent called Marquis Reagent, a drop of which is placed on a tiny scraping taken from the pill. If the pill contains MDMA or an MDMA-related substance, the chemical reaction causes a dark, almost blackish blue colour to appear. If it contains amphetamine, the colour change is to orange. If it contains 2C-B, the change is to green.

The Marquis Reagent test is, however, of limited value. It only offers an indication of the likely dominant ingredient of the tablet and it is entirely possible for other substances to cause exactly the same colour changes. It doesn't reveal how much of that ingredient is present and neither does it reveal what else might be in there. Most importantly for users trying to be sure that what they're about to neck is pure ecstasy, Marquis Reagent cannot distinguish between MDMA, MDA, MDE or any other similar substance. Indeed, the only certainty is when there is no colour change, meaning that no ecstasy-type substance, no amphet-amine and no 2C-B is present. What is present, though, is anybody's guess.

The next step in the Adviesburo Drugs test is to undertake a physical examination of the pill, noting the colour, shape and size (both diameter and thickness, which are measured using a micrometer), together with information about any logo. The physical characteristics are then cross-referenced with the Adviesburo's extensive lists of known tablets which have undergone laboratory analysis, lists which date right back to the earliest days of the organisation. For someone taking a pill to the Adviesburo stall at a rave, this is where the testing process ends, whereas those popping into the office throughout the week also have their tablets sent to a laboratory for further examination. As well as giving the user a clearer picture of what might be in store for them on Saturday night, the laboratory information is vital to continue building up the lists of known pills.

Herman-Louis Matser, who has been testing at Adviesburo Drugs since the off, claims the organisation has "a pretty much complete picture" of the pills doing the rounds in Holland. He is, however, careful to point out that a user is not told if their tablet is good or bad – "we can never be sure, we can only warn about the dangers," he says. Matser also notes that it's important to continually test because the components of the pills are con-stantly changing – two physically identical pills from the same source could contain 150mg of MDMA one week and 50g the next. And with a staff of only four people, this reality often translates into very long working hours. At least the nature of the work puts a different spin on the idea of 'just another day at the office'.

What is the legal status of tablet testing in Holland? Is it legal?
Herman-Louis Matser: "It's tolerated. The Adviesburo has a piece of paper from the Justice Department saying we're allowed to test. We're the only people allowed to do it, though. Officially, if someone hands a tablet to a tester, the tester handles it and then gives it back, there could be a problem of supply. If you look at the law literally, the user should take a scrape and measure the tablet themselves. Then there would be no legal problem at all."

If there are police officers at a rave where you are testing, how do they react?
"In general, they're happy we're there. They leave us alone. They have their job to do and we have ours. It's strange for them, maybe, because we ask raves to have a relaxed searching policy. We tell the police that it's better to let people keep the tablets they've bought from somebody they probably know. If you take tablets away from them at the entrance, they look to buy again when they get inside the rave and end up buying from somebody they probably don't know. That can be more risky."

Why does Adviesburo Drugs not test at clubs, only at raves?
"If you test at clubs, those clubs will soon be closed. They would get a reputation as a drugs club, because testing makes visible what otherwise stays hidden. Clubs are also smaller and different social controls are working. If a dealer sells bullshit in a club, everyone knows about it very quickly. But it's different for the bigger raves, when you have 10,000 or 15,000 people coming from all over Holland. Rave crowds are also usually younger, so it's an ideal place for someone to sell bullshit if they want to."

How many pills do you test in an average week?
"There are big changes in the number. At the office, anything from 30 to 100, maybe 200. If there are tablets with strange effects around, lots and lots of people will come. The same mechanisms are at work at a rave. For some people, though, it's a kind of ritual to have their tablets tested."

You charge a fee for the testing service, don't you?
"We charge two-and-a-half guilders [just under one pound] at raves and five guilders at the office. If we didn't charge, people would come back after half an hour and say, 'What was in that tablet I had tested?' If they pay, they listen."

And you test for dealers as well as for users?
"How can you see the difference? But if we test for one dealer, then we help more consumers than if we test for one consumer. If they are coming to have their tablets tested, then they are good dealers."

You try to make people good dealers, then?
"We try. Most dealers want satisfied customers, they want people to come back, so there's no logic in selling bad stuff. It's difficult, though, because the more popular a type of tablet gets, the more tempting it is to put in less and less MDMA or put in something else. Tablets often start with a high dose of MDMA but drop to a lower dose as the market for it grows. Sometimes it's the original producer and sometimes it's a counterfeiter.

157

People ask why don't we put our results on the internet, but then you give away all the information. Someone will say, 'Ah, this pill has a high dose of MDMA, so we'll make ours with that logo in that colour with those dimensions.' It's not difficult to do that. That's why we have to keep testing. In a sense, we're always behind. We can say how a tablet was yesterday, but we don't know whether it will be the same tomorrow. It changes very fast."

As well as picking out dangerous pills, is testing also a useful tool for opening discussions with people about their drug use?
"Completely. If it's somebody who's already obviously taken a few tablets, we can say, 'Hey man, what's the use of testing this pill? You've already taken so much. It's people like you who have caused this to be illegal.' They don't like that, of course. Also, if I find a nasty tablet, I will always give it back to the person. Always. It's up to them if they take it. I tell them, 'I wouldn't take this shit, it will make you trip out for two days – but if you like that, go ahead'. I've never seen anyone take a tablet after being told something like that. And if they do, it's their responsibility. You take drugs? Okay, but you're responsible."

Are most people responsible about their ecstasy use?
"A lot take it too easily. They take a pill and, if the evening was nice, the pill was good. No. That's much too easy. A pill doesn't guarantee a good feeling. People generally learn that, but it often takes too much time and too much ecstasy. That's unfortunate because the less ecstasy you take, the more it gives you. If you take a lot of it for a long time, you stop getting the ecstasy effect. You'll only get the stimulating effect and, because it's a small effect, you need more and more tablets to feel it. People who take a lot of pills are looking for that feeling, but it's not the ecstasy feeling. And when they have a tablet tested and they find out that it's amphetamine they'll say, 'Oh, I don't like that.' They'd rather take five or six ecstasy pills to achieve exactly the same result. That's remarkable."

You say that you always hand "a nasty tablet" back to its owner, but what happens if you find something really dangerous?
"We get the results from the laboratory on Fridays and we can then see what the pills contain. If we find something dangerous, we make flyers about it and take it to the rave that weekend. We keep the flyers under the table and, if we see these dangerous pills are around, we hand out the flyers. Within half an hour, people know what not to buy. As a last resort, we once stopped a rave to announce that a dangerous pill was out there. Warning campaigns are very strong weapons, though, so the less you use

them the more effective they are. If you warn people every week, they stop listening. It's often unnecessary, too. We'll tell the owner of the pill, 'Tell the guys behind this pill that we'll have big problems if it gets on the market. There will be pieces in the newspapers and that's no good for anybody.' We usually find that those tablets then disappear from the market."

What happens to them?
"They go outside of Holland. They go over the borders."

Including to the UK?
"Especially to the UK. People know they can sell the heavy stuff there."

In 1996, *Muzik* magazine invited its readers to take part in a simple telephone poll. The magazine posed the question, 'Do you think ecstasy testing should be introduced to UK clubs?' and printed two 0891 telephone numbers – a 'Yes' number and a 'No' number. Just under 1,000 people participated in the survey, with a massive 98 per cent supporting the idea of testing. While many who dialled the 'Yes' number probably had only limited knowledge of the activities of Adviesburo Drugs in Amsterdam, there's no denying the strength of their perception that the environment is safer for Dutch E users than it is for their British counterparts.

Although perhaps unknown to the majority of ecstasy users, tablet testing is now taking place in the UK. It is, however, extremely limited, both in terms of scope and of value. Release have been using the Marquis Reagent test at underground parties since 1998, checking around 20 pills on a busy night. The Green Party, whose manifesto calls for the possession of a small amount of drugs for personal use to no longer be a criminal offence, have been doing the same. Neither Release nor the Greens shout too loudly about what they are doing and their testers are careful not to handle drugs at any point in the procedure, making users take a scrape from the pill themselves.

As well as irregular Marquis Reagent testing at raves, it's also possible to buy home-testing kits in the UK. Possible and legal. The most popular is the commercially marketed E-Z Test. The Green Party, meanwhile, offer two testing kits, one consisting of Marquis Reagent and a micrometer, the other consisting of the reagent alone. The Greens' advise people to compare measurements taken with the micrometer against information on laboratory-analysed pills posted on Ecstasy.org, the internet website founded by Nicholas Saunders, the author of *E Is For Ecstasy* and *Ecstasy Reconsidered*, who died in a road accident in 1998.

The Greens' kits were launched at the end of 1997 with a press conference in London, the speakers at which included Nicholas Saunders and one-time dope smuggler Howard Marks. This was followed by a testing session outside The Fridge in Brixton. A few months later, George Howarth, the Home Office minister with special responsibility for drugs, confirmed to Parliament that the kits were legal and the government had no plans to change this. Howarth's announcement probably didn't go down well with Keith Hellawell, the Drug Czar, though. Hellawell has described the kits as "immoral".

Adviesburo Drugs' Herman-Louis Matser isn't a fan of these testing kits, either, pointing out that "the limitations should be made very clear, otherwise it gives a false sense of safety". He does, however, recognise that they have "some worth" in the absence of the kind of laboratory analyses available in Holland. Release and the Green Party are themselves both aware of the rudimentary nature of their testing work and, in order to help rectify this, the latter have called on the government to grant public access to the laboratory results of tablets examined by the National Criminal Intelligence Service (NCIS). They're probably not holding their breath, though. In the meantime, Release's Ciaran O'Hagan thinks much of the benefit of Marquis Reagent testing in clubs is as an educational tool.

"You can spark up some interesting conversations with people while you test their pills and get much more intimate work done than you would just handing them a leaflet," he explains. "We're able to say to people stuff like, 'This tablet isn't registering a colour change, which means it could be anything, so I'd advise you to question whether you should take it.' Or show them a colour change and say, 'This is coming up as an MDMA-related substance but, first, we don't know how much is in it and, second, MDMA itself is not safe, so make sure you do this and this as well.' We need to be able to get involved on that kind of practical level, to start talking about bodyweight ratio and so on. We need to get people thinking about their ecstasy use in a different way, rather than just throwing pills down their throats and crossing their fingers."

This is a key point. But even if the British government were to make NCIS laboratory information on pills available, would UK users react as positively to testing as *Muzik*'s 1996 poll suggested? Some drug experts think not. Mike Linnell from Lifeline is one of them.

"Just because tablet testing works in Holland doesn't mean that it will work in the UK," says Linnell. "The two countries are completely differ-ent cultures. The British consume alcohol in a different way and we consume drugs in a different way. The Dutch Antenna Project, which tries to monitor trends in drug use, has found that the average age of an Amsterdam heroin user is 39, whereas our lot are getting younger. They also monitor levels of cannabis use in Dutch schools. It's currently running at 26 per cent. It's double that in Manchester. We consume ecstasy in a different way to the Dutch, too. We've taken experienced drug users from Holland to British clubs and they've been shocked at what they've seen.

"We had a lad who died after taking E in Blackpool a few years ago. On the next day's television news, there was a man in a white coat in a laboratory. He was holding up a brown dove and saying, 'This pill has killed a young person in Blackpool and anyone who has this kind of pill should dispose of it immediately.' That weekend, our workers reported people were going round asking where they could get these brown doves because they'd heard they were really good. It was madness. But then the British are basically beasts. We lead the world in our ability to consume vast amounts of pills and booze – sometimes at the same time – and not give a fuck about it."

It's difficult to pick holes in this observation. But to Shane Collins, the Green Party's Drugs Spokesperson, accepting this line is defeatist.

"It's certainly true that hedonism is a great British tradition, but the only way to change that is by people having greater knowledge of what they're doing," counters Collins. "Yes, some people will neck anything, but if your mates know it's a dud pill, they'll say, 'You twat.' And if you feel ill after taking it, they'll say, 'Serves you right, you twat.' That's how some people learn. While I accept Mike Linnell's point, I think we should try to change it. Let's not just leave it as it is."

(P)

30

Beyond The Gateway I: Ketamine, GHB, 2C-B And Methamphetamine

Anti-drug lobbyists have often used the theory of 'gateway drugs' when fighting decriminalisation. The gateway theory being that once a person tries an illicit substance, and crosses the threshold of the law, an entire world of illegal drugs opens up to that person. That this person will be more likely to essay other drugs, possibly harder drugs. For years, those on the drug-tolerance side refuted this. For the longest time, the so-called 'gateway drug' was identified as cannabis. Throughout the Sixties, Seventies and Eighties pro-pot activists pointed to the many people they knew who only smoked spliff and had no interest in becoming heroin addicts or speed freaks, thank you very much. The gateway theory just sounded *uninformed*. However, in the Nineties with ecstasy as the new first-drug-tried for many, it began to seem less so. One need only to look at the bulging pharmacopoeia of today's clubland to understand why. In the Nineties, a Pandora's box had clearly been cracked. Something had to have opened it.

It could well have been E. There is no question that the MDMA boom of the Eighties created a whole new generation of drug users who, by the next decade, were looking for other drugs to try. Because of curiosity. Because of E burn-out. Because of the realisation that drugs might not be the devil. That drugs might be fun, liberating, helpful even. They'd tried ecstasy – a Class A, a Schedule I – and the sky didn't fall. It just became prettier.

Yet pinning the 'gateway' charge on E alone is blinkered. Even if the 1988 Summer Of Love had never happened, the Nineties internet revolution still would have. And the internet immediately gave marginalised data prominence and space. It has served as an incredible portal to information about an alphabet soup of illegal drugs – substances which, prior to the www.world, few outside the laboratory, the psychedelic community or the DEA would have heard of. The internet gave drugs culture its own phone line and anyone could call. Sometimes you could even use your credit card to order in.

The roster of illegal and controlled substances which achieved a new prominence during the last decade of the 20th century is seemingly endless. The four drugs detailed below are synthetic substances which can be seen as 'post-E' in terms of more than marginal usage: drugs which became popular on the Nineties club and rave scenes, and can be considered novel, but only for their inclusion in the mainstream dance context. In addition to these, it should be noted that, both inside and outside the nightlife environment, the use of more established illegal substances such as cocaine, acid and speed also rose to unprecedented heights in the Nineties.

Ketamine (ketamine hydrochloride)

Street names: K, special K, vitamin K, ket, cat valium

Legal status: Unauthorised supply illegal in the UK (under the Medicines Act), Schedule III in the US

First synthesised in America in 1962, ketamine is a hallucinogenic, dis-associative anaesthetic related to phencyclidine (PCP). Today, it is commonly administered as a human anaesthetic in the Third World and regularly used by veterinarians in many countries to anaesthetise house pets and farm animals. It was initially used recreationally by those on the Sixties 'neuroconsciousness frontier'. "Ecstasy hinted at how powerful the mind could be, that once first gear was mastered, there was a second gear, and a third," wrote Jay Stevens in *Storming Heaven: LSD And The American Dream*. "Compared to MDMA, vitamin K was 10th gear."

Ketamine found its way onto the gay club scenes of big American cities like New York and Los Angeles in the Seventies, and emerged palpably in Britain in the late Eighties, sometimes being sold as ecstasy at raves. By the early Nineties, it had come into its own on the UK clubscape, often gaining popularity in times of ecstasy drought. K remains a fairly common drug on the UK club and rave scenes, an extremely prominent drug on the US scenes, and a staple of the international gay dance circuit and among psychedelic devotees.

Almost all of the ketamine which reaches the street is diverted from medical and veterinary sources. In the Nineties, a rash of vet burglaries on both sides of the Atlantic were the result of escalating K use. Pharmaceutical ketamine (such as Ketalar, produced by Parke-Davis) is an odourless, colourless liquid meant for injection, but much of the K used recretionally is in powder form (the liquid boiled down) and is taken by snorting 'bumps' (short lines) of the substance. Users may also inject re-liquified K intramuscularly, take it orally by mixing it with fluids, or shoot the drug up the rectum, using a syringe with the needle removed. The psychedelic line dose for ketamine is around 1.8 to 2mg per pound of body mass. The effects last from 20 to 40 minutes.

Ketamine acts on many different systems in the brain, but some of the key effects are believed to be due to its blocking of NMDA (N-methyl-D-aspartate) receptors. These receptors play a role in memory, motor activity and thinking. By blocking them, the drug creates a wall against 'incoming data' and the brain then fills the empty space inside the wall with data collected from the chasms of the mind, rather than the outside world. The slang term 'K-hole' refers to the sometimes nightmarish place a person can reach through this process. Certain psychotherapists believe that ketamine's ability to unlock embedded thoughts or memories may make it a valuable tool for therapy.

Because K is a disassociative, its most consistent effect is that it separates the physical experience from the mental: many users report that they feel as if their physical body belongs to something or someone or somewhere else – that their view of their own physicality is third person-like. Classic disassociative phenomena include out of body experiences, celestial or cosmic voyages, time travel and perceptions often associated with near-death experiences. Like many other anaesthetics, ketamine can also cause extreme nausea and vomiting. Motor skills may be all but lost, speech may be extremely tricky, and the substance isn't particularly kind to music.

In anything but minimal doses, K is a long way from a social drug. Barring the undeniable escapist qualities, it's an oddball inclusion on the dance pharmacopoeia – something as simple as walking, never mind dancing, can be both difficult and dangerous while high. In New York, the term 'K boots' is used to describe the lead-footed motions of someone trying to walk while on the drug. Ketamine can also depress breathing when injected intravenously and shouldn't be used with other respiratory depressants, such as alcohol or GHB. In large doses, K has caused temporary psychosis, which can mimic schizophrenia, and has been known to induce trance-like states with odd physical movements. The drug can be psychologically addictive, too. Little is known about the long-term effects on the brain of regular use.

GHB (gamma-hydroxybutyrate)

Street names: G, soap, liquid ecstasy

Legal status: Unauthorised supply illegal in the UK, tightly controlled but not scheduled in the US

GHB, an anaesthetic with pseudo-steroid properties, was first synthesised in the Sixties by Dr H Laborit and was originally intended as a sleeping aid. GHB has been medically administered as a general anaesthetic, as a treatment for insomnia, narcolepsy and alcoholism, and as an aid in child-birth. In the Eighties, it was widely available in American health food shops - its ability to stimulate pituitary growth hormone release made it a popular body-building drug.

GHB became common on the American club and rave scenes in the mid-Nineties, when it was often seen as a cheaper ($10 a hit) and easier-to-handle alternative to ecstasy. It has also proved a resilient addition to the international gay dance pharmacopoeia. It made a brief appearance in UK clubs in the mid-Nineties, with users often procuring it from sex shops, but the interest of the UK clubland hasn't been sustained.

The substance is usually sold as a clear liquid in a small vial or, more rarely, as a powder. A vial of GHB is usually poured into a drink and then sipped. Both the odour and taste of the drug can be slightly plasticky. A dose hits within 10 to 20 minutes and yields a one to two-hour buzz.

The drug gives a recreational high by storing up levels of the neuro-transmitter dopamine, the brain chemical which is believed to play a large part in feelings such as pleasure and reward. In the brain, some GHB is converted into GABA (gamma-amino butyric acid), a neurotransmitter in the central nervous system which helps to stop nerve cells from firing too fast. Overactive nerve cells can cause tension, anxiety and physical conditions like muscle spasms or epileptic fits.

In low doses (generally 0.5 to1.5g), GHB has an uninhibiting effect which many users have likened to that of MDMA. Others say the light, euphoric, often prosexual buzz of low dosage GHB is like being tipsy on alcohol. In higher dosages, these effects intensify and the drug can cause vomiting and extreme vertigo. High doses can also induce a sudden, deep sleep (hence its effectiveness as a sedative) and, in rare cases, a coma. It should further be noted that concentrations of GHB vary wildly. In addition, the dose-response curve of the substance is extremely steep: one person's pleasant buzz can be another's overdose.

Mixing the drug with some other substances can turn GHB from a rather lamb-like drug to a potential leveller. GHB can cause respiratory depression and using it with other substances which depress breathing, such as alcohol, can result in respiratory arrest. GHB mixing has caused several deaths in both America and Europe. In the US, problems with people collapsing after mixing GHB have prompted some of the first visible signs of 'official' drug recognition in rave-generation clubs and events – usually posters and flyers with messages like 'Don't Mix GHB' or 'GHB = Danger!'

2C-B (4-bromo-2,5-dimethoxyphenethylamine)

Streetnames: Nexus, twocees, ceebees

Legal status: Class A in the UK (under the Misuse Of Drugs Act), Schedule I in the US

2C-B was first synthesised by Californian chemist Alexander Shulgin in the Seventies. This highly psychedelic substance is classed as a phenethylamine – the same drug family as MDMA, MDA and MDEA. Other phenethylamines include DOB (2,5-dimethoxy-4-bromoamphetamine), a strong psychedelic stimulant called 'golden eagle' or '100X' on the street (users say it feels 100 times stronger than ecstasy), and PMA or 4-MA (4-methoxyamphetamine), a substance sold as 'chicken yellow' in the Eighties and 'flatliner ecstasy' in the Nineties. PMA is highly toxic and has led to several deaths (hence the grim 'flatliners' tag), including 12 fatalities in Australia in 1997.

2C-B is a less volatile substance than either DOB or 4-MA – its strength and effectiveness are more compatible with MDMAs. In the early Nineties, when 2C-B was still legal in many parts of the world, it was marketed by a German company called Drittewelle under the name of Nexus. Advertised as an aphrodisiac, Nexus was available for purchase in health food and sex shops in the US and parts of Europe. Now banned pretty much everywhere, 2C-B has often been fallaciously sold as ecstasy. By the mid- Nineties, though, it had come in to its own as a moderately popular club drug in Europe and in large American cities, sometimes taken in conjunction with E.

The effects of 2C-B fall between the tactile properties of ecstasy and the hallucinogenic properties of LSD. Unlike many other psychedelics, 2C-B can have a touchy-feely effect. In low doses (5 to 10mg), the drug gives a 'body buzz' and a heightened awareness to sensual stimuli such as light and taste. In higher doses (10 to 25mg, although some seasoned users use up to 40mg) these effects are enhanced and the drug can also become highly hallucinogenic, but not as terribly introspective as LSD can be.

Many users say a 2C-B high is manoeuvrable, in that it can be steered to an extent. Some say the high is largely positive, but 2C-B is not considered to be empathogenic the way ecstasy is and users sometimes take it with MDMA to guide their experience in a more empathogenic direction. Bad 2C-B trips, complete with nightmarish hallucinations, are not uncommon and, because the drug enhances physical sensations, it can highlight any physical discomforts, which can be very unpleasant. 2C-B can also cause vomiting, diarrhoea, stomach gas and bloating. The drug has an onset of 45-75 minutes and the effects last four to eight hours. Little is known about the long-term effects of 2C-B on the brain.

Methamphetamine (d-N-methylamphetamine)

Street names: Crystal meth, meth, crystal, crank, Mexican speed, redneck coke, poor man's coke, tina, crypto, cryptonite, ice (smokeable methamphetamine only)

Legal Status: Class A (if prepared for injection) or Class B in the UK, Schedule II in the US

Methamphetamine, commonly known as crystal meth on the street, is thought to be the strongest of all amphetamine analogues. A central nervous system stimulant first created in 1919 by Japanese chemist Dr A Ogata, it has been prescribed under the commercial name Desoxyn for a variety of medical conditions, including obesity and narcolepsy, and in the treatment of Attention Deficit Hyperactivity Disorder.

Methamphetamine gained prominence as a recreational substance during the Sixties, when it was mainly distributed in the US by motorcycle gangs, and has been described as one of the chemicals to ruin the San Francisco hippy community love vibe at the end of the decade. In Seventies and Eighties America, it had an unshakeable reputation as a redneck drug due to its popularity with night-shift blue collar workers and truck drivers.

Synthesised using readily procurable chemicals extracted from products like household drain cleaners and allergy medications, methamphetamine has been illegally produced in clandestine labs in rural parts of America since the Sixties. It is rarely diverted from medical sources in the US, as controls on pharmaceutical methamphetamine are extremely stringent. In the late Eighties, production of the drug began in illegal 'superlabs' in Mexico and, by the Nineties, use in America rose to what the DEA called epidemic proportions, transcending all social and racial boundaries. Methamphetamine isn't so widely used in Europe, though. In Britain, it's most prevalent in the north of England and in Scotland. It is, however, an exceedingly popular drug on the international gay dance circuit.

The drug comes as white-ish powder (which is usually snorted or injected), as a pill (taken orally, or crushed and snorted or injected) and as a translucent rock. Rocks or crystals are the most potent form and are often smoked through glass pipes or broken-off light bulb tops, or using tin foil and straws. On the street, a crystal meth dose usually costs less than half the price of an E or a comparable cocaine dose. It hits quickly (seven seconds when smoked) but metabolises slowly: one hit lasts four to eight hours.

Unlike other stimulants, such as cocaine, methamphetamine doesn't simply block the reuptake of neurotransmitters by the brain's nerve cells. It also enters the storage vesicles of cells and forces neurotransmitters such as dopamine and norepinephrine to leak out. Metaphorically speaking, it plugs up the drain and turns on the tap. Ingesting the substance instigates the body's 'fight or flight' response, the neurological state often reached at times of extreme emergency, such as life-or-death situations. Some meth users have said the drug feels like cocaine, ecstasy and speed combined, bringing intense confidence, euphoria and boundless energy with no need for sleep.

Methamphetamine can also provoke extreme restlessness, long-lasting insomnia, and feelings of panic, anxiety and paranoia together with hallucinations. In high doses, it can induce a pattern of psychosis marked by severe aggression, or confused or repetitive behaviours, such as compulsive scratching of skin or masturbation, often leading to deep lacerations. Some users have stated that the drug provokes a strong need for sexual gratification. Methamphetamine is highly psychologically addictive – in addictive qualities, it ranks higher than cocaine. The drug has been known to inspire bingeing and some abusers (known as 'tweakers') have been admitted to hospital after staying continuously awake and high for up to one month straight.

The physical effects of methamphetamine include increased pulse, blood pressure, temperature and respiration. Users are advised to stay cool and hydrated. The use of the drug alone can lead to stroke, convulsions or heart attack. This danger is exacerbated by mixing with other drugs, especially other stimulants, including ecstasy. Many of the dangers involve the behaviours crystal meth induces, which can be violent or reckless. The psychosis which can result from over-use of the substance can be fairly long-lasting (and can mimic schizophrenia), but seems to completely dissipate with time. Little is known about any long-term effects on the brain.

31

Beyond The Gateway II:
Legal And Prescription Drugs

One of the greatest myths concerning drugs has long been that legal drugs, the things doctors prescribe, are safe. Illegal drugs, the things Joe Blow sells on the street corner, are dangerous. Legal drugs are our friends – they treat sickness and ailments. Illegal drugs require a 'war' against them. Yet the fact remains that, in both the UK and the US, more people die every year as a result of taking prescribed and over-the-counter medications than from all illegal drugs combined.

The legal drug myth has travelled well into club culture: words like 'pharmaceutical' are often equated with words like 'safe'. In actuality, this falls very short of the truth. According to UK government figures, between 1993 and 1998, the drugs most implicated in deaths in Scotland were legal tranquillisers like Valium and temazepam – both of which were rife on the recreational black market during this period.

The boom in ecstasy use in the Nineties created a demand for complementary chemicals: chemicals to take with, before, after or as an alternative to E. Yet it's no new phenomenon that many in this chorus of substances came from the medical and health industries. Drugs diverted from hospitals or bought at the pharmacy have always had a place in musical youth culture: just think of jazz hipsters in the Twenties using benzedrine asthma inhalers for a dance-all-night buzz, or mods in the Sixties raiding their mum's stock of 'mother's little helpers' to induce sleep after a speed binge.

The drugs detailed below include some similarly recontextualised substances which have become popular in the post-E era. They are not necessarily 'lighter' than many illegal drugs, though. In terms of 'lightness' or 'heaviness', they are drugs which have simply been spared an early letter or a low digit in the highly subjective art of drug scheduling. Sometimes because doctors believe their medical use is indispensable. Sometimes because they are big money-makers for the pharmaceutical industry. And

169

sometimes because the authorities are unaware of the double lives certain substances lead.

Benzodiazepines (temazepam, Rohypnol)

Benzodiazepine medications are prescribed by doctors for insomnia, anxiety, severe agitation, panic attacks and seizure disorders. The first benzodiazepine made commercially available was Librium (chlordiazepoxide), which was put on the market by the Swiss drugs company Hoffman-La Roche in 1960. Other benzodiazepines available on prescription in America and Europe to help cope with everyday anxieties include Valium (diazepam), which was particularly popular with housewives in the Sixties. They were often called 'mother's little helpers'. Today, benzodiazepines are among the most commonly prescribed drugs in Britain, where one in seven people take them at some point during the course of every year.

Benzodiazepines work by binding to GABA neurotransmitter receptor sites, keeping the receptor sites open longer and allowing more nerve-calming GABA to flow in. Benzodiazepine medications have an average onset of 20 to 30 minutes and the effects of a prescribed dose can induce sleep, relaxation or a feeling of comfort. The drug can gently loosen inhibitions, and cause light-headedness and dizziness, but taking too much can increase excitability and behaviour may become exaggerated, aggressive or hostile. Benzodiazepines can also affect motor skills and judgment (driving is an extremely bad idea).

It is very uncommon for people to OD on benzodiazepines alone, but mixing with other substances, including alcohol, can depress breathing and lead to severe or lethal consequences. Benzodiazepines are physically addictive and withdrawal symptoms include anxiety, sleeplessness, panic attacks, tremors and sometimes hallucinations, which can persist for weeks after stopping use. An abrupt withdrawal from high doses of the drug can cause convulsions and fits, and should be undertaken with medical supervision.

In the Nineties, benzodiazepines were a popular and inexpensive way to come down from ecstasy or to temper strong E. The illegal use of benzodiazepines became big news, not least in the media, in the form of two medications: temazepam, one of Britain's most prescribed sleep medications, and flunitrazepam. The second of these is better known by its brand name, Rohypnol.

Temazepam medications are commercially available as Restoril, Normison or Temazepam (the brand name under which it is produced by Mylan). Street tags include 'jellies', 'tems' and 'eggs'. The drug was extremely problematic on the Scottish rave scene in the mid-1990s, with some users injecting the substance with heroin to intensify the latter's 'blot-out' effect. Injecting temazepam gelcaps can lead to gangrene, sometimes resulting in amputations. Temazepam is a Class C drug in the UK (under the Misuse Of Drugs Act) and a Schedule IV substance in the US.

Rohypnol, a benzodiazepine produced by Hoffman-La Roche, has street names which include 'roofies', 'roofinol', 'rope', 'rib' and 'rapers'. It is much stronger and acts for longer than temazepam, and some recreational users claim it is extremely prosexual. In the US, the substance has found popularity in scenes ranging from the rave circuit (often taken with or after E) to country & western bars and also on college campuses (often used as an alcohol enhancer, as it can make a person feel more drunk).

Rohypnol has been at the centre of several media scares since first being identified as a 'date rape drug' by the American press in the early Nineties. It has reportedly been ultilised by 'bar rapists', who drop the tasteless, easily dissolved pills into the drinks of unsuspecting victims and then take advantage of the resulting drugged or sometimes unconscious state. Rohypnol can also have an amnesiac effect (it's hard to recall what happened by the next day), which makes it a particularly effective 'rape drug'. In the US, the authorities have issued general warnings about leaving drinks unattended in public places and accepting beverages from strangers, and there have been recent reports of Rohypnol-assisted rape in the UK. Hoffman-La Roche added a blue dye to Rohypnol in 1998, to make the drug more detectable in drinks. Rohypnol is classified as a Schedule IV drug in the US, but is Schedule I in certain states. Supply of the drug is controlled under the Medicines Act in the UK.

DXM (dextromethorphan hydrobromide)

A cough suppressant, DXM is often referred to as 'Robo' in the States, after the over-the-counter cough syrup Robitussin, in which the drug is the main active ingredient. The recreational ingestion of DXM is usually through large doses of cough syrup or cough capsules containing the chemical, which was first used in these medications as a non-narcotic replacement for codeine in the Sixties. The chances are that the street use of DXM was discovered by those already drinking cough syrups recreationally for the codeine content.

By the Eighties, the drug had become popular with high school students and also with punks in the US hardcore scene, mainly due to its easy accessibility and cheap price. In the Nineties, the use of DXM gained momentum through internet word-of-mouth. The drug remains extremely popular with teenage American ravers, for whom ecstasy may be too expensive. Pure DXM is now sometimes sold by US drug dealers in a powder form, probably diverted from pharmaceutical chemical suppliers.

DXM is related to substances in the opiate family, such as morphine and codeine, although its recreational dose effects are more ketamine-like than opiate-like. As with ketamine, DXM blocks NMDA receptors, which play a part in mental and motor activity. It also blocks the reuptake of dopamine neurotransmitters by brain nerve cells. In low dosages (100 to 200mg), the drug is slightly psychedelic and gives a feeling of mild euphoria. Some users say it makes them feel speedy. Many say music sounds wonderful and dancing is extremely pleasurable. Higher dosages (over 200mg) can have a disassociative and memory unlocking effect close to that of ketamine and can cause extreme hallucinations. The onset of the drug is between 30 and 90 minutes. Effects generally last four to six hours.

Recreational doses of DXM carry many dangers and possible side effects. Some cough medications containing DXM also contain acetaminophen (paracetamol), which can be fatal in high doses. Some also include gauifenesin, which can cause extreme vomiting in high doses, and nasal decongestants or antihistamines, which can cause severely adverse reactions. Some of the dyes, thickeners or other inactive ingredients in cough preparations can cause allergic reactions and intense itching is said to be a common side-effect of cough med tripping. Other physical side effects can include nausea, stomach cramps, gastric disturbances, diarrhoea, profuse sweating, facial swelling and hypertension.

DXM is not known to mix well with other substances. Mixing with illegal drugs such as ecstasy, with legal anti-depressants, or with 'non-drowsy' antihistamines can cause serious complications and can be fatal. Regular abuse of DXM may cause long-term cognitive damage.

Smart drugs (nootropics) and legal alternatives

Smart drugs are sometimes called 'nootropics'. They are also known as cognitive enhancers (the 'noo' in 'nootropics' is from the Greek 'nous', meaning mind), although some substances popularly considered to be nootropics deviate from this original designation. Many nootropics are organic, such as the gingko biloba plant (said to aid cerebral circulation, mental alertness and overall brain functioning), but others are synthetic, such as the nutrient Piracetam (said to enhance memory, attention and intelligence).

Nootropics have long been a staple on the New Age circuit and also with body-builders, as some can assist in the building of muscle mass and in sustaining the kind of energy needed for intense workouts. They also feature heavily in the artillery of medications prescribed in what Western doctors often call 'alternative medicine', such as Chinese medicine. Nootropic substances can be bought at health food shops, fitness centres and alternative drug stores. The internet is another possible source.

Smart drugs rose to great popularity in the Nineties American rave scene, often taken as an adjunct to ecstasy. Many US raves included 'smart bars', offering fruity drinks with names like Fast Blast and NRG Elixir. Some smart drinks had genuine nootropic ingredients, such as ephedrine (a stimulant found in the ma huang herb and also one of the main precursor chemicals to amphetamine and methamphetamine) and L-phenylalanine (an amino acid which can affect certain neurotransmitters depleted by stimulant drugs). These drinks were also not always nootropic in make-up, though. More often than not, the mixtures included primary substances like caffeine and vitamin C. Sometimes they included nootropic substances which were only thought to be effective after regular use, such as the controversial hormone DHEA (dehydroepiandrosterone), which some believe has an anti-ageing influence.

Experimentation with nootropics has also occurred on the British club and rave scenes. Herbal anti-depressants such as St Johns Wort (which affects serotonin) have been used as 'preloaders' to ecstasy, said to prevent an unpleasant E comedown.

One notorious nootropic concoction which reached both the UK and America in the mid-Nineties was a combination called Herbal Ecstasy, produced by a company named Global World Media Corporation. Herbal E included ephedrine, guarana (an unprocessed herb similar to caffeine) and nutmeg (a herb which is psychoactive in high doses), along with ingredients such as ginseng and green tea. The pills were essentially a stimulant and the effects ranged from extreme nausea to amphetamine-like speediness.

Most smart drugs are legal in both Britain and America. In the US, 'nutrients' and 'dietary supplements' fall beyond the charge of the Food & Drink Administration (FDA) as long as they are not marketed as 'drugs', which is why nootropics are frequently sold in bottles which do not describe the substance's therapeutic effects. This, together with the fact that nootropics are often natural plant or herb extractions, or nutrients already found in the body, has led many people to assume they are completely safe highs. This is a misconception: many nootropics are extremely potent, some are hazardous or deadly in large doses (there have been several high-profile ephedrine deaths in the US in the Nineties) and some are volatile when mixed with other drugs.

The difference between a nootropic and a 'regular drug' can come down to a question of semantics. A good example is GHB, which was generally considered a nootropic nutrient until it was banned in the US by the FDA in 1998, after which it has been continually referred to as a 'hard drug'. The prohibition of GHB had a knock-on effect, though, and boosted smart drug sales on the internet. Since the ban, many smart drug sites have offered 'legal GHB alternatives' like Reviverant, Blue Nitro, Enliven and Renewtrient – mixtures which include GBL (gama-Butyro-lactone), a substance which is converted to GHB in the body when ingested orally. GBL thus carries many of the same dangers as GHB, including GHB's volatility when mixed with other drugs. In 1998, there was one American death associated with the ingestion of a product containing GBL.

Lifestyle drugs (Prozac, Viagra)

The term 'lifestyle drug' was coined in the Nineties to describe drugs said to enhance 'quality of life' rather than treating or controlling sickness. Although mostly prescribed by medical practitioners, many lifestyle drugs are marketed by pharmaceutical companies using aggressive direct-to-consumer advertising strategies – they have sparked an unprecedented trend in using television and print adverts to target potential patients rather than only doctors.

Lifestyle drugs run the gamut from impacting cosmetic conditions like male pattern baldness (Propecia) to brain functions like memory (Aricept), physiological problems like erectile dysfunction (Viagra) and, bearing in mind the direct-to-consumer marketing, even mental conditions such as depression (Prozac, Zoloft and Paxil). In some ways, they have shrunk the gap between why people take prescription drugs and why people take illegal drugs like ecstasy (quality of life; happiness) – and highlighted the subjectivity with which substances are labelled good or bad. Prozac, for instance, the anti-depressant prescribed to over 10 million people in the world. It is the fifth-best selling drug in the US, where it's nicknamed 'bottled sunshine', and has provided more adverse reaction reports (including deaths) than any other drug in the history of the FDA.

While some users of recreational drugs may also take lifestyle drugs by prescription, few lifestyle drugs have reached the recreational black market. Prozac, which is a selective serotonin reuptake inhibitor (SSRI) and works by blocking serotonin reuptake, takes four to six weeks until its effects are felt in any perceptible way and although some drug dealers have tried selling SSRIs as 'E enhancers', the practice has not sustained as the pills are useless as a one-off. The only lifestyle drug to have truly penetrated the recreational black market is the anti-impotence Viagra.

In 1999, Viagra was the fastest-selling prescription drug in pharmaceutical history. Launched by Pfizer in 1998 for men experiencing erectile dysfunction, the drug costs $7 to $13 in the US when prescribed. This price can double when bought illegally and increasing numbers of recreational drug users, notably in the gay scene, are taking the drug to counteract the flaccid-inducing effects of the likes of ecstasy and LSD. Viagra, which comes as blue, diamond-shaped pills, works by blocking the enzyme that causes the muscles around the penile arteries to contract. These muscles then relax and blood can flow through easily, leading to engorgement.

The effects of Viagra are completely physiological – a case of hydraulics. Nonetheless, the drug is often sold in clubs and raves under the fallacious pitch that it is an 'aphrodisiac'. It is also increasingly purchased illegally by women thinking the drug will make them horny. Studies have shown that Viagra can lead to engorgement of the vaginal area, but that these effects are not pleasurable or even noticeable to most women, other than those experiencing difficulty with vaginal lubrication due to the effects of menopause or hysterectomy operations.

Viagra is not recommended for those with heart conditions. It causes a dip in blood pressure and is known to be extremely dangerous when mixed with nitrites such as poppers or nitrous oxide, as nitrites also lower blood pressure. On its own, Viagra has caused priapism (a painful erection which lasts over six hours and can lead to permanent penile damage or impotence), and other side effects can include blurred vision, headaches, blackouts and coital coronaries (mainly suffered by those with pre-existing heart conditions). Combining the drug with protease inhibitors (AIDS medications) such as Ritonavir can cause an 11-fold increase in amounts of Viagra in blood and is strongly warned against by Pfizer. According to *Harper's* magazine, Viagra was implicated in a worldwide total of 130 deaths during the six-month period between November 1998 and May 1999.

32

Ecstasy And The UK Press III

The drug in the news, 1995–1999

6 April 1995

The Times

'Scientist Made Ecstasy In Error'

An Essex scientist who manufactured an estimated £400,000 worth of ecstasy walks free from Snaresbrook Crown Court after "persuading a jury that he had been trying to make a hayfever cure". James Edgar claimed that he'd received a lot of interest in his hayfever cure, Airborne Ten, the chemical formula of which was MDMPA, but "an inexplicable chemical reaction" had occurred in the production. Which is why a bath tub full of MDMA was found at his laboratory. After his acquittal, the judge tells Edgar he can sue the police for the return of the confiscated drugs.

Summer 1995

The Herb Garden

'Fresh Fruit From Foreign Places'

E causes haemorrhoids. Several well-known DJs are apparently sufferers. "Surely, when you go for a crap and start turning inside out, it's time to acknowledge that it's all over," says youth culture's answer to *Private Eye*.

August 1995

Mixmag

'Catch The Pigeon'

Mixmag's readers' contact adverts page includes an entry from Pete, Berkshire: "Alison from Essex, we met at Final Frontier 9/6/95. I shared a heavy burden with you. Thanx 4 listening. I'd love to hear from ya."

7 October 1995

NME

'Confusion Reigns Over CJA Prosecutions'

An independent report reveals that under 10 per cent of the 493 arrests made under the Criminal Justice Act during the first 12 months of the legislation resulted in prosecutions. Of the total number of people arrested, only 10 were identified as ravers, compared with 154 hunt saboteurs, 113 football fans and 71 road protestors.

17 November 1995
The Times
'Leah Is Dead But It Is Bearable Because She Can Help Others'
At Broomfield Hospital in Chelmsford, Essex, the life-support machine which Leah Betts has been on for five days as a result of taking ecstasy at her 18th birthday party, is turned off. Her organs are donated for transplants and a photograph of her is later used alongside the words, "Sorted. Just one ecstasy tablet took Leah Betts" in an anti-drugs poster campaign.

19 November 1995
Independent
'The Revolution Is Happening And It's Down At Raquel's'
Picking up on the fact that the tablet which killed Leah Betts was bought at the mainstream Raquel's club in Basildon, Essex, *Independent* columnist Decca Aitkenhead says E has "rendered the very phrase 'drug culture' meaningless". She describes how, each weekend, "profoundly conventional people without a subversive thought in their heads dress up in Top Shop clothes to dance to *Top Of The Pops* tunes in clubs like Raquel's – and take a highly illegal drug."

4 February 1996
Sunday Telegraph
'Leah's Photo Hijacked To Back Ecstasy'
Agit-pop group Chumbawamba use the Leah Betts 'Sorted' photo for a postcard reading: "DISTORTED. Statistically, you're as likely to die from swallowing a bayleaf as from taking an ecstasy tablet. So why do we have to put up with a media dealing in shock, not truth? What we need is information, not scare stories." Paul Delaney, a director of the advertising agency responsible for the 'Sorted' campaign, accuses the band of "staggeringly bad taste", but Chumbawamba counter that they are simply demanding more information be made available to people taking drugs.

July 1996
Eternity
'E For Ecstasy'
Eternity's regular monthly analysis of ecstasy doing the rounds in clubland

publishes photos of five tablets. One has a faint dove symbol: "MDEA 172 milligram. Very heavy dosage! One tablet is plenty, two is most definitely NOT healthy. It is suggested that half at a time is adequate, more than this is quite dangerous as it speeds the heart up far too much."

17 January 1997
Mirror
'Ecstasy Shock Issue'
The Mirror print a picture of a huge white tablet on its front cover. Below are the words: "A million young people take E every weekend. East 17 pop star Brian Harvey caused outrage yesterday by claiming the drug 'makes you a better person'. It can also make you a dead person."

March 1997
Muzik
'Everything Starts With A P'
Holes, white sweets which Nestlé Rowntree claim are made from the middles of Polo mints, spark uproar in school playgrounds across the UK. Teachers are said to have been "horrified to discover that children were in possession of small white 'pills' marked with the letter P, L or O, fearing they were new types of E!"

27 April 1997
Daily Telegraph
'Doctors In Transplant Row "Were Guilty Of Euthanasia" '
Margaret Pirie accuses doctors at Edinburgh Royal Infirmary of refusing to conduct a liver transplant operation on her granddaughter, 15-year-old Michelle Paul, because she had become ill as a result of taking ecstasy. Michelle had taken half a tablet at a rave near Aberdeen in November 1995. She died three weeks after being admitted to the Edinburgh hospital. "As I saw it, what they had done was to commit euthanasia," says Margaret Pirie.

20 June 1997
Scotsman
'Life Support Switched Off For Ecstasy Boy, 13'
Doctors at Monklands Hospital in Airdrie, Scotland, turn off the life support machine which 13-year-old ecstasy victim Andrew Woodlock has been on for five days. He had been given three pills by another young teenage boy, who found the tablets at the home of 23-year-old Alexander McFarlane. McFarlane is later jailed for six years. Andrew Woodlock is the youngest British ecstasy fatality.

15 January 1998
Mirror
'Shame Of Di Ecstasy Tabs'
E pills are being stamped with the names of Princess Diana and Dodi
Fayed on one side, and 'RIP' on the other: "Drug experts say the pills are
a marketing ploy by cynical pushers eager to increase sales."

June 1998
Mixmag
'This Man Smuggled 25 Pills Through Customs (And Got Caught)'
Journalist Mark White flies into Heathrow Airport from Amsterdam with
a plastic bag containing 25 paracetamol tablets strapped to his leg as part of
his research for an article about UK Customs. He's stopped by customs
officers and, despite letters from British and Dutch lawyers explaining the
tablets, subjected to a strip search. "I take my clothes off, noticing ruefully
that my white CKs aren't quite so white any more," he writes.

30 October 1998
Guardian
'Ecstasy "Injures Brain For Life" '
The *Guardian*'s Science Editor, Tim Radford, reports on the latest research
into the effects of ecstasy on human brain cells. "Our immediate concern is
that people who use MDMA recreationally are unwittingly putting themselves at risk of developing brain damage," says Dr George Ricaurte, one of
the world's most respected neurologists.

20 November 1998
Independent
'Three Die From New Designer Drugs'
Police issue warnings about two new "derivatives of ecstasy", DOB and
flatliners. DOB is "up to 33 times" stronger than E, while flatliners –
"which look like cream-coloured headache tablets" – have been linked
with three deaths in the UK in recent months and two further fatalities in
Holland.

9 February 1999
The Times
'Ecstasy Woman Wins Hospital Damages'
North Middlesex NHS Trust agree to pay £250,000 damages to 25-year-
old Lorraine Leighton, who says she wasn't properly treated when admitted to hospital in Edmonton in 1995 after collapsing as a result of taking
ecstasy at a club. Her counsel, Duncan Pratt, tells the High Court that the

severe neurological problems experienced by Lorraine during the last four years, including having to relearn how to speak, read and write, were due to the hospital staff failing to carry out a blood test and giving her the wrong type of fluid in a drip.

27 February 1999
Daily Star
'Fish Lands In Jail'
John Moriarty – "a top angler nicknamed 'The Fish' " – is jailed for 17 years for conspiracy to supply drugs. He'd been arrested as he loaded boxes containing 143,400 ecstasy pills into a van near his south London home. He told the court that he thought the boxes were "a cheap batch of maggots he'd been offered by a stranger".

30 August 1999
Daily Mail
'The Night I Took Drugs On *Top Of The Pops*'
Blur singer Damon Albarn reveals that he and bassist Alex James took ecstasy before performing 'There's No Other Way' on *Top Of The Pops* in 1991. He claims they were given the pills by the head of their record company.

September 1999
Mixmag
'Drugs Of The Decade'
Mixmag lists the 50 most talked-about drugs of the late 20th century. No less than 16 are 'brands' of E, including the entire Top Five. Number One are Mitsubishis – "responsible for reviving the popularity of ecstasy in a club scene worn down by poor-quality pills" – followed by doves, double doves, pink calis and rhubarb & custard. Coke, speed, ketamine, methamphetamine, 2C-B, GHB, Valium, absinthe and Tippex also make the list.

33

Q&A: Dealers And Manufacturers

Drug manufacturers and dealers don't like talking about their activities. However, with the help of Herman-Louis Matser at the Adviesburo Drugs information service in Amsterdam, six European ecstasy manufacturers and large-scale dealers agreed to anonymously answer questions designed to shed some light on their part in the E story. The questions were faxed to Herman-Louis Matser, who then collated the manufacturers' and dealers' responses.

Where are ecstasy pills manufactured? Do they come from any particular countries?
Pills are made anywhere there is a pill pressing machine – which is almost everywhere. You can smuggle pills, but you can also smuggle ecstasy powder and make pills where you need them. Both happen. The powder has to be made somewhere you can get the necessary substances and have a quiet laboratory, but you can also do that in lots of different places.

In what kind of places are ecstasy laboratories usually housed? In people's homes? In garages or sheds? Or somewhere purpose-built?
All of such places are possible. You can make ecstasy in the back of a van, if you want to. You don't need very much space. Having somewhere purpose-built is not common, though, because it's more easily noticed. In the Eighties, it was sometimes made in pre-existing laboratories, maybe at night, but that's now an unlikely scenario.

Why has the street price of E come down over the years – from £25–50 a tablet in the UK in the mid-Eighties to £10 or less by the late Nineties?
Competition and economies of scale. In other words, because more people are making it and more people are taking it.

If a person pays a high price for an ecstasy pill, is it more likely to have a higher MDMA content?
On a large scale, perhaps. If a dealer wants a certain dosage and is prepared

to pay for it, he'll probably get it. This doesn't happen if someone is buying a small quantity of pills, though. When it comes to buying a single tablet in a club, for example, the price gives the buyer no indication of any of the ingredients.

What are the different stages of manufacturing a tablet?
There are four stages. First, the ecstasy powder is manufactured. The powder is then mixed with other substances which go into the tablet and the mixture is weighed out. The final stage is the manufacture of the actual tablets. All of the process can be done in one place, but it is usually split up and done in different places.

What quantity of ecstasy might be produced at any one time?
It's possible to make very large amounts of the drug, but a manufacturer would then need to have a large laboratory set-up. It's not logical to do that. It's better to have five places making five smaller amounts than one place making one large amount.

Do manufacturers 'specialise' in ecstasy only, or do they also make other drugs?
Most specialise. A manufacturer will buy a recipe and instructions to make one drug. But that is all he can make. If he wants to make something else, he'll need to get a new recipe. And they are expensive. Also, if you are making money in a particular business, you'll stay in that business.

Why is E sometimes sold as a capsule rather than a pressed pill?
Using a capsule-making machine is a lot cheaper and easier than using a pill press – especially if you don't want to produce a large amount of the drug. Capsules suit the small-scale businesses. The problem is that a capsule can be opened and something else can be put in. A capsule should always be completely filled with powder – the machines completely fill the capsules, they don't half fill them. If a capsule isn't full, there's a potential problem.

The drug is increasingly sold as powder. Why is this? Does it mean it's more refined?
If you are smuggling, you only have a certain amount of space and powder takes up less space than pills. So you can smuggle a bigger quantity of drugs. Also, at times when pills have a bad name, powder looks more pure. The truth is that powder can actually be more easily cut with other substances. It's also more unpleasant for the user to take.

What sort of people manufacture E? Scientists? Drug cartels? Are these people in any way less criminally motivated than those making, say, cocaine and heroin?
Scientists, yes. Drug cartels would probably do better business with other drugs. But if there is a lot of police activity in a certain place or at a certain time, it's generally only the heavier people who will be involved. More 'normal' types of people will step out of it.

Do dealers usually know the composition of the pills they sell?
Dealers in Holland can know because they can have tablets tested. In a lot of countries, though, they don't know. They can only find out by testing it on people.

How many dealers might there be between the manufacturer and consumer?
It depends on local conditions. The more repression from the authorities there is, the more people there are in between. In the beginning, the lines were very short. Now they are longer.

How are large quantities of pills moved between different countries?
The old methods are known. The new methods nobody talks about.

How are large-scale amounts of pills distributed within a country?
Probably in a car.

What does a dealer do if he gets a dangerous or ineffective batch of E? Would a manufacturer ever destroy batches of such pills?
A dealer can return it to where he got it from and try to get his money back. Or he can sell it, usually in one go and usually somewhere far away. If a manufacturer finds his tablets have been badly mixed or too highly dosed, they can be crushed and re-made.

Can a manufacturer be 'blacklisted' by dealers?
Of course. And it happens. But a manufacturer can always find somebody to put their drugs on the market and, of course, it's hard to trace the source.

34

Superclubs And The Mainstreaming Of E Culture

Debbie stands in front of the full-length mirror in her bedroom. She's holding two different stringy lycra tops up against her naked chest. "Black or white?" Her sister Emma looks up from the electric hair straightener she's fiddling with. "White. Definitely."

It's 9pm on a Saturday night and the sisters are listening to pumpy pumpy house on Radio 1 as they get ready to go out clubbing. Debbie, 25, skinny, strawberry blonde hair, glitter on temples, a college drop-out temp secretary, says she is "really up for it tonight" because she "really needs a shag – a right proper shag". Her sister Emma, 18, baby fat not yet all lost, sausaged into a mauve corset bustier, a shopgirl who would rather be a hairdresser, murmurs in agreement. "You said it, girl." The sisters have a resilient habit of saying "girl" after every phrase uttered. Emma notes it's not "like a feminist thing or anything".

Emma only started clubbing six months ago, but she says she's already "a true clubber". Debbie, six years older, goes one up on her sister and calls her own self "a clubbing cliché". Sounding rather like the type of house record she loves dancing to, Debbie says she "lives for Saturday night". Emma gives her a high-five. "You said it, girl." Both sisters giggle. As a prelude to the E they will take tonight, they have been snorting long lines of cocaine off Debbie's "Ladies And Gentlemen . . . The Best Of George Michael" CD case since 6pm. "I'm getting fucked-up, girl." "Me too, girl."

On this unexceptional Saturday night in the spring of 1999, Debbie and Emma pay £20 to enter the 'superclub' they visit every weekend. On this unexceptional Saturday night, Debbie and Emma – extraordinary only for their ordinariness – each ingest amounts of drugs and stay up amounts of hours which, a dozen years before, would have seemed extreme to say the least. Several lines of coke, several spliffs and a couple of ecstasy tablets apiece. At 2pm the next day, shortly before going to bed, Debbie swallows a Valium. "My friend's brother went to India and brought back loads," she says, looking haggard. "I am not looking forward to this week," she adds, anticipating the chemical comedown which will follow her to work on Monday, and maybe even Tuesday and Wednesday. "I wish it was next weekend, like, *tomorrow.*"

In 1995, *Mixmag* deputy editor Andy Pemberton coined a term to describe a new breed of club: the 'superclub', the focal point of what *Mixmag* often referred to as 'corporate clubbing'. The superclub was the epicentre of the great mainstreaming of ecstasy culture – the process which had, by this point, gone into high gear and propelled E into places it had never been before. Namely, into the offices of Big Business UK.

"These clubs were elevating themselves above the others in that they were becoming empires," says Pemberton, now the editor of Q magazine. "The likes of Ministry Of Sound in London, Cream in Liverpool and Renaissance in the Midlands were putting out platinum-selling mix CDs. They had lots of merchandising and their logos became very important devices. They opened DJ agencies and travel agencies. They started radio shows. They were doing club tours around Europe, to bring the idea of their club to new places and to create hype back home. They [attracted] big corporate sponsors, like Pepsi and Sony, which was a very new thing for British house clubs. The superclubs were more than just places to go and pop a pill and dance at. They were brands which commodified ecstasy culture to the point where everyone could have a piece if they wanted it, regardless of whether they went to these particular clubs or not."

Superclubs made the culture of ecstasy easier to get hold of and they cleaned it to a shine for mass consumption. Superclub developers took cues from both the suburban multiplexes of America, which hold 52 movie screens, a bowling alley, a skating rink and a food court, *and* companies like Calvin Klein, who know that putting their logo to a blender makes that blender instantly desirable. The superclubs aimed to provide everything their punters might want – from clothes to music to travel – and put it all within reach. The idea was to create a clubby insta-mega-culture. A Total Leisure Concept. A concept which abolished the urban club scene's former status of subculture.

The owners of superclubs intoned that they were bringing a never-before-realised legitimacy to the business of clubbing. They shunned the back-door tactics, bouncer protection rackets and other under-the-table-isms which have been the age-old property of the nightclub owner. Their hands were clean. Their businesses sound. But every superclub experienced one huge, glaring problem in the legitimacy department. A massive pill-shaped paradox which was growing bigger and bigger by the year. Because at the centre of their shining corporate empires, in the middle of their Saturday night, lay ecstasy. Not just E the idea, but E the chemical. An illegal drug. A Class A. Something not the least bit permissible in corporate la-la-land.

It was something most other corporations and companies commodifying ecstasy culture didn't have to worry about, really. A major record label could licence an E anthem without fear of hundreds of party people crashing their offices and snorting crushed doves off their glass table tops. A soft drink company could create an E-tastic commercial without their actors getting as high as kites. But could a club designed around the pleasures of ecstasy – the sounds, the lights, the podiums – survive without people actually experiencing the effects of the drug within its confines?

No way. People clearly feel the need to take drugs in clubs. In this sense, superclubs are no different from their minor league competitors. What's more, the superclubs need people to take drugs on Friday and Saturday nights. So that when Monday rolls round, the company can sell those people flashbacks: remember how good you felt dancing to that set the DJ played? Here's the CD, you can feel that way again at home. What superclub companies peddle is their vibe. And their vibe simply wouldn't be there if countless thousands weren't taking E every weekend. Some superclubs – especially Cream in Liverpool – have dealt with the E paradox in new and constructive ways. Others – especially Ministry Of Sound in London – haven't.

James Palumbo, Ministry Of Sound's big cheese, has suggested that there are no drugs in his club, no E even, because his security is tight. But to anyone who knows anything about the dance scene, about ecstasy culture, the thought of an E-free nightclub is unrealistic. For a start, it doesn't allow for the fact that some clubbers pop pills before they get anywhere near the entrance.

The Eton and Oxford-educated Palumbo, the son of former Arts Council chairman Lord Palumbo, only intended to invest a small amount of money in the Ministry Of Sound project. By 1992, after the club had been open for just one year, he had left his job in the City and was running the place. Before Ministry, Palumbo had never been to a club. An opera and classical aficionado, he had little interest in dance music. As someone who had never taken an illegal substance in his life, he is reported to have believed drug users were degenerates. In 1995, he even lent his support to Crimestoppers' SNAP (Say No And Phone) anti-drugs campaign, which encouraged users to inform on dealers by warning "if you get hooked, you will have to steal to get enough money to pay for your drugs. There is nothing wrong in telling tales on criminals. We need to put them away."

James Palumbo ran the business of Ministry the way he knew best – the established, City way of running a business. Target the market. Keep the quality high. Create a brand loyalty. Start on crossover ventures. Within 18 months of Palumbo grabbing the wheel, the club's profits were in the millions (by 1997, the Ministry's turnover was £20 million). Palumbo then posted signs in the Ministry offices, bearing the company's new call to arms: "We are building a global entertainment business, based on a strong aspirational brand, respected for its creativity and quality. The Ministry Of Sound team will be more hard-working and innovative than any other on the planet."

The youth press – so ready to pounce on any story involving ecstasy, so ready to pooh-pooh the government's drug policy or praise the work of clubby drug awareness organisations – have maintained something of a collective silence on the Ministry's attitude towards E. If the issue is picked up at all, it is with gilded tongs. Journalists let in to talk to Palumbo whispered to friends that the club had an 'inner sanctum' where Labour minister Peter Mandelson and other politicians hung out. They wrote about Palumbo's impressive glass office and his silent-but-strong demeanour. They wrote about the cool Tiffany & Co penknife he carried. But few said anything about his club's stance on drugs.

"[It's] because the Ministry is powerful," says Andy Pemberton, "because magazines, especially the youth culture magazines, rely on the Ministry's advertising." And also probably because Palumbo didn't talk about the subject much. "Ministry Of Sound does not and never has gotten involved in discussions about drugs," says the club's press officer. Which would be fine if their entire "aspirational brand" wasn't based on a culture not just inspired by, but fuelled by a pill.

The biggest superclub company in the north of England – Cream in Liverpool, founded in 1992 by James Barton and Darren Hughes – have an altogether different take on the role of ecstasy in a corporate environment. At Cream, the drug is almost seen as a part of the company's commercial image. "We accept that, not only has the culture of ecstasy become a mainstream leisure industry, but that the chemical itself has mainstreamed as well," says Jayne Casey, Cream's head of communications. "We accept that people do drugs in our club! Of course they do! Those drugs are an integral part of the culture we are involved in. Following on from that, we just try to make the club as safe an environment as possible."

Cream is understood as a cool community leader in Liverpool. The club's owners have dealt responsibly with drugs – by installing a first aid area from day one and paramedics from day two, after the highly publicised death of Essex teenager Leah Betts. By co-operating closely with the police and the drug services, they have managed not to let drugs be the fall of their empire, the way it was at The Hacienda in Manchester.

Even after the police pursued a 10-month undercover investigation at Cream, leading to the arrest of 23 people in connection with supplying drugs at the club in 1996, their pristine reputation remained unscathed. The police said they knew the management were not involved.

"Cream are the good guys," says Ben Turner, editor of *Muzik* magazine. "They've proved you can be big business and yet understand ecstasy culture at the same time. And their crowd is incredibly dedicated because of it. Their crowd will buy anything with the Cream logo on it because of it." Driving around Liverpool, it's certainly true you see the famous three droplets logo everywhere. On cars. On rucksacks. In record shops, clothing stores and travel agencies. On skin, even, in the form of tattoos: permanent badges proudly worn by some of the club's regulars. "Cream has become a total obsession for many people in the north," concludes Ben Turner. "It has achieved the ultimate goal of the superclub. Total brand loyalty. Kids would literally give their lives for Cream."

One of Cream's recent advertisements, seen on the back of many magazines, features a photo of a guy in his early twenties posing in his work togs. He's a plasterer, not a model, and he was spotted dancing on a Cream podium one Saturday. In the advert, his clothes are caked and splattered with plaster. He limply holds up the tools of his trade like a woeful Masonic Jesus. His eyes are heavy-lidded. Set across the middle of the photo, the selling caption reads: "It's why I work all week." The Cream logo appears just below the caption.

Jayne Casey says the advert represents everything Cream is about. "The campaign is saying what our whole fucking culture is all about," she declares. "Ordinary kids who work all week and live for Saturday night."

Maybe so. But looking at the photograph you can't help thinking that the plasterer doesn't look too happy.

(MS)

35

Ecstasy And Other Drugs
On The American Gay Circuit

Palm Springs is an oasis in the deserts of southern California. A lush, hot place, nestled beneath the monumentally high, snow-capped San Jacinto mountains, it is one of America's more prestigious resort towns. Like so many other warm holiday destinations in America, the town has the strange idiosyncrasy of containing a transient gay population, a humongous number of senior citizens and an enclave of tennis culture aristocrats – all groups which either ignore or play unaware of each other. It's an immaculately greened-up clustering of richy-rich country clubs, Golden Age early-bird dinner specials, and gay spas and underwear shops. Driving in from any side, there's nothing but scraggly desert for miles, and then suddenly a well-watered paradise of intense leisure, full of grass, flowers, and trees fastidiously trimmed to look any shape but tree-shape.

Palm Springs is the site of one of the largest gay 'circuit parties' on the planet. Every spring, up to 40,000 gay men visit the resort for the Annual White Party celebrations. A weekend of shared hotel rooms, pool parties, club nights and tea dances, all buttressing the huge ball where everyone wears white and dances the night away to hi-NRG and house music.

D is a self-confessed 'circuit queen'. A Los Angeles accountant, he is tanned, trim, wealthy, and travels to approximately a dozen circuit events every year. The Palm Springs White Party remains his favourite, though. "I always go extra-nuts at the White Party," he says. "I always have too much work in the spring. And with my kind of job, you need to go crazy and get raunchy every now and again. You know, release the pressure."

At the 1998 White Party weekend, D took four ecstasy tablets in one 12-hour period. "I took one driving in, just as I entered Palm Springs city limits. Like, 'OK, I'm ready!' I went straight to this little party and, by the time I got to the big event, I had taken three Es. I was flying and all I wanted to do was have sex. I wanted to have sex for, like, 10 hours

straight." D's dealer in LA had told him that the pills were Mitsubishis –
"something new and special from Europe."

"Mitsu-whatever Es . . . Yeah, those were good. They turned me into,
like, the biggest *slut* in the history of the universe. I was dancing with this
terribly handsome, ripply, muscle-god guy, in the middle of the dancefloor, crammed between all these other boys. We were practically doing it
on the dancefloor. God, I was rushing. We went to his car in the parking
lot. Actually, it was a big Jeep thing. A monster truck! We pushed down
those bucket seats, split my last pill and we fucked. And we fucked and we
fucked. It was sooo naughty. I know some men can't get it up on E but,
honey, we had no problem that night."

D visited a private AIDS clinic two weeks later, scared rigid. His sex with
Mr Monster Truck hadn't been safe. He promised himself he would never
take drugs and never go to another circuit party again in his life. D got his
results within a few days. He was still negative. He says he cried out of relief,
out of joy. "And then I went to a circuit party the next month. Ha! You
know, someone should start a new service called CQA – Circuit Queens
Anonymous. Because, my God, those parties, that lifestyle? Too addictive."

Gay America is dancing hard again. In the era of ecstasy, in the era of AIDS,
gay America is dancing harder than it has danced since the days of disco.

The events which form the gay male circuit, a linking of approximately
60 annual or one-off DJ-dance events, make up the mainstream of gay
dance culture in America today. The scene – its independently promoted
parties neatly arranged so that the hardcore circuit boy can fly to a different
city every weekend – has grown exponentially since it began gaining
prominence in 1991-92. An estimated half a million men flock to North
American circuit events every year, and satellite circuit scenes have started
cropping up outside America as well, most notably in Australia and New
Zealand. Some have called circuit parties 'gay raves', as circuit culture and
rave culture are very similar at points. Yet unlike rave culture, which in
the grand scheme has remained largely apolitical, the circuit is involvedly
political by definition: approximately 80 per cent of all circuit events are
AIDS fundraisers.

The modern circuit is a two-sided coin. On one side, it can be seen as
falling within the tradition of gay self-help: with the spread of AIDS in the
early Eighties, newly formed grass roots organisations like New York's
Gay Men's Health Crisis (GMHC) began exploring different ways of
gathering funds to fight the disease that the American government seemed
intent on ignoring at the time. DJ-dances held in clubs or in open-air spots
like the beaches of Fire Island – where the GMHC began holding their
annual Morning Party in 1983 – proved to be a good way to raise both

money and consciousness within the community.

On the other side, the Nineties' circuit is the direct descendant of the drug-sex-'n'-hi-NRG-loving Saint disco scene which peaked just before AIDS hit America's gay consciousness: in Eighties New York, the Saint club threw several official 'special parties' every year. They weren't fundraisers for anything, just big-themed balls that were calendar highlights for the club's patrons. These parties and similar events at West Coast clubs like The Probe superdisco in LA, led to an elite knot of men who would fly back and forth between New York and California, enmeshed in what increasingly became called a 'gay circuit'.

The world of the contemporary circuit seems unbelievable from the outside and, to many on the inside, even more wondrous. It's an exclusive, ideal, super-male world, quite like The Saint, only a zillion times bigger and with soft drink, condom and airline sponsorships. It is a place where beauty and youth abound. Where professional, well-heeled circuit queens – the direct progeny of the Saint clone, with perma-tans, masculine muscles, designer-everything and voracious drug appetites – party guiltlessly. Where everybody can afford a ticket to go and hear Junior Vasquez or Danny Tenaglia or DJ Buc in Miami or Toronto or Perth, plus a hotel room for the three nights it takes to visit the many parties surrounding a circuit event.

But over and above the money and glamour, circuit punters – who, it should be noted, are almost always white – will tell you that the best thing about their larger-than-life society is the feeling of well-being and unity imbued in their floating scene. How the scene symbolises, if only by its size and prosperity, the liberation of the modern gay man. How it represents his entry into the mainstream. In other words, acceptance. "A circuit party gives us the chance to escape the pressures of our day-to-day existence and to enter the altered world where man-to-man sex is not only accepted, but is celebrated," proclaims the magazine *Circuit Noise*. "When the circuit comes to town, that town becomes an instant gay ghetto full of hot men who are behaving as queer as they care to be."

Drugs are an integral part of the circuit experience. And while GHB, crystal meth and ketamine are popular, ecstasy remains the drug de choix on the scene. In many ways, the reasons men on the circuit take ecstasy is no different from why anyone in any other branch of club culture does: "to escape day-to-day existence" and to reach an "altered world". But unlike, say, the rave scene, where these aspects of the E trip are considered beneficial at best and harmless at worst, many gay activists view them as far from harmless for contemporary gay men. They view them as closer to calamitous.

191

"Ecstasy and all those drugs, they have the effects of something like a time-travel pill for many men on the circuit," says Canadian gay activist Matthew Hays, who has written about the scene for magazines like *The Advocate*. "You go to these parties and they're all about forgetting and pleasurable excess. There are these bodies all around you, you are taking mind-altering substances, you feel fantastic, you forget, your emphasis shifts from the present-day reality and – boom! Before you know it, you are back to the kind of carefree-ness that characterised the disco era. When you didn't have to worry about wearing a rubber. When you didn't have to worry about your friends dying. When you didn't have to worry about you yourself being sick." A time many circuit boys may be too young to even remember, but might dream about anyway.

"There is an AIDS fatigue floating around the gay community now," continues Hays. "People are sick of thinking about illness, so this kind of nostalgia is very potent. There are now men who will only rent pre-AIDS porn. There is the cult of barebacking [a network of men who deliberately and continuously have anal sex without condoms – an extremely marginal practice. Men who have unsafe sex 'by mistake' should not be considered barebackers]. There are men who wrongly believe that the new combination AIDS medications, the protease inhibitors, are a cure, when they are really only very effective life-prolongers."

Some activists now believe the primary danger for gay men on the circuit isn't what E will physically do to their bodies. "But rather, what some will do with their bodies while on drugs like E," says Hays. "Especially the younger boys, who haven't seen so many friends die."

"Hogwash!" says Steven Baird, the chairman of Miami's Winter Party. "These critics don't know what they are talking about. This whole question of E leading to unsafe sex is useless! Lots of men I know, I'd say most, can't ejaculate or can't even get it up on ecstasy, and so I don't think ecstasy, a drug which so many circuit-trashing [critics] have demonised, is any problem at all. It will just get a buncha guys hugging and dancing – not having sex. Ecstasy almost acts as a chemical condom. So, tell me this: when you have all these guys on E and they can't penetrate, how, just how are they going to give each other this disease?"

B is a designer for a large sportswear company. A gay man in his late twenties who lives in New York City's 'gay ghetto' of Chelsea, he travels to approximately 10 circuit events every year. When at home in New York, he likes going to circuit-style clubs like the popular muscle-bound danceteria Splash. He attended his first circuit party and swallowed his first ecstasy tablet in 1996 – at Montreal's Black & Blue Festival, the largest annual circuit event on the North American continent. The Black & Blue

192

features over 20 parties in one long weekend every October, and is so established that it's even substantially sponsored by the City of Montreal and the Montreal Tourism Bureau.

"I had a friend at work who was always accusing me of being a 'straight gay'," says B. "He was a circuit boy and he invited me to come see what it was all about in Montreal. I was nervous. I was a bit of a late [starter] with drugs. I had smoked pot, even tried acid when I was at college, but I never got too interested in all that stuff. I never quite fitted into the gay scene back then. Until I started working the circuit, you could say I was a bit shy and awkward. I wanted to be social, but I felt I didn't know how to do it properly.

"Ecstasy changed my life," he continues. "After that Montreal week-end, which was sooo fabulous – like, I had never seen so many beautiful boys together in one place – I began coming out of my shell. It was like metamorphosis! I started going to the gym, I bulked up, and I became very conscious of my body and the sexiness of my clothes. It sounds superficial, but I had a whole new lease on life. Men who would never look at me before, who I would have never dared talk to, were suddenly paying me all sorts of attention. I made new friends and felt, for the first time, like I was part of a gang. I was in a crazy whirlwind."

It was at a circuit party in Chicago in 1998 that B began worrying that his whirlwind was slowing. "There I was, at yet another party full of topless, over-buff boys, and I wasn't having it. I was having a lame time. By then, my [ecstasy intake] had upped to three pills a party, sometimes more. But even on so many pills, I just couldn't get to where I wanted to be. E just started feeling sinister and boring, like it was an old drug. I had always stayed away from crystal meth, it seemed a bit low to me or something, but loads of my circuit friends were total crystal queens and always raved about it . . . Like, how you could have great sex on crystal, how it kept you hard for hours, how you could ejaculate over and over again, and how it was the best 'up' around, a real confidence-gainer. I did it at this party, I smoked just a tiny, tiny bit, and suddenly ecstasy seemed like child's play."

Crystal meth is crystal methamphetamine – methamphetamine in the form of a crystalline rock. It is smoke-able, shoot-able, snort-able, you can sprinkle it on food, and it is cheap. At about $15, a single hit (usually approximately 1/64 of an ounce) can last anywhere from eight to 16 hours. This very potent type of speed is also popularly dubbed 'crank' or 'ice' and could be considered the fastest spreading illegal drug in America today. Almost 90 per cent of all illicit drug laboratories seized in America in 1998 were crystal meth labs. Often synthesised using fairly easily procured ingredients (ephedrine from allergy medicines like Sudafed, for instance) in 'mom'n'pop' clandestine labs (usually in rural or suburban areas), it is a Schedule II drug in the United States – a drug considered to have little medical use and a high potential for abuse.

In America, crystal has a 'white trash' stigma to it, mainly due to the rednecky places it is produced and its popularity with night-shift workers and truck drivers. The stigma is misleading. Throughout the Nineties, it has increasingly become among the most classless drugs in America, used everywhere from factories to Ivy League campuses to Wall Street to raves and the gay scene. "I would think that the reasons crystal became big on the circuit and on the [American] rave scene are pretty much the same," says West Virginian DJ Buc, one of the top circuit DJs. "People start taking it when they get tired of E, when E doesn't work for them any more." Crystal is also more easily available in certain parts of America than E is and, during ecstasy dry spells, some may try crystal as an alternative. "The problem is that crystal is addictive in ways that E isn't," says Buc. "I know about this, I got to shooting up two-and-a-half grams of crystal a day. And now there is so much crystal on the circuit scene – I mean, some people are using the word epidemic."

Some men on the circuit who have used crystal say the drug instantly puts them in a good mood. Some say it pulls their self-esteem up, makes everything seem better. Some say it allows them to dance for hours on end. Many also say that the drug has a hypersexual effect so strong that it's sometimes uncontrollable.

In his six-month stint as a crystal meth 'tweaker' before he went into treatment, B says he smoked up to four grams of crystal a week. B began keeping his stash in the oak cabinet in his front vestibule, the place where he put his keys, right by his front door. That way, he could smoke the hit he always smoked immediately before going out at night, and leave his flat in seconds. "This became my standard ritual," he says. By doing this, he says he seriously decreased the compulsion to masturbate when the drug hit, and the likelihood of staying at home jacking off until his penis was raw at daybreak.

"Now take that kind of compulsion, that kind of insane impulse to gratify your cock, and put it in the setting of a circuit party, where everyone is looking for some action," says B. "Imagine the consequences! The give-it-to-me-now sexual impulse of that drug is so strong, you forget about everything else – literally forget. All those years of education, all your morals, are gone – bang! Everything becomes about, like, *I want pleasure now! Now! Now!* In that kind of condition, being safe is just impossible. Even if you have HIV. Unfortunately, I am speaking from experience here."

In 1996, the number of gay men with AIDS in major American cities like Miami and LA increased for the first time in about 10 years. In one 1996 study conducted by Dr William Darrow on the gay population of Miami's

South Beach – one of the main circuit cities in America – 75 per cent of all men questioned said they had participated in anal sex without a condom within the previous year. The question of whether the AIDS fundraising circuit was actually helping the spread of AIDS became a heated debate. Steven Baird from Miami's Winter Party says that the circuit should not be blamed for instigating "bad behaviour" among its patrons. "Like, don't shoot the messenger. If it wasn't happening on the circuit, it would be happening anyway. In nightclubs or whatever. That's a fact."

This laissez-faire stance has seriously aggravated many gay activists. Some have run campaigns to shut certain parties down. Some parties have shut down. But as the history of ecstasy culture proves, stern voices on the outside will, in the long run, do little to stymie practices on the inside. So it's much more important to note that this infuriating 'boys will be boys' attitude has gotten the goat of a good portion of men inside the circuit, too.

"We have arrived at a Teflon-coated place where we are criticised but nothing sticks, where leadership disappears (or overdoses) when the going gets tough and where, left to our own devices, we will rot on the vine if we do not make wine, and quickly," wrote pro-circuit sage Alan Brown on his Electric Dreams website in 1998. "Clearly, we have a lot of prevention and healing work to do [on the] party circuit. People are hurting themselves with drugs and excessive partying, and shopping for self- esteem at the gym. We cannot just accept this as a fact of life, or as some sort of trade-off for fabulousness, and keep partying like nothing is wrong."

Compared to the UK, drug safety campaigns within the North American club and rave scenes have been pitifully thin. Besides the odd often ill-informed flyer typed up and Xeroxed by a do-gooder scenester or renegade mad mother, ventures in effective club outreach work remain next to zilch. In this environment of negligence and blind-eye-ism, the considerable efforts recently taken by some on the circuit should be seen as both extremely brave and entirely ground-breaking.

Ground-breaking, because the circuit's attack on drugs has gone beyond being a post-ingestion clean-up job. Of course there are free condoms, safety leaflets, flyers and posters coming out of the wazoo, of course there are first aid areas. "But that's not enough for us, we must have something of a wider stance," says the Black & Blue Festival organiser, Robert Vezina. "I think the new overall attitude on the circuit has been that this is a social problem, not a physical problem, that this is a shared problem, not this person or that person's problem. And our plan of action has been designed accordingly. We can't just tell people to drink lots of water."

Before the Gay Men's Health Crisis cancelled their annual Morning Party in 1998 (a GMHC press release read: "While it is painful for us to

195

end this Fire Island tradition, it is more painful that the Morning Party's reputation for drugs undermines GMHC's year-round efforts to educate people about substance abuse and how it relates to HIV infection"), they had been offering drug abuse seminars on Fire Island during Morning Party week. And seminar attendance was growing steadily every year. Now other circuit promoters are carrying this torch, offering similar platforms for education on drugs, packed seamlessly between their military balls and tea dances. "There is no reason that this oppurtunity of getting so many gay men together should be wasted," says Robert Vezina. "This was the point of the original circuit parties – group education about things people are afraid to talk about."

On 6 October 1996, a British gay man named Philip Kay died after attending a London nightclub. Following an autopsy and toxicological investigations, the cause of death was determined to be an MDMA overdose. Kay had taken two and a half ecstasy tablets, but the levels of MDMA in his blood were astonishingly high – as if he had taken 22 tablets. While on holiday a few weeks earlier, Kay had used some of the same ecstasy pills, with no adverse effects. However, since returning from his vacation, Kay had started taking the drug Ritonavir – a protease inhibitor produced by Abbott Laboratories – as part of his anti-AIDS therapy.

Philip Kay's boyfriend, Jim Lumb, was sure that the Ritonavir had contributed to the death of his lover. In 1997, bereaved but determined, he sought an inquest into the effects of combining the protease inhibitor with MDMA. The investigations proved that the 10-fold increase in levels of MDMA in Philip Kay's body were indeed the result of ingesting Ritonavir and then ecstasy: the pathway in the liver which metabolises Ritonavir also metabolises MDMA. When Ritonavir is metabolising, this pathway becomes blocked, and the MDMA is forced to 'wait' in the bloodstream. Where it can build up to fatal levels.

At the time of writing, while Abbott Laboratories accept that Ritonavir could theoretically have been an accomplice in the death of Philip Kay, the company are hesitant to make information about mixing Ritonavir and E directly available to patients on packaging. They fear it will make them look like they are condoning the use of illegal drugs. Yet there are signs that pharmaceutical companies like Abbott may soon budge. If they do, it will be the first time legal drug packaging has made any mention of illegal drugs. Until then, though, the circuit itself has taken on the task of filling the gap in the transmission of information.

"*Everybody* on the circuit knows about mixing protease inhibitors and E, *Nobody* on the AIDS drugs will take illegals anymore," says B, who was diagnosed with HIV in 1998 and has been using AIDS combination therapies. "It's like there was a major push [on the part of circuit party organisers] to get this information out. It's shown that where there is a will to change behaviour, there is a way. Of course, there is still a long way to go. But at least these particular preventable deaths are now being prevented."

And the other preventable dangers? "The cause of those are deeper," says B. "But I've seen things on the circuit lately that are heartening. I've seen men using buddy systems to make sure nobody does anything stupid. A kind of web of self-help is generating. Gay men can act stupidly, we can think with our cocks all too often. But when things turn, we always come together and fight whatever needs fighting. Our history attests to that. Drugs have always been a part of our culture. And AIDS has been part of our culture for what seems like forever now. But these things won't be the end of our culture. We just won't let that happen."

(MS)

36

The Drug Czar And "A Better Britain"

One of the first actions of Tony Blair's Labour government after its land-slide election victory in May 1997 was to announce the creation of the post of UK Anti-Drugs Co-ordinator. Or Drug Czar, as the position soon became known. With an annual salary of around £100,000, the post was advertised in the summer of 1997 and attracted applications from Leah Betts' father Paul Betts, ecstasy guru Nicholas Saunders and reformed dope smuggler Howard Marks, among others. One of those others was top cop Keith Hellawell, then Chief Constable of West Yorkshire. The odds-on favourite from the off, Hellawell's appointment to the post of Drug Czar in October 1997 surprised nobody. Least of all Saunders and Marks, probably.

Keith Hellawell's confirmation as Drug Czar came after 36 years service as a police officer. He'd joined the West Yorkshire Constabulary in 1961, after five years working as a coal miner at the Emley pit near Huddersfield. Hellawell rose through the ranks fast, becoming the youngest sergeant in Britain at the age of 24 in 1965 and, the next year, the youngest inspector. In 1990, he was promoted to Chief Constable, firstly of Cleveland and then, in 1993, of West Yorkshire. He is also the one-time drug spokesman for the Association of Chief Police Officers, a trustee of the National Society for the Prevention of Cruelty to Children and holder of the Queen's Police Medal for Distinguished Service. Not bad for someone who quit school on his 15th birthday with a leavers' report which read "Keith excels at sport and little else".

Some drug experts were disappointed at Tony Blair's choice of Keith Hellawell as Drug Czar, whose chief responsibility is to co-ordinate all those employed to deal with drugs in the UK, from the police, courts and prisons, to health workers and youth workers. They had been hoping for an appointment which signalled that the new government would be taking a fresh approach to the drugs issue – someone with a background in drug treatment or education rather than law enforcement. But although Hellawell had been a police officer, he'd never fitted the stereotype. He'd talked about legalising cannabis – and had done so on national television. He wasn't personally at all in favour of the idea, but that didn't make him blind to the possibility that it might one day happen. He'd talked about legalising prostitution, too.

Moreover, Hellawell's pragmatic approach to policing had often displeased the tabloids – as illustrated by an incident in the early Eighties, when he was involved in the final stage of the Yorkshire Ripper investigation. In a profile of the Drug Czar for the *Guardian* at the beginning of 1999, journalist Colin Hughes describes how Hellawell visited the Ripper, Peter Sutcliffe, at Broadmoor Hospital, the high security mental institution. It was Christmas and, in an act of spontaneity, Hellawell took a greetings card from his briefcase, signed it and gave it to Sutcliffe. A Broadmoor staff member who witnessed the event informed the press, resulting in the policeman suffering widespread condemnation. "It was just part of the rapport thing, that was all," Hellawell told Colin Hughes.

As a copper, Keith Hellawell was considered pretty good at "the rapport thing". In the wider public capacity of the Drug Czar, though, some think that he is poorly qualified. According to "a senior academic in the drugs field" quoted in the *Independent* in mid-1999, Hellawell is "aloof, uninspiring and out of touch. Worst of all, he is out of his depth. He's simply not bright enough. He can't hold all the balls up in the air." But such cutting criticism has been far from universal and many who believed that the focus of his agenda would fall on law enforcement have been proved wrong. The description of him as "aloof" doesn't square with his willingness to meet and listen to drug users themselves, either.

During his first six months as Drug Czar, Hellawell and his deputy, Michael Trace, formerly director of the Rehabilitation for Addicted Prisoners' Trust, consulted with over 2,000 individuals and organisations. Their findings formed the backbone of *Tackling Drugs To Build A Better Britain*, a government White Paper which outlined a 10-year strategy on drugs and set four key objectives:

1. A reduction in the proportion of people under 25 using illegal drugs
2. A reduction in the levels of repeat offending among drug offenders
3. An increase in problem drug users' participation in drug treatment programmes
4. A reduction in the availability of drugs to five- to 16-year-olds

Tackling Drugs To Build A Better Britain was published in April 1998, at a time when, in the words of the document itself, "the number of addicts is going up, and availability and drug-related crime is increasing". The

White Paper referred to a 1997 UN report which estimated that drugs accounted for eight per cent of total international trade – the same as oil or world tourism – and talked about "record levels of drug seizures". It also noted how "the average age of first drug use is becoming younger" and how the latest British Crime Survey indicated that 48 per cent of 16 to 24-year-olds in the UK had used illegal drugs. No less disturbing was the rise in the number of deaths in the UK attributable to the misuse of drugs, up from just over 1,000 a year in the early Nineties to just under 2,000 in the latter part of the decade.

And it wasn't just the human cost which was spiralling. In 1993–4, £500 million a year was spent trying to combat drug use in the UK. By 1997–8, that figure had almost tripled to £1.4 billion. Hellawell didn't think that money was always wisely utilised, though. Almost two-thirds of it was what he termed "reactive expenditure", going to the police, the courts, the prisons and the probation services. Only 13 per cent of the drugs budget was spent on treatment and only 12 per cent on prevention and education, and addressing this imbalance was a central aim of the White Paper. "We must now shift our emphasis from reacting to the consequences of drug misuse to tackling its root causes," Hellawell wrote in his introduction.

Other shifts were also apparent in *Tackling Drugs To Build A Better Britain*. Again in his introduction, the Drug Czar talked of the "misconceptions" of drug use: "All young people do not take drugs; all drug takers are not addicts; all drugs do not kill; all drug takers do not commit crimes; illegal drugs are not the unique preserve of people from particular social or ethnic backgrounds." For the first time, too, there was political recognition of the fact that "enjoyment" was one of the reasons why people took drugs – an unthinkable idea under successive Conservative administrations. As was the suggestion that the often-voiced "war on drugs" might not ever be fully won. "I think it would be pie in the sky for me to recommend that we will create a drug-free society," Hellawell told journalists at the White Paper's launch. "I would like that to be the case as a parent and as a grandparent, but we have got to be sensible, we have got to be realistic."

To monitor the 10-year strategy, the Drug Czar was asked to produce an annual report. The first of these, published in May 1999, set stiff targets for cracking down on the estimated 100,000 to 200,000 heroin and crack cocaine addicts in the country. The number of young people using these two drugs would be cut by 25 per cent by 2005 and 50 per cent by 2008, said Hellawell. The immediate emphasis was placed on the younger drug users, with plans to cut the number of 11- to 16-year-olds using Class A drugs by 20 per cent by 2002. By 2002, too, every school in the UK would be running an anti-drugs programme. Experts questioned whether the £217 million which the Drug Czar had been allocated to pay for all this would be enough, though, particularly given the *Guardian*'s claim that UK drug services were "already overloaded, with many agencies reporting that they were finding it difficult to meet current demand levels".

Hellawell's focus on heroin and crack addicts was undoubtedly because of their links with crime. Users of these two drugs were said to be behind 30 per cent of all crime in the UK and the *Tackling Drugs To Build A Better Britain* document referred to a survey of 664 addicts who had committed a whopping 70,000 offences in a period of only three months. But in addition to such figures, there was also evidence from Professor Howard Parker, a drug expert at Manchester University, that purer and cheaper Class A drugs were increasingly available in Britain. By mid–1999, a wrap of cocaine cost £10 compared to £30 three years earlier and a wrap of 40 per cent pure heroin cost £10. There were reports of the price of ecstasy dropping, too – down to as little as £5 a tablet in some places.

For ecstasy users, the implications of Labour's 10-year strategy are unclear. Although *Tackling Drugs To Build A Better Britain* noted that "a majority of illegal drug users do so for so-called 'recreational purposes' ", the document contained few clues to what the government proposed to do about cutting the numbers of these people. Nor what statutory provisions might be made for them in the meantime. In terms of ecstasy, there was nothing in the White Paper about Safer Dancing-type harm reduction campaigns, for example, despite a positive comment on the impact of harm reduction in relation to heroin.

Keith Hellawell's 1999 *First Annual Report & National Plan* suggested that one way the government is hoping to tackle ecstasy use in the earliest years of the 21st century is by trying to clamp down harder on the supply of the drug. The Drug Czar was clearly enthusiastic about Barry Legg's Public Entertainments Licences (Drugs Misuse) Act, which gave local authorities the power to revoke a club's licence if drugs were supplied or consumed at or near the premises and had only come into effect in May 1998. Hellawell also referred to a White Paper on the private security industry, published a couple of months before his report, which announced strict new regulations on club door staff, some of whom the government thought were "involved either directly or indirectly in drug dealing in clubs".

But what of E users themselves? Some anti-drug lobbyists have expressed fears that the adoption of a tougher stance towards those dealing in ecstasy could be a prelude to a more relaxed attitude towards users – as is the situation in Holland, where supplying ecstasy is a serious offence but the possession of a single tablet is considered merely a misdemeanour.

That Britain is about to emulate Holland seems unlikely, though, not least because of comments made by Keith Hellawell a few days after his appointment as Drug Czar. While he sympathised with people addicted to drugs, he thought that recreational users simply should know better. "It would appear, particularly within the rave scene, that people are taking no notice at all of the health message and the damage they may cause themselves," he said. "They are cautioned if caught at the moment, but perhaps it's time to prosecute them. If people will not listen to reason, maybe they ought to listen to the law."

If, as this suggests, exercising tighter controls on E and other recreational drug users is in the pipeline, a number of experts believe the focus of such controls will be drug screening. One of the actions recommended in *Tackling Drugs To Build A Better Britain* was to "implement drugs in the workplace initiatives", encouraging employers to screen people for drugs, in other words, as is increasingly common in the United States. The roadside testing of car drivers the police suspect of having taken drugs is another of the government's favoured ways of picking up on recreational users. Initially prompted by a 1997 survey which showed that drugs were involved in 16 per cent of fatal road accidents in the UK, roadside screening was piloted in several parts of the country during 1998.

As MDMA can be detected in urine for between two and five days after it has been ingested – and the higher the quantity of MDMA taken the longer the substance can be detected – some drug experts believe that screening is the government's strongest weapon against ecstasy. In the event of the introduction of widespread workplace and roadside screening, the authorities would undoubtedly hope that it would act as a deterrent, but that would partly depend on the consequences for somebody tested positive. And despite Hellawell's stern warning to ravers, putting E users in the dock does not square with the government's more treatment-oriented approach to heroin and crack cocaine users. It may even undermine that approach by bizarrely making those substances more attractive propositions than E or other recreational drugs.

To compound the authorities' difficulty in dealing with ecstasy is the fact that traditional detoxification treatment orders are utterly pointless. How do you detox someone of something which is in their bodies for a few hours perhaps only once or twice a month? It might be that a counselling programme of some kind would be appropriate for habitual E users, but developing such a programme or programmes does not appear to be a government priority.

With all this in mind, the government's best hope of cutting the number of ecstasy users over the next few years turns on its twin ability to stop young people taking the drug in the first place and get those who are already committed to taking it to stop of their own volition. Although the former task is well underway via anti-drugs school programmes, achieving the latter will require some very lateral thinking in the Drug Czar's office. *Tackling Drugs To Build A Better Britain* notes the importance of efforts to "make the misuse of drugs less culturally acceptable to young people", but forcing even the thinnest of wedges through the 10-year plus link between ecstasy and the club scene is an almighty challenge. One perhaps more suited to someone called Hercules rather than Hellawell.

(P)

37

Report From The Research Lab

Ecstasy casualties. No, not Leah Betts. Not the ones who became statistics.

Ecstasy casualties like that geezer who always stands in the same corner of the club, his eyes so big they look like they're gonna walk right outta his skull, his jaw mashing through a couple of packets of gum a night. Sure, you know the guy. The one who starts nodding his head when he's queuing to get in and is still nodding as he gets his coat at the end of the night. He was in that dance magazine – in that 'Gurner Of The Month' photo thing. Yeah, yeah, yeah, that's him. Fucking nuts or what? Too many Es, man. That guy's mind is fried. To a fucking cinder, man.

Whether or not ecstasy causes long-term harm to the brain has been the big question for what seems like forever – for the medical world, the political world, the media and, most importantly, for users. The claim that MDMA is neurotoxic, that it damages the brain, goes right back to the very earliest days of recreational use of the drug. It was one of the main topics for discussion at the public hearings which followed the Drug Enforcement Administration's decision to make MDMA an illegal substance in the US in 1985.

One slightly soiled E Generation on, there's a growing body of evidence to suggest that the drug does have an effect on the way the windmills of the mind turn. But the extent of that effect and whether it amounts to actual brain damage remains a highly contentious issue.

Research into the effects of MDMA on the brain has taken place in just about any country where anybody has waved a lightstick – from European countries like Germany, Switzerland, Italy and Spain, to Israel, Australia, Canada and, of course, the US. Since the mid-Nineties, though, attention has been focused on the work of one research in particular – Dr George Ricaurte, an American medical bigwig and no mistake. How big a wig? Associate professor of neurology at Johns Hopkins University Medical School in Baltimore, Maryland, which forms part of Johns Hopkins

Medical Institutions, one of the biggest and most respected medical research centres in the world.

Dr Ricaurte has been investigating MDMA since joining Johns Hopkins during the late Eighties, mainly looking at the effects of the drug on the neurons (or nerve cells) which produce serotonin, the brain chemical believed to play an important part in shaping mood, thought processes, sleep patterns, eating patterns, and motor activity. Serotonin is a neurotransmitter, transferring messages across the synapses (or gaps) between adjacent neurons. It is produced by a nerve cell and is then released into the synapses from the end of tentacle-like extensions called axons, transporting information to another cell before being absorbed back into the first in a process known as reuptake. MDMA provokes a flood of both serotonin and dopamine, another neurotransmitter, into the synapses and also disrupts the reuptake process.

Ricaurte's interest in neurotransmitters began with investigations into the effects on dopamine of MPTP (1-methyl-4-phenyl-1,2,5,6-tetrahydropyridine), a contaminant substance formed in the sloppy production of a synthetic heroin called MPPP (1-methyl-4-phenyl-4-propionpiperidine, also known as meperidine). Some of the people who had taken MPTP had developed Parkinson's disease, the shaking condition caused by a degeneration of dopamine neurons in the brain. By testing MPTP on squirrel monkeys, it was discovered that there was a marked similarity in the neuropathology of Parkinsonism in human and non-human primates. The findings suggested much could be learned about Parkinson's disease in humans by the study of MPTP-dosed monkeys.

George Ricaurte's initial work with MDMA involved squirrel monkeys and also rats. The animals were given doses of the drug matching those often taken by human users, the doses formulated by interspecies scaling methods which take into account the differences in body mass between the human and animal subjects. At low doses of MDMA, the animals were found to suffer decreases in their levels of serotonin. At higher doses, Ricaurte and his team observed changes to the animals' serotonin transporter nerve fibres and axons – changes which Ricaurte interpreted as damage. However, because the apparent destruction was to the nerve fibres and axons, but not the cell body itself, there was clearly a potential for regrowth. Was the change, or damage, only temporary, then? Could the brain, an intricate and often extremely resilient organ, repair itself?

"After a period of about a year, we found there was some recovery in some areas of the brain, but not in others," says Dr Ricaurte. "Our concern wasn't just that the recovery wasn't complete, but that the regrowth which did occur was often aberrant, it was often abnormal. In a few instances, we actually observed an overgrowth. There was effectively an abnormal rewiring. Another important observation was that the aberrant regrowth was mainly in the non-human primates."

The fact that monkeys seemed to be more sensitive to MDMA than rats worried Ricaurte. Bearing in mind the similarities discovered in MPTP-induced dopamine degeneration in human and non-human primates, he wondered if this meant humans might also be particularly susceptible to the effects of MDMA. Ricaurte began trying to answer that question in 1994, when he compared the brains of a group of MDMA users with those of non-users. The results suggested that his fears were not without foundation: humans did indeed appear to be vulnerable to the same kind of neuronal changes seen in squirrel monkeys. These findings have since been supported by further research undertaken by Ricaurte, most notably a 1998 study involving a group of nine men and five women who had all reported heavy use of MDMA.

The eligibility criteria for the users recruited for the 1998 study was that they'd taken MDMA on at least 25 occasions – "although the 14 users taking part said they'd taken it between 70 to 400 times, with an average of 228 times," notes Ricaurte. The average duration of use was 4.6 years and the average frequency was six times a month. The average dose of MDMA ingested was 386mg. A control group of 15 people who had never taken MDMA was also recruited, with the two sets matched on age (late twenties) and education levels. All of the 29 participants agreed to abstain from psychoactive drugs for three weeks prior to the study and were screened to ensure they hadn't broken that agreement.

The participants' brains were then studied using a neuroimaging technique known as positron emission tomography (PET) with a radioactive ligand – "a chemical tag which sticks to serotonin transporters and lights up healthy serotonin synapses on a scan," translates Ricaurte. The "chemical tag", which was administered intravenously, allowed Ricaurte and his team to look directly at serotonin neurons in the living human brain by effectively isolating them from the millions of other nerve cells. What they saw wasn't what most E users wanted to hear.

"The people who'd never used MDMA had normal levels of serotonin transporters, but the MDMA users had a lower density of transporters in all brain areas," says Ricaurte. "Not only that, but the greater the use of the drug, the greater the extent of the deficiency."

The details of George Ricaurte's PET study were first published in *The Lancet*, the prestigious British medical journal, but subsequently made newspaper headlines around the world. In the UK, most sections of the media presented Ricaurte's findings as conclusive evidence that ecstasy causes brain damage. The response from the medical science world, however, was more cautious.

In recognition of this, in April 1999, *The Lancet* printed half a dozen letters expressing doubts about various aspects of Dr Ricaurte's PET study. The letters were crammed with medical gobbledygook – mRNA expressions and Logan-Patlak plots, for example – but Dr John Farnill-Morgan from the Department of Psychiatry at St George's Hospital Medical School in London was more straightforward in stating his belief that Ricaurte and his team were "over-eager to wring meaning from their findings".

Among the points raised by the *Lancet* letters was the possible inaccuracy of the information which the people participating in the study gave Ricaurte about their drug habits. One problem especially pertinent to ecstasy was the fact that, as Dr Karl Jansen of the South London & Maudsley NHS Trust and Professor Robert Forrest of the Department of Forensic Pathology at Sheffield University noted in their letter, an 'ecstasy' tablet doesn't always contain MDMA. It may contain one or more of a whole range of other substances. In his reply to *The Lancet*, Dr Ricaurte agreed this was the case, but said that because only MDMA and MDMA-related substances "have been shown to cause serotonin neurotoxic injury" the effects of any other drug wouldn't have had any impact on his study.

Some of *The Lancet* correspondents, including Dr Jansen and Professor Forrest, also talked about the link between serotonin and personality. Maybe low levels of serotonin transporters in MDMA users are pre-existent, they argued, giving rise to personalities which make taking pleasure-stimulating substances more attractive to those people than to others. Put simply, rather than the use of MDMA causing a low level of serotonin transporters, perhaps a low level of transporters causes people to seek out drugs like ecstasy.

"There might be pre-existing genetic, neurochemical, personality differences between those inclined to try ecstasy, those who like it, those who hate it and those who would never contemplate taking it," expands Karl Jansen, a psychiatrist at South London & Maudsley's Chaucer Centre. "Those who have a strong drive to take large quantities of stimulants and psychedelics might have inherited an under-functioning of, for example, the dopamine pleasure system, as has been proven for some types of alcoholism. It could increase the likelihood of depression, anxiety, fear of immobility and commitment, and a sense of dissatisfaction which is rarely appeased. It could also create a drive towards seeking a higher level of novelty and stimulation."

With this in mind, Jansen believes that a group of MDMA users should be compared against a group of non-users who have not taken the drug simply because it's never been available to them, rather than because they have elected not to take it for personality or other reasons. He also thinks that a comparison of a group of heavy MDMA-only users and a group of heavy cocaine users would yield valuable information. He says that cocaine is a stimulant often sought out by people with an under-functioning of serotonin and dopamine brain systems, yet it is not known to cause changes to serotonin fibres and axons. "So if heavy cocaine users proved to show similar changes in serotonin transporter mechanisms to MDMA users, we could conclude that the deficits, relative to non-drug use, are pre-existing and not caused by MDMA," wrote Jansen and Forrest in their letter to *The Lancet*.

Rick Doblin, who led the fight against the DEA scheduling of MDMA as an illegal substance in 1985, similarly believes that the personality of the participants may have had a confounding effect on Ricaurte's PET study results. Like some of the medical experts who wrote to *The Lancet*, Doblin also has doubts about the reliability of PET imaging. He notes that it's still a new technique and there could be 10 to 15 per cent variability between two scans on the same person. Ricaurte, however, while allowing that "Dr Jansen and Mr Doblin raise some interesting points", is unswerving in his opinion that MDMA induces a loss of serotonin transporters in humans. He believes the evidence is too strong to suggest otherwise, particularly if the human research is viewed together with the animal findings.

"In terms of any possible influence of personality and the accuracy of PET imaging, I think the key is to look at the work we've done with non-human primates, which has been going on simultaneously with the human studies," says Ricaurte. "The animal studies have helped us to know how to approach human subjects and how to assess human data. They also provide us with verification. PET imaging has been used on non-human primates as well as humans and we decided to sacrifice some of the non-human primates, in this case baboons, to conduct post-mortem studies on their brain tissue. What we found verified the PET scan results we'd previously obtained with them."

Anxiety, depression, panic attacks, persistent perceptual changes, persistent hallucinations, insomnia, nightmares, flashbacks, paranoia, grandiose delusions, a feeling of being unreal, a feeling that the world is unreal, post-traumatic stress disorder, fragmentation of the personality, mania and suicide. Karl Jansen describes the list of psychological conditions which have been associated with ecstasy use as a "catalogue of distress". But he calls it "suspiciously long and diverse", too.

"When widespread use of a drug results in a problem list covering a large section of psychiatry, we may just be seeing the illnesses which exist in the population rather than specific drug effects," he explains. "In other words, the link with drug-taking may be coincidental. The user is searching for an understandable cause for their problem and mind-altering drugs are a popular choice. It's a way of avoiding the stigma which is still attached to some forms of psychiatric disorder. It is to the mind of the user, as well as to the brain, that we must sometimes look."

Yet despite doubting the extent of the psychological difficulties linked to ecstasy and the exact role of the drug in those difficulties, Karl Jansen doesn't believe users' minds are unaffected – at least in the short-term. He points to what clubbers call 'the midweek blues': a short period of depression or perhaps irritability which usually occurs two to four days after taking a tablet. According to Jansen, "almost all persons who have taken an effective dose of MDMA experience this", although he adds that frequent users may be less likely to do so as they will have developed a tolerance to the drug. Jansen also notes how post-E depression is sometimes "masked" by the use of other drugs, such as cannabis and alcohol. "Those who say they have never experienced a post-E dip are probably also those who use copious amounts of other drugs every day," he says.

As well as the kind of neurological examinations undertaken by George Ricaurte, E users have also been the subject of numerous mood, behaviour and functionality research studies. Several of these have taken place in Britain, including a 1997 study conducted by Valerie Curran from University College in London. Curran spent several Saturday nights at a London club recruiting a total of 24 people, 12 of whom claimed they had taken ecstasy while the other 12 said that they had consumed only alcohol. She ran a series of mood and memory tests on all 24 subjects at a makeshift laboratory which she set up at the club, and then tested them for a second time at their homes the next day and for a third time the following Wednesday. Curran reported that the two groups were similarly generally depressed and irritable on the Sunday, but the anxiety ratings of the ecstasy users were double those of the alcohol users on the Wednesday. The E group also performed twice as badly as the alcohol group in memory tests on the Saturday night and the Sunday. Although their memories had improved by the Wednesday, they still fared poorly compared to alcohol users.

The results of such research studies certainly suggest that ecstasy causes a change in the way the brain functions, but both Karl Jansen and Rick Doblin question whether this equates to long-term damage. Like Jansen, though, Doblin doesn't claim the drug is free of psychological risk.

"The unblocking effect of MDMA can bring up difficult issues from the user's past," says Doblin. "If they could cry, if they could let out their feelings, it might be fine. But because they're often at a club with a bunch of friends and everybody else is having a fun time with the drug, they try to stuff their emotions down. That's often when you see people having a physical reaction, throwing up and so on, or feeling incredibly lonely, feeling there's something wrong with them. It's sometimes because they don't have the maturity to handle the drug – the younger that someone uses MDMA, the more likely they are to get into trouble. If the onset of use can be postponed, people may end up having fewer problems with it."

Karl Jansen also talks about the "unblocking effect" of MDMA. "While no lasting harm may result and defences may rebuild themselves as the drug wears off, it is possible that some of the liberated material cannot be pushed back in," he says. "This may lead to anxiety, nightmares, low moods and other problems." Jansen calls this "the Pandora's box syndrome". But he also points out that the uninhibiting effect of the drug was precisely why it was once so highly valued as an aid to psychotherapy.

"Throughout human history, it has always been understood that some substances can be used either as beneficial medicines or harmful poisons, depending on the context," he explains. "What MDMA does depends on the set and the settings. In favourable settings, the results might be therapeutic. In unfavourable settings, the results might be harmful. It's the yin-yang, the negative-positive – the most fundamental law of being."

Indeed, long after the DEA banned all use of the substance in the US, the use of MDMA in therapy is still recognised as having potential benefit by some American medical figures. Dr Charles Grob, Associate Professor of Psychiatry and Associate Professor of Pediatrics at the UCLA School of Medicine in California, for example, who has been researching the possible use of the drug in helping terminally ill cancer patients come to terms with their illnesses since the mid-1990s. Dr George Greer, the therapist whose work with MDMA in the early 1980s formed the backbone of the Doblin-led case against the DEA's 1985 scheduling of the drug, has maintained his belief in the drug's potential therapeutic value, too. In 1998, Greer published a research paper in the Journal Of Psychoactive Drugs in which he described how, with government approval, he'd used MDMA to bring relief to a man suffering from multiple myeloma, a type of cancer with no present known cure, and a woman suffering problems resulting from her family's experiences in the Holocaust.

E has frequently been described as "a timebomb". Despite most users saying the drug has no lasting psychological effect on them, some medical experts claim that hospital psychiatric wards will be full of E victims in 20 or 30 years time. Karl Jansen is dismissive of this scenario, though, viewing it as essentially a myth perpetrated by the media. He draws a comparison with the press reaction to E and the reaction to LSD in the 1960s.

"The profound mental effects of LSD led to an expectation that it must

210

damage the brain," he says. "But repeated injections of huge amounts of the drug into animals had no lasting impact upon brain hardware and it is now accepted by most specialists that LSD has relatively unremarkable long-term effects. One disproven media theme was that LSD could damage chromosomes and another issue was flashbacks. Yet despite intense media interest in flashbacks in the past and high levels of LSD use in the present, they no longer seem to be common. Although the UK government official report for 1998 noted that a staggering 10 per cent of people under 30 had taken LSD, the drug has largely vanished from the pages of both the tabloids and the medical journals."

Over at Johns Hopkins University in Maryland, though, Dr George Ricaurte doesn't view the ecstasy timebomb scenario as simply a media myth. He thinks it's a totally realistic possibility.

"Part of the problem is we still don't know too much about serotonin," says George Ricaurte. "We do, however, know that levels of dopamine decrease as people age – there is a natural decrease of eight to 10 per cent per year. Which is not usually a problem, because there's sufficient dopamine in reserve for it not to matter. For some people, though, this is not the case and one of the effects is for them to exhibit the symptoms of Parkinson's disease.

"Now the question is, does the same kind of natural decrease occur in serotonin? And what level of serotonin decrease is needed before there is an effect? We still don't know. But if serotonin does decrease and somebody has already experienced a significant drop in serotonin as a result of taking ecstasy when they were younger, there is a possibility of them falling below the threshold level at an earlier age."

The uncertainty of it all is clearly another major worry for E users. The simple fact is that, despite Dr Ricaurte's work, despite Dr Jansen's considered criticisms and theories, and despite the fact that many other medical experts throughout the world have been investigating MDMA since the late 1980s, none of them still knows for 100 per cent sure what the long-term effects of the drug on the human brain are. As Jansen says, "it's early days for brain science".

Within that one big question of whether ecstasy causes long-term brain damage, then, are countless other questions. Ricaurte's work looks set to continue for some time yet. It may not be until well into the 21st century, perhaps 20 or 30 years after the start of widespread recreational use of the drug in the late 1980s, that the one big answer will be revealed. For now, it still lies with the geezer in the corner of the club. And you know the state he's usually in.

(P)

38

Gatecrasher Kids And Candy Ravers

If there was such a thing as a UK clubland HQ, an E culture office block from which all the British clubs and record labels and best-selling record-ing artists and big-name DJs and television shows and magazines ema-nated, it would have been a glum place to visit at the beginning of 1998. It would have been full of people holding their breath and packing their bags and cushioning their arses for a fall they felt was inevitable. For in early 1998, the quiet consensus of many of those packaging and selling ecstasy culture to the masses was that the scene had run its course.

Sure, there were chart hits and heaving clubs and more punters than ever going to Ibiza for the summer. But the faculty in the mythical HQ feared that a ceiling had been reached, that the scene couldn't grow any bigger. It could only shrink. The underground creativity, the fuel which had regenerated the E environment for the past decade had dissipated, they said. We've commercialised it into oblivion, some admitted. It had been 10 years since acid house and many on the cultural supply end agreed that a decade is a mighty long time for a drug, and a culture spawned by a drug, to remain in demand. Plus, there were all the books – books on the history of rave, the history of house – and history books don't get written unless something is, in fact, history. Or soon to be.

The people packaging the E experience still liked saying that the drug had changed their generation. That line made it into lots of the books. But however true, the words probably began feeling flat and tasteless in their mouths. Because the drug's culture had become vocational food for them: it had become their work. And because their generation had grown into 30-somethings, or almost 30-somethings, it was getting harder to really, honestly care about the ins and outs of clubs'n'drugs'n' E'd-up hugs, what with bills to worry about and baby showers to go to.

The enduring nature of British E culture had created the weirdest phe-nomenon – a huge generation gap within a single drug scene. In 1999, this gap became glaringly obvious through a group of clubbers in the north of England who called themselves Gatecrasher kids, or Crasher kids, after the superclub in Sheffield to which many of them pledged allegiance. They were 18, 19, sometimes 20 years old. They were four, five, six years old when, in 1985, *The Face* published the first UK magazine story about ecstasy. When Shoom opened, they were trying to read books without pictures. During the hardcore rave era, they were spending their pocket money on their first records. When Leah Betts died at the age of 18 in 1995, she was still older than any of them.

In 1999, finally of age and very familiar with the idea that loads of people do drugs at weekends, normal people and that's-just-a-fact, they began to partake themselves. For them, a pill at a club may have been as regular a rite of passage as a pint down the pub had been to their older siblings. So they did their first E, remembering the stuff about dehydration that that counsellor bloke who visited their classroom one day had talked about. Weathering their first door-frisk, they entered clubland and went straight to the bar to buy a bottle of water. For them, this night – the first night they took E! The best night of their lives!! Hugging strangers and shaking hands with, ohmygod, the DJ!!! – was just the beginning.

It was only a short time until it became quite clear that these newbie teens seemed to enjoy the ecstasy experience more than the Nineties clubbers who'd come before them. It was all marmalade skies for the Gatecrasher kids. No kinks to work out, no skins to grow into, no questions, no problems, no fear. They'd grown up with drug culture fluttering around them. They knew how to do the ecstasy thing almost instinctively, just as they instinctively knew how to use computers. They didn't need to read the manual or click on any 'help' function. And what the old heads – who thought E culture was going to die when their generation got married - didn't realise was that, with or without a fertile underground, the Gatecrasher generation felt it was their God-given right to do the E thing, more than anyone, like, ever.

So what did these kids do with E and Saturday night and dance music? Nothing new and at the same time something completely new. The Crasher kids swapped all the old, crotchety pretensions of 'cool' for an upped quotient of 'fun'. They took the bits they liked best from clubland's past 10 years – maybe the most obvious bits – and sewed them together. They took the over-the-top brotherly love and hip-to-be-happy expressionism of 1988, but clipped it of its political t-shirt doodles. They took the "It's why I work all week" superclubber's stance and made it less morose: "It's why I work all week and it's worth every gruelling hour and I wouldn't have it any different, thanks!" They took trance music from the crusty scene, the Goa traveller's bag, and cleaned it up to a sparkling shine, turning it into their fave sound of 'power trance'. They took the more-

213

is-better, all-is-forgiven-here, lampshade-headed fun-fun-fun attitude of the Ibiza summer massive and transported it back to sooty Britain.

More than anything else, though, they took their cues from rave's high era, from the 1992–1994 hardcore era – the ecstasy moment anyone who was a kid in the Nineties was bound to remember best. Because it was the most literal. Because it had big fluorescent letters painted all over it, just like *Sesame Street*. Because it was the loudest, the most colourful, the most humongous, the car-ayyy-zeee-iest, the kiddiest. Because its people played with toys and sucked dummies and wore orange boiler suits on *Top Of The Pops*. When you're 11 years old, that'll get your attention.

At Gatecrasher in Sheffield, Sundissential in Birmingham, Passion in Coalville and any big club which would allow it, the toys were just the beginning of the new ravers' kindergarten of the future aesthetic. There were stuffed, yellow happy face cuddlies, teddy bear rucksacks, flashing doodlybugs, jelly-filled balls, pop-up bubble wristwatches, foam letters, string spray, inflatable aliens and SuperSoakers. There were McDonald-land puppets and Tinky Winkies and Hello Kitties and Marvin The Martians. There were pink plastic address books in which to take down new friends' telephone numbers and e-mail addresses. There were home-made banners and flags. There was hair in all colours but brunette or blonde or ginger, fashioned into pinhead-style spikes or wrapped into tin-foil dreads or clustered into hundreds of tiny pigtails with orthodon-tist's elastics. There were children's undershirts with little robots on them and musical socks and edible necklaces and sparkle-encrusted face-masks and stick-on stars and fluorescent face paint, nail polish, lip gloss. And there were dummies. And lightsticks, glow-sabres, glow-balls and glow-tape. If someone had taken the roof off one of these places, the dancefloor would have been visible from the moon.

One of the resident DJs at Gatecrasher, Judge Jules, an old London head who rose to fame DJing in the jurassic acid house era, was appalled. Using his Radio 1 show and the dance music press as his platform, he called for a ban on toys in clubs. He called the clubs which allowed them irresponsi-ble, and said lightsticks were a return to the old rave days, meaning the hardcore days – days he thought were terrible. "Schoolyard lunacy," he sniffed in an interview with *Muzik* magazine. The Crasher paraphernalia went against everything he believed clubbing should be about: appreciat-ing music, revering the DJ and, to an extent, being cool.

Amazingly, the Gatecrasher floor didn't clear the next time Judge Jules got on the decks. The crowd didn't really care that much: he was only the guy playing records and, despite 'We Luv U' banners often being unfurled to greet a favourite DJ, the Crasher kids' clublife was primarily about the punters, not the 'star' behind the turntables. "It was quite unexpected," says Bethan Cole, the first journalist to write about the Gatecrasher kids. She called them "the mental generation". "After years of the youth media and corporate club culture banging it into heads that the DJs were the gods, because E culture needed saleable figureheads, the Crasher Kids took it all back to these almost quaint ideas of going out to meet people and make new friends and 'everyone is a star here'. People like [Judge Jules] just couldn't get into that. It was very far from what he knew by then."

"A lot of the older DJs and promoters didn't really understand the Gate-crasher thing," agrees former *Muzik* editor Ben Turner. Aged 25 in 1999, he considered himself old then, too. "There was this feeling of, like, who *made* these people? It was all so insane. So bizarre. So far out. Where did all this kiddie stuff suddenly appear from? Was it the Mitsubishi pills? Maybe it was the Mitsubishis. I think, yes, it was the Mitsubishis . . ."

Throughout the Nineties, novel new brands of ecstasy appeared in the UK almost monthly. These brands usually all meant the same thing – a hodgepodge of chemicals pressed together into a pill, stamped with a logo for the sake of fancy, sold as ecstasy and swallowed with the hope that it contained at least a shred of MDMA. By 1997, E users' confidence in anything pill-shaped had waned tremendously. Some manufacturers responded to this by changing the format of the drug. Capsules, once the absolute sign of 'dodgy E' had reappeared, this time hawked as 'more pure': "There ain't none o' that binding shite in here, mate!" E in powder form, nose ecstasy, was also becoming increasingly popular. Much of the snortable E on Britain's streets was actually the same old pills crushed into powder by savvy dealers (and probably then cut again, with baking soda or something similarly cheap). Yet the trend for inhaling powdered E soared, because users bought the pitch that the loose condition of the drug meant it hadn't been adulterated.

At the end of 1997, users' trust was at an all-time low. Then, sometime early the following year, a brand of E embossed with the triple diamond logo of the Japanese Mitsubishi corporation – perhaps some drug pro-ducer's ha-ha commentary on 'corporate clubbing' – began streaming into the UK from a Low Country manufacturing base. Many who tried these 'Mitsubishis' said there was something different about the pills. Those who remembered the rush of pure or close-to-pure MDMA said Mitsubishis were, astoundingly, the 'real deal'. First-time users, or younger users who wouldn't have previously known an MDMA molecule if it waved hello and introduced itself, agreed. These pills *did* feel like nothing they'd ever had. Empathetic, not aggressive. Huggy, not hallucinatory. Clean, not dirty. Warm, open and uninhibiting, not speedy or harsh or dark or icky or yucky: "So this is why they call it 'ecstasy'!" It was. Pure bliss.

Although it's quite clear that the original Mitsubishis did have an uncommonly high MDMA content, it's less obvious why the original man-ufacturers of the product suddenly decided to export such 'high quality' tablets. Was it some kind of philanthropic decision? Or did these manufac-turers have the same fears as the people in the mythical clubland HQ? Did they too fear a ceiling had been reached? Were they worried that mass ecstasy consumption was on the brink of collapse? Were Mitsubishis some drug producer's masterplan to keep E culture alive and kicking and filling the coffers?

The technicolor crowds taking the drug at clubs like Gatecrasher didn't care a jot. Even the death of a Gatecrasher clubber in April 1999 didn't slow down the Mitsubishi mania. And the Crasher kids weren't just taking Mitsubishis – they also wore the Mitsubishi logo on any stitch of clothing they could sew it. They attached triple diamond cut-outs to the ends of the springs and pipe-cleaners twirled in their hair. They painted signs with messages like "MITSUBISHIS: NEVER ENOUGH AND WE'RE FUCKIN' LOVIN' IT!" and waved them in front of the DJ booth all night. They refused to use any batteries for their flashing toys other than those branded Mitsubishi. To this generation, the logo became what the smiley had been to the acid musketeers of 1988: a badge of druggy certifi-cation, even camaraderie. See someone on the bus on a gloomy Tuesday and they've got a Mitsubishi logo painted on their rucksack, you give that person a smile, a wink, a thumbs-up – "I know how you feel. I was there, too. See you next Saturday."

Of course, it wasn't long before Mitsubishis were degraded and imitated and "not what they used to be." By mid-1999, the make-up of the bulk of the pills stamped with the triple diamond had reverted to chemical cock-tails which may or may not have contained MDMA. But the Gatecrasher phenomenon continued to grow. The Crasher kids continued to dress like toddlers on Halloween, continued to be overly friendly for the sake of friendliness, continued to make the kind of connections which they said they'd never made before in their lives, not ever. Taking this into account, then, it's hard to believe this movement happened only because a batch of pills coasted into Britain bearing more MDMA than usual. It's hard to swallow the Mitsubishis theory as a total explanation. Not least because in America, where the triple diamond wonders never arrived in bulk, a very similar sort of scene had unfurled its multicoloured wings.

At 17, Leya was just one of tens of thousands of 'candy ravers' skipping across the American nightscape in 1999. Just one in a great, dancing, teenage mob which was multiplying with uncanny speed. Just one of the thousands to leave a poem on one of the dozens of candy raver websites on the internet, too, the sites serving as a communication link between candy ravers across the vast North American continent. Leya's poem is called 'The Raver: A Pilgrimage Poem'. The following is a clipped version of it:

"Today is the day, it's Saturday
Tonight is the night, when friends unite
Leaving the comfort of my home
I drive to the party like a lil' drome
We don our brightly coloured Polo, Nautica, Tommy Gear
& 80 inch pants
Then dive into our self-induced trance
Only 17 years old
And my soul's been sold
To the warmth of drugs
And the coldness of stranger's hugs
I love myself & the way i feel
When i've bought drugs & i know they're real . . .
The objects in my bag represent me
As odd and different as they may be
Lotions, potions, stickers and toys
It's the lil' things that bring us joy
Maybe it's a representation of lost childhood
We've been our own parents, playmate & best friend
Because we are left for ourselves to fend
Driving home extremely cracked out
I still do not know what life's all about"

By the year 2010, there will be 35 million teens in the US, the largest number of teenagers in the history of the nation. There were 31 million of them in 1999 – that's 31 million Americans born in the Eighties.

The kids of the economically booming, hugely middle class and upper middle class America of the first days of the new millennium have spent most of their leisure time engaged with not just one idiot-box, the television, but with several: the VCR, the computer, the game console, the CD player, the Discman, the portable phone, the cellular phone, the interactive pager, the MP3 player, the digital camera and, of course, the mega-cable-enhanced TV, with an average of 150 channels to choose from. They have lived their years in a state of electronic, not human, interaction. School days are now taken up with screen time – computers are an integral and multi-levelled part of the education system and classes taught by televisions (with commercials!) have increasingly become the norm – and after-school kicking the can-type neighbourhood games have been replaced by lots of sitting down pressing buttons on many different machines, often alone.

There is much less plain ol' hanging out going on. Less park-crawling, yard-sitting and block-walking. Loads less time spent outdoors in general. There's a lot more time spent in ceilinged, consumerist environments, in megaplexes and laserdomes and leisure centres and shopping malls. There is tons more ingestion of information, coming from all sides, all screens, all media. Not surprising, then, is the fact that American youths have fewer conversations – less talk – than ever before, even with the people they live with: one study in the mid-Nineties claimed that the average American teen spoke with his or her mother for an average of seven minutes a day, and with poor old dad for two minutes less than that. Other studies suggest today's American teenagers are more stressed-out than they have ever been in the history of such research. Their concerns are often the concerns of adults – they fear for their futures (getting into good schools), for their health (AIDS, pregnancy), for their safety in an increasingly violent society (school shootings, date rape). A carefree kiddieland this is not. A mega-informed, hyper-processing, über-consumerist generation of kids who know too much to 'act their age'? But are anxiety-ridden and feel isolated, because they *are* their age? Yes, that's more the thing.

Only in an environment such as this could hugging be seen as a total act of rebellion. Only in this context could loving your fellow human being be considered incredibly defiant. Only under these circumstances could 15-year-olds think themselves really kooky for wanting to go somewhere to play and talk and connect and interact, person-to-person.

"The whole thing about candy ravers is their, like, friendliness and human[ness]," says Amy, aka Aim-E, an 18-year-old candy raver from Los Angeles, California. "It's like, of course you don't want to go out of your way to give someone you don't know a lift to the party, but when you are a candy raver you do that kinda thing. You force yourself to help and be nice." Candy sites on the internet, which often feature databases of photos and profiles of ravers, organised according to city or state, are indeed full of requests and offers of lifts to parties. "Also, if you're a candy kid, you give people you don't know hugs and buy candy to give out to strangers at the rave, because, like, I dunno, there is no room to do that kinda thing in REAL LIFE, you know?" continues Aim-E. "In real life, taking candy from strangers is like, a really bad thing, right? So in the candy rave thing, we've made the opposite true."

The term 'candy raver' was first used in North America during the early Nineties, when the rave scene was just beginning to spread from the west and east coasts into the middle of the continent. It was originally derogatory: to the US rave elite, a candy raver meant a fabric-softened kid, usually under 20, usually from the 'burbs, usually affluent, who had cottoned onto the American dance scene and used ecstasy, but had no clue why. Candy ravers just went out to have fun and bounce around. They didn't go out to develop the scene, or pull America out of its aged rock'n' roll-ism, or 'expand their minds', which to the we-must-educate-the-crowd ideology-obsessed American rave glitterati of the time was just not good enough. In the earlier Nineties, the candy raver was the American version of the British 'cheesy quaver' – a vulgar scene ruiner – only with much more green in pocket and mom's Acura keys in hand.

But they proliferated. And in the later 1990s, when the elite went off to get adult, get a 'real job', get into a good graduate programme, the multiplying candy teens chomped into a good deal of the Ameri-rave platform. As in Britain, the elite said it was the death knell of the dance scene. As in Britain, all that actually died was an ecstasy culture which had hardened into bourgeois, 30-something-ish ideas of 'taste'.

So what did *these* kids do with E and Saturday night and dance music? With less E culture lore available to them than the Crasher kids (most kinds of club culture still fall a good deal left of the mainstream in the US), basically anything they wanted. "And what they wanted, obviously, was a place they could be children in," says Matt Massive, co-publisher of Midwest anti-candy rave zine *Massive*. "A place where they could be soft and cuddly like stupid little bunnies dancing to stupid childish music."

The present-day candy raver wardrobe would make that of the Gatecrasher patron seem downright adult. Everyday fare can include fun-fur XXL overalls, baby-blocks made into necklaces or wallet-chains, leisure suits fashioned out of hundreds of stuffed animals, huge trousers which make the wearers look like cartoon characters come to life, teddy bear backpacks and, of course, dummies, toys, light-things and glow-things (there are candy web sites which specialise in selling these all-important accessories). Compared to Britain, there's always been less allegiance to one kind of sound-of-the-moment in American rave. But if the representative candy genre had to be chosen, it would be happy hardcore, a marginalised, violently gleeful, hyper-ecstasy-fied and incredibly fast kind of rave music which grew out of the kiddiecore side of early UK techno. "Silly music, silly talk," continues Massive. "Candy ravers always [talk] this bullshit PLUR garbage. Something about it is really fuckin' sad, man."

PLUR is the candy ravers' favourite buzz phrase. It stands for Peace Love Unity Respect – it's pretty classic E speak – and they all say it and type it and wear it on their sleeves, a whole lot. "PLUR!" says an excited Aim-E. "I didn't know what it meant and then, in 1998, I went to my first rave, did my first you-know-what, and suddenly I understood the whole rave thing and PLUR and why PLUR was important. Like, 'OK, you feel bad? You feel lonely? You feel weird or something? That's OK, I do too! I mean, would I dress like this if I felt normal? No! But everyone is my friend here, 'coz we're at a rave. Everything's cool here, we're all friends here and all that bad stuff from the world doesn't exist here! Like, let's share this drink! Want some? Lets hug!' PLUR!"

Ecstasy use in America has not yet become as overtly mainstream as it has in Britain. The reason for this is largely due to draconian zero tolerance laws, puritanical 'Just Say No' campaigns, and successive US governments treating illicit drugs and their users in much the same way they dealt with communists in the Fifties. The Cold War comparison might seem a bit far-fetched, but try speaking to many Americans – even ravers – on the phone about drugs and they are uncomfortable with anything but coded language when talking about personal use. They'll call ecstasy "you-know-what". As if their lines are tapped. As if the police will burst in and cart them off to jail.

Their fear is understandable – the connection between drugs and criminality in the American social conscience seems an unbreakable tradition – and even filters into the US ecstasy culture-inclined media. In the UK, the letters pages of clubby magazines are filled with glamorised stories of over-the-top drug excess. *Muzik* even has a hip-to-be-fucked section called 'Casualty Ward'. In comparable Stateside magazines, like *Urb* or *Mixer*, the letters pages will often include a sorrowful communication from someone who is in jail, often incarcerated for simple possession of narcotics. British club magazines talk about new drugs as if they are the hottest new band or DJ. In America, interviews with US rave celebs usually offer statements like the by-now classic "our scene is about music, not drugs."

The American environment of fear and necessary deception (if *Urb* launched a 'Casualty Ward'-type page the publication would immediately be removed from many shop shelves) means practical information about E is hard to find. In the US, ecstasy outreach today means reaching out and sending users to the slammer. Club owners and rave promoters will not generally pick up the harm reduction baton, as admitting that some people *might* be taking drugs at their events could endanger them. Someone like a candy raver then, who may say their scene is all about PLUR but still pops an E to set the words in motion on a Saturday night, has but one place to look for the straight dope on their pill of choice: the world wide web.

The internet is America's premier lawless zone. And Americans have undoubtedly been a pioneering force in getting information about illegal drugs up on it. Websites like The Vaults Of Erowid and Hyperreal contain huge archives of drugs data, including molecular diagrams, cultural overviews, safety tips and responsible users' guides. But the sites are not aimed at people like Aim-E. The products of the neuroconsciousness frontier and the psychedelic scene rather than of the kiddie ravescape, the sites are high-talking, loaded with words like "techno shamanism" and "quantum psychoalchemy". Besides, Aim-E's never heard of them. She says the sites she likes visiting most are candy raver sites, the ones with raver profiles on them.

Aim-E's knowledge of ecstasy is a seemingly bottomless stockpile of erroneous information. She says E "usually has heroin in it". She warns against drinking too much water when doing E because "your insides can drown". She claims that the energy drink Red Bull – a dehydrator – should be taken with ecstasy "to give you strength". She also says that mixing E with "natural drugs", like the stimulant ephedrine, a combo popular with "some people [she] knows", is "pretty safe" compared to mixing with "weird chemical drugs".

A scan of some of Aim-E's favourite candy raver websites proves disquieting. Candy Kids Central, for instance, probably the most popular site of the lot, has an ecstasy review page, on which different brands of tablets are evaluated. "None of these pills have actually been tested in a lab," it reads. "The contents of the pills are only a speculation made by various experienced E users. Candy Kid Central does not condone drug use in any way. We merely provide information that may prove useful in assuring a safe ecstasy experience." All the tablets assessed get rather good reviews. There are no warnings, even about those Candy Kid Central believes to contain the famously hazardous PMA. Seven of the 15 brands reviewed are said to contain heroin – which is more than a little unlikely. Which could mean that ravers who took these pills and liked them, and later read they supposedly have heroin in them, may be less wary of trying heroin proper. This is precisely what happened in Orlando, Florida – with frightening results.

"The forces that are supposed to serve and protect have blood on their hands," says Orlando rave promoter Bevin O'Neil. "Kids don't know their asses from the elbows when it comes to doing drugs in this country. They just know they want to do drugs. If half the kids in Orlando knew what they should've known, my thinking is there would have been less tragedies. But the police, the government, the Mr and Mrs Right-wing-anti-drug-lobbyist-pieces-of-shit? They respond by laws, slogans and shut-downs. Does it work? No! Band-Aid solutions! Still more kids doing more E and more stuff than ever. The kids are going to do this – America's going to have to deal."

It will be interesting to see if America does "deal". If new and widespread harm reduction campaigns will be launched in America as they have been in Britain. At the time of writing, in January 2000, it seems like the US rave drugs scene is becoming more critical. It's not the first time it has felt this way. With each new wave of ravers comes a honeymoon period, of course, but then there's also an inevitable descent into recklessness, problems, darkness.

The candy-coating of the latest American rave phase is presently beginning to show signs of cracking. The causes are not new: simple E use turning to polydrug habits, including the use of crystal meth, the fastest spreading drug in America, and the use of the incredibly unmixable GHB; ravers going from optimism to negligence when they're not rainbow-swooped to an entirely better life; and a fracturing of responsibility as the scene grows ever bigger and more unwieldy. The response of the US authorities has been predictable, too: "Band-Aid solutions", moral outcry, political brouhaha and punishment by useless crackdowns after the fact, instead of useful sorts of intercession before.

As with the Gatecrasher kids in the UK, there have been candy deaths and they are incredibly poignant because the average age of a candy raver is probably something like 17. There were a number of fatalities in 1999: 18-year-olds overheating to death, 15-year-olds suffering fatal heart attacks. However, the most publicised deaths of the year were also the most *Americana* of the fatalities: in August 1999, five California teenagers, aged 15 to 18, plunged to their deaths over a cliff when driving home on a winding hilltop road from a rave cheerily called Juju Beats. The party had been thrown by the princes of California candy promotion, B3 Cand-e, at the Snow Crest ski resort. Witnesses say it seemed like the driver had accidentally stepped on the gas instead of the brake. Coroners reports showed all five youths had ingested both MDA – presumably bought as ecstasy – and methamphetamine.

"I felt so bad about the people who died," says Aim-E. "Because they were people I could have known. But also 'coz I know they took whatever they took just to have a good night. I think that's why everybody takes [ecstasy]. To feel good and special. Not to be bad or weird or anything. But they died because of it. And that's terrible, 'coz all they probably wanted was, like, happiness – like, you know, bliss? That's why so many kids wanna rave. I know I'm just a kid, I'm not mature, but I still think there are a lot of people who get some good things out of doing this stuff. Like, when I have kids, I maybe wouldn't mind if they wanted to do it. I could understand it. Does that sound, like, crazy?"

Yes. No. Possibly. Depends who you speak to. But from the mouth of an average middle-class California high school student, one who tried out for the cheerleading last year, a girl who "sucks at math" and "loves shopping at the mall", there is no denying the words have some shock

222

value. If only because, from a mouth like Aim-E's, they sound so new. Think about it – she supports the use of a synthetic, illegal substance. She "maybe wouldn't mind" if her children took it. She has an unproblematic acceptance of the idea that this substance can bring happiness, true happiness. That it can be life-enriching. Just a couple of decades ago, it was only people on the cultural fringe who thought like this in the US. Now, as in the UK, it's the people in the middle, too.

Aim-E says the reasons people do E has something to do with "bliss" and she's spot on. Bliss has always been what the ecstasy quest is all about. Whether or not Aim-E's children – the children of the millennium – will want to continue this quest is, however, unclear. Perhaps something more attractive than E will come along. Perhaps conditions will change and people will no longer want to experience the kind of feelings E provokes. But with more ecstasy users than ever now, not only in Britain and America but also in many other parts of the world, and with the culture still spreading, still morphing, still vibrant, there's little to suggest that the multi-climaxing story of this drug has reached any sort of conclusion yet. For better or worse, the grand saga of E may only be just beginning.

(MS)

Bibliography

"56 People Held In Acid House Raids." *The Times*, 7 November 1988.

"100 Of The Best Things To Happen This Year." *i-D*, December 1987.

"1988–99: Ten Years Under The Influence." *Muzik*, March 1998.

Aaron, Charles. "Drums And Wires." *Spin*, September 1996.

Abcarian, Robin. "Come On, Put On A Happy Face." *Dallas Morning News*, 26 October 1988.

Abrams, Fran. "Mandelson Defends Right To Go For Chauffeur-Driven Spin." *Independent*, 23 December 1996.

"Acid Burns Up Tabloids." *NME*, 29 October 1988.

Adderley, Jonty. "Ecstasy: The Debate." *Muzik*, April 1996.

Adler, Jerry, Pamela Abramson, Susan Katz and Mary Hager. "Getting High On 'Ecstasy'." *Newsweek,* 15 April 1985.

"Agony Ecstasy." Mirror, 17 January 1997.

A Guide To Acid House Parties. Pay Party Unit report, 1990.

Aitkenhead, Decca. "The Revolution Is Happening And It's Down At Raquel's." *Independent On Sunday*, 19 November 1995.

   "Too Large For Their Boots?" *Independent On Sunday*, 19 January 1997.

Altman, D. *The Homosexualization Of America.* Boston: Beacon Press, 1985.

Alvarez, Maria. "Survival Of A Superclub." *Daily Telegraph*, 8 December 1997.

Anthony, Wayne. *Class Of 88: The True Acid House Experience.* London: Virgin, 1998.

Arlidge, John. "Temazepam Controls 'Too Weak'." *Independent On Sunday*, 14 January 1996.

Armstrong, Stephen. "Pretend That We're Cred." *The Face,* August 1996.

   "Sonic Boom." *The Face*, August 1996.

"Bad Acid." *Melody Maker*, 28 October 1989.

"Bad Medicine." *The Face*, June 1998.

Bailey, Brad. "New Year's Eve Runs The Gamut." *Dallas Morning News*, 1 January 1985.

Baird, Steven K. "Bitter Table For One? A Defense Of Circuit Parties." *Miamigo,* February 1999.

Barron, Jack. "Biology Lessened." *NME*, 28 October 1989.

Bauer, Esther M. "Designer Drugs Trial Dropped On Technicality." *Dallas Morning News*, 24 July 1986.

Beadle, Jeremy J. *Will Pop Eat Itself?: Pop Music In The Soundbite Era*. London: Faber & Faber, 1993.

Becker, Michael. "US Acts To Ban Sedative Rohypnol." Reuters, 5 March 1996.

Bedding, James. "Travel: Dancing The Night Away." *Daily Telegraph*, 8 August 1998.

Bennetto, Jason. "Drug Factories Become Britain's New Illegal Cottage Industry." *Independent*, 28 June 1999.

"Three Die From New Designer Drugs." *Independent*, 20 November 1998.

Benney, Paul. "Dave Beer: I Did It My Way." *Jockey Slut*, August 1997.

Benson, Richard. "Over The Rainbow." *The Face*, March 1996.

Benson, Richard, ed. *Night Fever: Club Writing In The Face 1980–1997*. London: Boxtree, 1997.

Betts, Janet and Paul Betts with Ivan Sage. *The Party's Over: Living Without Leah*. London: Robson, 1997.

"Bizarre." *Sun*, 12 October 1988.

Borges, Walter. "Designer Drugs Sales Questioned." *Dallas Morning News*, 20 December 1985.

Braddock, Kevin. "A Normal Life . . ." *The Face*, September 1999.

Braunstein, Peter. "The Last Days Of Gay Disco." *Village Voice*, 24 June 1998.

Brennan, Fleur. "Brian Had So Much . . . Ecstasy Ended It All." *Woman*, 10 August 1992.

Brewster, Bill and Frank Broughton. *The Manual: The Who, The Where, The Why Of Clubland*. London: Headline, 1998.

Brinkworth, Lisa and Chris Dawes. "Jesus Saves!" *Soho News*, 2 November 1988.

British Crime Survey 1994. The Home Office, 1994.

Broughton, Frank. "Chicago: Still Rockin' Down The House." *i-D*, April 1995.

Brown, Ethan. "Clear And Present Danger." *New York*, 22 November 1999.

Bruni, Frank. "Drugs Taint An Annual Round Of Gay Revels." *New York Times*, 8 September 1998.

Budd, Lawrence. "Shooting From The Lip." *Orlando Weekly*, 9 October 1997.

Byron, Howard. "The Future Of Clubbing." *Independent On Sunday*, 30 August 1998.

Cannabis: The Scientific And Medical Evidence. House Of Lords Select Committee report, 1999.

"Car Accident After Cali Party Sparks More Rave Controversy." *Mixer*, October 1999.

Cassidy, Carol. *Girls in America: Their Stories, Their Words.* New York: TV Books, 1999.

"Catch The Pigeon." *Mixmag*, August 1995.

Chamberlin, Daniel. "Are We Too High?" *Urb*, September 1999.

Chamberlin, Daniel with Tommy Nguyen. "Teenagers' Deaths Lead To Anti-Rave Sentiment." *Urb*, November 1999.

Champion, Sarah. "Kids In America: From Rockers To Ravers." *i-D*, September 1995.

Champion, Sarah, ed. *Disco 2000.* London: Sceptre, 1998.

Disco Biscuits. London: Sceptre, 1997.

Charters, D. "Agonising Over Ecstasy While The Rave Goes On." *Liverpool Daily Post*, 3 February 1992.

Cheeseman, Phil. "The History Of House." *DJ*, 22 April 1993.

Cheshyre, Tom. "Travel: Mile-High Raves Get Ready For Take-Off." *Daily Telegraph*, 18 October 1998.

Choyke, William J. "Judge Wants Ecstasy OK'd For Medical Use." *Dallas Morning News,* 24 May 1986.

Clark, Alisson. "Drugs, Music Dominate Rave Scene." *Gainesville Sun*, 25 July 1999.

"Close Disco Of Death Pleads Tragic Sister." *Daily Mirror*, 22 August 1994.

Cocoran, Cate C. "Dancing On The New Edge." *San Francisco Bay Guardian*, 9 October 1991.

Cole, Bethan. "The Deranged Generation." *Muzik*, June 1999.

"High In The Basement." *i-D*, August 1996.

"One Nation Under A Groove." *Muzik*, March 1998.

Coles, Joanna. "10 Years In Jail For Acid House Party Organiser." *Daily Telegraph*, 11 November 1989.

Collin, Matthew. "European Electronic Community." *i-D*, December 1991.

"Party On!" *i-D*, February 1991.

"Saturday Night Fever." *The Face,* July 1996.

Collin, Matthew with John Godfrey. *Altered State: The Story Of Ecstasy Culture And Acid House.* London: Serpent's Tail, 1997.

Concar, David. "After The Rave, The Ecstasy Hangover." *New Scientist*, 21 June 1997.

"Blow Your Mind." *New Scientist*, 8 November 1997.

"Deadly Combination." *New Scientist*, 12 July 1997.

"Confusion Reigns Over CJA Prosecutions." *NME*, 7 October 1995.

Controlled Substances Act [US], 1970.

Cook, Emma. "The Ecstasy And The Agony." *Independent On Sunday*, 12 October 1997.

Cook, Miranda, Tom Whitwell, Alexis Petridis and Nicky Wilson. "Drugs Of The Decade." *Mixmag*, September 1999.

Cook, Samantha, Tim Perry and Greg Ward. *USA: The Rough Guide. London: The Rough Guides*, Penguin, 1998.

Corless, Frank. "Flake Girl Rachel Set For TV Comeback In Hair Gel Ad." *Daily Mirror*, 3 June 1993.

Cramb, Auslan. "Doctors In Transplant Row 'Were Guilty Of Euthanasia'." *Daily Telegraph,* 29 April 1997.

Criminal Justice & Public Order Act [UK], 1994.

Crysell, Andy. "Irresistible Force." *DJ*, 24 November 1994.

Curran, Frank and Julia Peat. "What A Dope!." *Daily Star*, 29 January 1992.

Curtis, Jake. "Dance Radio: Has it All Gone Pete Tong?" *Jockey Slut*, April 1997.

Curtius, May and Michael Ybarra. "Gay Party Tour: More Harm Than Good?" *Los Angeles Times*, 13 October 1997.

Curvin, Laura and Darren Ressler. "Orlando: The Next Magical Musical Kingdom?" *Mixmag* [American edition], December 1996.

Darch, Marianne. "Scientist Made Ecstasy In Error." *The Times*, 6 April 1995.

DaSilva, John. "The Whole World Is A Disco." *DJ*, June 1992.

Dass, Ram. *The Only Dance There Is*. New York: Aronson, 1976.

Davidson, Ros. "For Drug Pioneers, Their Way Still The High Way." *Guardian*, 14 December 1997.

Davies, Peter. "Trading On The Ancient Appeal Of Ecstasy." *Daily Telegraph*, 3 August 1987.

"Drug Czar To Target Clubbers." *Muzik*, December 1997.

"Drugs And Nightlife: E Is For England." *The Economist*, 8 June 1998.

"Drugs Raid On Club UK." *Muzik*, December 1995.

"Drug Tsar Begins Work In Earnest." *Independent*, 5 January 1998.

Drug Use In England: Results Of The 1995 National Drugs Campaign Survey. Health Education Authority, 1996.

Dunlap, David W. "As Disco Faces Razing, Gay Alumni Share Memories." *New York Times*, 20 August 1995.

"Interview With Robbie Leslie." *Stardust*, May 1983.

Dunn, Janice. "The Secret Life Of Teenage Girls." *Rolling Stone*, 11 November 1999.

Dyer, Clare. "£250,000 Award For Ecstasy User." *Guardian*, 9 February 1999.

Dyer, Richard. "In Defense Of Disco." In Kureishi, Savage, *The Faber Book Of Pop*.

E, Barbara. "Voodoo Rave." *NME*, 8 July 1989.

"Ecstasy – Editorial Comment." *Muzik*, March 1997.

"Ecstasy Claims Its First British Victim." *Daily Mail*, 30 March 1989.

"The Ecstasy Debate – You Decide." *Muzik*, March 1996.

"Ecstasy Shock Issue." *Mirror*, 17 January 1997.

"Ecstasy – The Latest Narcotic Menace." *Daily Telegraph*, 1 May 1985.

Edwards, Jeff. "Cops Smash Acid House Drugs Ring." *People*, 4 December 1988.

Eisner, Bruce. *Ecstasy – The MDMA Story*. Berkeley: Ronin, 1989.

Ellerton, Kate. "Off On An E." *Observer*, 2 October 1988.

Entertainments (Increased Penalties) Act [UK], 1990.

Eshun, Kodwo. "Outing The In-Crowd." In Kureishi, Savage, *The Faber Book Of Pop*.

Everbach, Tracy. "Starck Goes Out In Style." *Dallas Morning News*, 12 July 1989.

"Everything Starts With A P." *Muzik*, March 1997.

Evison, Sue & Peter Willis. "Evil Of Ecstasy." *Sun*, 19 October 1988.

"Fashion Models In Ecstasy Drug Raids." *Daily Mail*, 14 May 1987.

Fenton, Ben. "Drug Fears At Acid House Parties Spark Clampdown." *Daily Telegraph*, 4 November 1988.

Finn, Philip. "How The Evil Of Ecstasy Hit The Streets." *Daily Express*, 25 April 1985.

"First Ecstasy Death." *The Times*, 30 March 1989.

"Fish Lands In Jail." *Daily Star*, 27 February 1999.

Forsyth, AJ. "Places And Patterns Of Drug Use In The Scottish Dance Scene." *Addiction*, April 1996.

Fowler, Dave. "A-Z Of Trance." *Muzik*, September 1999.
   "Northern Lights." *Muzik*, July 1999.

Frith, Simon. *Performing Rites: On The Value Of Popular Music*. Cambridge: Harvard University Press, 1996.
   "The Suburban Sensibility In British Rock And Pop". In Silverstone, Roger, ed. *Visions Of Suburbia*. London: Routledge, 1997.

"Fury At Sex Guide To E." *Sun*, 29 January 1992.

Garratt, Sheryl. *Adventures In Wonderland: A Decade Of Club Culture*. London: Headline, 1998.
   "Club Classism." *The Independent*, 25 November 1996.
   "Ill Communication." *The Face*, March 1998.
   "Pills 'n' Thrills." *The Face*, May 1995.

"The We Generation." *The Face*, December 1989.

Garret, Laurie and Jesse Mangalman. "A Deadly Epidemic Of Denial." *Newsday*, 30 May 1995.

Garvey, Geoff. "Killer Ecstasy Pills Flooding Into London." *London Evening Standard*, 9 January 1992.

Geller, Brian. "Precautions Bring Tamer All-Night Parties." *Gainesville Sun*, 22 August 1999.

Gendin, Steven. "They Shoot Bare Backers, Don't They?" *Poz*, February 1999.

Godwin, Stephen. "Drugs-Related Deaths Double In Glasgow." *Independent*, 10 December 1998.

Goldstein, Amy. "Viagra's Success Fuels Gender Bias Debate." *Washington Post*, 20 May 1998.

Gordon, Pat. "Authorities Fear Nationwide Spread Of 'Designer Drugs'." *Dallas Morning News*, 12 May 1985.

The Government's Proposals For Regulation Of The Private Security Industry In England And Wales. The Stationary Office, 1999.

Gray, Louise. "The Island Of A Thousand Dances." *Independent On Sunday*, 23 August 1998.

Greer, George and Requa Tolbert. "Subjective Reports Of The Effects Of MDMA In A Clinical Setting." *Journal Of Psychoactive Drugs*, October/December 1986.

Grylls, James. "The Rave Of Death." *Daily Mail*, 3 May 1994.

Guidelines For Good Practice At Dance Events. Scottish Drug Forum report, 1995.

"Gun Gangs Force Nightclub To Close." *Independent*, 31 January 1991.

Haden-Guest, Anthony. *The Last Party: Studio 54, Disco And The Culture Of The Night*. New York: William Morrow, 1997.

Harlan, Christi. "Drug Agents Seize 31,200 Ecstasy Tablets." *Dallas Morning News*, 30 July 1985.

"Five Charged With Conspiring To Distribute Ecstasy." *Dallas Morning News*, 31 July 1985.

Harris, Collette and Pascal Wyse. "Sex, Drugs And Rock 'n' Roll." *Independent*, 28 January 1996.

Harris, Daniel. *The Rise And Fall Of Gay Culture*. New York: Hyperion, 1997.

Harrison, Melissa, ed. High Society: *The Real Voices Of Club Culture*. London: Piatkus, 1998.

Harvey, Steven. "Behind The Groove." *Collusion*, September 1983.

"Get That Perfect Beat." *The Face*, October 1983.

Haslam, Dave. "DJ Culture." In Redhead, Steve, ed. *The Club Cultures Reader*.

Hays, Matthew. "Dancing On Our Ashes." *Montreal Mirror*, 30 June 1994.

Headon, Jane. "Drugs And The Army." *Mixmag*, July 1994.
   "Prisoners Of Ecstasy." *Mixmag*, September 1994.

Headon, Jane and Dom Phillips. "Sorted?" *Mixmag*, February 1996.

Henderson, Sheila. *Ecstasy: Case Unsolved*. London: Pandora, 1997.

Hermes, Will. "Garage Shock." *Spin*, September 1996.

Hill, Dave. "Boystown Nights." *The Face*, September 1984.

Hills, Gavin. "Whatever Happened To The Likely Lads?" *The Face*, December 1991.
   "Wonderland UK." *The Face*, January 1993.

Holleran, Andrew. "The Twelfth Floor." In Kureishi, Savage, *The Faber Book Of Pop*.

Hooley, Peter. "Ecstasy Drug Epidemic." *Daily Express*, 22 September 1992.

Horsnell, Michael. " 'Leah Is Dead But It Is Bearable Because She Can Help Others.' " *The Times*, 17 November 1995.

House, Chris. "Police Raid River Acid Parties." *Sunday Mirror*, 6 November 1988.

House Of Commons Parliamentary Debate [Crime and Punishment (Scotland) Bill]. Hansard, 5 November 1996.

House Of Commons Parliamentary Debate [Entertainments (Increased Penalties) Bill]. Hansard, 27 April 1990.

House Of Commons Parliamentary Debate [Public Entertainments Licences (Drug Misuse) Bill]. Hansard, 17 January 1997.

House Of Commons Prime Minister's Questions [regarding Brian Harvey]. Hansard, 16 January 1997.

House Of Commons Statement [regarding "Tackling Drugs To Build A Better Britain"], Hansard, 25 May 1999.

House Of Commons Written Reply [regarding ecstasy and alcohol death figures in England and Wales]. Hansard, 16 December 1996.

House Of Commons Written Reply [regarding various drugs death figures in England and Wales]. Hansard, 7 July 1998.

House Of Commons Written Reply [regarding various drugs death figures in Scotland]. Hansard, 29 April 1998.

House Of Lords Written Reply [regarding the Advisory Council On The Misuse Of Drugs]. Hansard, 2 February 1997.

Hughes, Chris & Lucy Turner. "I'm So Stupid." *Mirror*, 17 January 1997.

Hughes, Colin. "A Fair Cop, Guv'nor." *Guardian*, 16 January 1999.

Hughes, Walter. "Feeling Mighty Real: Disco As Discourse And Discipline." *Village Voice Rock And Roll Quarterly*, Summer 1993.

Hunter, Flora. "Leah's Photo Hijacked To Back Ecstasy." *Sunday Telegraph*, 5 February 1996.

James, Mandi. "Ecstasy." *The Face*, November 1991.

Jansen, Karl L. "The Brain Drain." *The Face*, April 1997.

Jenkins, Milly. "Man From The Ministry Works To Get The Youth Vote Out." *Independent On Sunday*, 2 February 1997.

Jones, Fabio. "Uprising." *XLR8R*, issue 16.

Judge, Elizabeth. "Ecstasy Woman Wins Hospital Damages." *The Times*, 9 February 1999.

"Just Say Noel." *Melody Maker*, 8 February 1997.

Kartohadiprodjo, Yudha. "Paying Devout Homage To The Ministry Of Sound," *Jakarta Post*, 19 December 1998.

Kellaway, Robert and Simon Hughes. "Spaced Out!." *Sun*, 26 June 1989.

Kelso, Jann. "In Pursuit Of Idlewild: Debs Make Their Entrance." *Dallas Morning News*, 27 October 1985.

Kim, Lillian Lee. "Date Rape Drug Made Easier To Identify When It's Dropped Into Drink." *Minneapolis Star Tribune*, 24 September 1998.

Kirsch, Irving and Guy Sapirstein. "Listening To Prozac But Hearing Placebo." *Prevention & Treatment*, 26 June 1998.

Kleinburg, Eliot. "Starck Club Raided." *Dallas Morning News*, 9 August 1986.

Kleinman, Mark and Sally Satel. "Meth Is Back And We're Not Ready." *Los Angeles Times* [Washington edition], 1 May 1996.

Knapp, Mike. "Soccer Drugs Menace." *Daily Star*, 5 September 1989.

Kureishi, Hanif and Jon Savage, eds. *The Faber Book Of Pop*. London: Faber & Faber, 1995.

Lebrecht, Norman. "The Arts: Labour Loves Rock." Daily Telegraph, 1 April 1998.

Lee, Martin and Bruce Shlain. *Acid Dreams: The CIA, LSD And The Sixties Rebellion*. New York: Grove Press, 1986.

Leppard, David and Jon Craig. "Police Arrest 31 At Acid House Parties." *Sunday Times*, 6 November 1988.

Letters Page [regarding effect of MDMA on brain serotonin neurons]. *The Lancet*, 10 April 1999.

Letters Page [regarding "Chill Out" leaflet]. *Liverpool Echo*, 4 February 1992.

Letters Page [regarding acid house]. *NME*, 30 July 1988.

Levin, Steve. "When Drug Abuse Begins At Home." *Dallas Morning News*, 1 April 1986.

Lewis, Kevin. "Was This Man The Best DJ In The World?" *Jockey Slut*, January 1998.

Lewis, Lynette A and Michael W Ross. *A Select Body: The Gay Dance Subculture And The HIV/AIDS Pandemic.* London: Cassell, 1995.

Lim, Dennis. "The Chemistry Set." *The Face*, August 1998.

Local Government (Miscellaneous Provisions) Act [UK], 1982.

Lodge, Bill "Two Jailed In Crackdown On Drug Ecstasy." *Dallas Morning News*, 10 July 1985.

MacDonald, Victoria. "BBC Promotes Ecstasy Song Despite Drug Alert." *Sunday Telegraph*, 6 September 1992.

Maclin, Jeff. "Danger In Euphoria." *Dallas Morning News*, 25 August 1986.

MacWhirter, Ian. "It's Time To Choose Reality On Drugs." *Scotsman*, 6 August 1998.

Mahoney, John. "Acid House Mr Nasty Says 'Parties Go On'." *Daily Star*, 5 November 1988.

Marks, Kathy. "This Man Is Paid £106,000 A Year To Stop Britain's Youth Taking Drugs – Is He Worth It?" *Independent*, 26 May 1999.

Marsa, John. Untitled editorial on Orlando club scene. *Orlando Business Journal*, 11 April 1997.

Mead, Helen. "Tune In, Turn On." *i-D*, August 1992.

McBean, Sharon. "Club Sues Orlando Over Rave Shutdown". *Orlando Sentinel*, 1 January 1998.

McCan, Paul. "Youth Culture: Dangers That Lurk In The Shadows Of Clubland." *Independent*, 17 September 1997.

McCann, Una, Z Szabo, U Scheffel, R Dannals and George Ricaurte – "Positron Emission Tomographic Evidence Of Toxic Effect Of MDMA (Ecstasy) On Brain Serotonin Neurons In Human Beings." *The Lancet*, 31 October 1998.

McClellan, Jim. "Spiritual Highs." *The Face*, October 1995.

McClelland, Susan. "The Lure Of The Body Image." Maclean's, 22 February 1999.

McCready, John "Promised Land." *The Face*, August 1997.
"Working On A Building of Love." *The Face*, May 1997.

McDermott, Peter, Alan Matthews and Pat O'Hare. "Ecstasy In The UK: Recreational Drug Use And Cultural Change." In Heather, Nick, Alex Wodak and Ethan A Nadelmann, eds. *Psychoactive Drugs And Harm Reduction – From Faith To Science.* London: Whurr, 1993.

McGowan, Patrick. "New Designer Drugs Menace." *London Evening Standard*, 19 November 1998.

McJannet, John. "Ecstasy Mega Bust." *Daily Star*, 17 February 1992.

McKay, George. *DIY Culture: Party And Protest In Nineties Britain.* London: Verso, 1998.

McNiffe, Mike. "Flying Squad Smashes Acid House Drugs Lab." *Daily Star*, 21 July 1989.

Meier, Stacy. "He Set The Standards In Guests And Jeans." *Dallas Morning News*, 15 July 1986.

   "Rob Lowe And Jim Belushi Stalk The Starck Club." *Dallas Morning News*, 6 October 1986.

Melvin, Ann. "So Who Needs Euphoria?" *Dallas Morning News*, 19 April 1985.

Miles, Tim. "Shoot These Evil Acid Barons." *Sun*, 1 November 1988.

Milloy, Courtland. "Sending Mixed Messages On Drugs." *Washington Post*, 6 May 1998.

Moodie, Dave and Maureen Callahan. "Don't Drink The Brown Water." *Spin*, October 1999.

Moore, Jane. "Ecstasy For Sale!" *Sun*, 14 April 1987.

Moore, Ralph. "Toy Story." *Muzik*, August 1999.

Morgan, Alister. "After Dark: Sony's Games Theory Pays Off." *Independent*, 22 December 1997.

   "Clubs: Creme De La Cream." *Independent*, 18 April 1998.

   "Northern Exposure." *Independent*, 21 February 1998.

   "Take The High Road." *Independent*, 13 June 1998.

Morgan, Piers. "George's Hell On Ecstasy." *Sun*, 6 September 1990.

Morton, Roger. "Ministry Of Unsound." *NME*, 30 April 1994.

"Muzik Readers In Favour Of E-Testing." *Muzik*, May 1996.

Nasmyth, Peter. "MDMA We're All Crazy Now." *The Face*, October 1985.

Newsome, Rachel. "Ecstasy Testing Hits The UK." *Muzik*, February 1998.

Niven, John and David Gill. "Fresh Fruit From Foreign Places." *The Herb Garden*, Summer 1995.

Noon, Mike. "Freaky Dancing." In Kureishi, Savage, *The Faber Book Of Pop*.

Oakenfold, Paul. "Bermondsey Goes Baleric [sic]." *Boy's Own*, July 1988.

O'Hagan, Sean. "Passing Poison." *Observer Life Magazine*, 9 October 1994.

   "Raving Madness." *The Times Saturday Review*, 22 February 1992.

"Overdue For Appeal." *The Times*, 24 July 1992.

Owens, Sherri M. "Raves: Is Party Over Or Just Relocating?" *The Orlando Sentinel*, 15 September 1995.

Oxford, Esther. "Sleeping Pill Being Used As Courage Drug By Criminals." *Independent*, 13 January 1994.

Palmer, Alun. "The Night I Took Drugs On Top Of The Pops." *Daily Mail*, 30 August 1999.

Palmer, Tamara. "Coming Of Age." *Urb*, July/August 1998.

Papp, Leslie. "Viagra To Hit Drug Stores Soon." *Toronto Star*, 10 March 1999.

Park, Jan Carl. "Interview With Warren Gluck." *Stardust*, March 1983.
"News From The Saint." *Stardust*, March 1983.

Peat, Julia. " 'E' Kids Dog-Gone On Worm Tablets." *Daily Star*, 3 September 1992.

Pecora, Ted. "Tribute To Roy Thode." *Stardust*, May 1983.

Pederson, Rena. "Drugs Scene: How Bad." *Dallas Morning News*, 27 March 1985.
"Ecstasy: Call For Information." *Dallas Morning News*, 1 May 1985.
"Ecstasy On Campus." *Dallas Morning News*, 31 July 1985.
"Summer And Smoke." *Dallas Morning News*, 14 September 1985.

Peltier, Michael. "Florida Bans 'Date Rape' Drug." *Reuters*, 26 June 1996.

Pemberton, Andy. "Has Jeremy Healey Gone Too Far?" *Mixmag*, April 1986.

Perlman, Shirley E. "MD Guilty Of Drugging, Raping Women." *Newsday*, 15 January 1993.

Petridis, Alexis. "Weedkiller For Your Brain." *Mixmag*, August 1996.

Phillips, Dom. "Electronic Listening." *Mixmag*, August 1993.
"Going For The Pound Note." *Mixmag*, November 1996.

Phillips, Lisa. The American Century: Art & Culture 1950–2000. New York: Whitney Museum Of American Art/WW Norton & Company, 1999.

Pierce, Kim. "Ecstasy Goes Underground." *Dallas Morning News*, 1 July 1985.
"Federal Government Cracks Down On The Use Of Ecstasy". *Dallas Morning News*, 7 January 1985.

Pithers, Malcolm. "Police Criticised Over Acid House Raid." *Independent*, 23 July 1990.

"Police Seize Ecstasy." *The Times*, 22 July 1989.

"Police Storm Acid Rave." *Melody Maker*, 28 July 1990.

"Police Swoop On Club UK." *Mixmag*, December 1995.

"Police Target Club Dealers." *NME*, 28 October 1995.

Public Entertainments Licences (Drugs Misuse) Act [UK], 1997.

"Press The Panic Button." *New Scientist*, 25 January 1997.

Price, Simon. "We're Not Out To Shock People." *Melody Maker*,
    27 March 1992.
Puccia, Joseph. *The Holy Spirit Dance Club*. New York: Liberty Press,
    1988.
Push. "Crocus Pocus." *Melody Maker*, 18 April 1992.
    "For Fac's Sake!." *Melody Maker*, 23 May 1992.
Push and Andrew Smith. "The Great Rave Debate." *Melody Maker*,
    10 March 1990.
Push, The Stud Brothers and Paul Mathur. "The Road To Utopia."
    Melody Maker, 20 August 1988.
"Quote Of The Year 2." *Boy's Own*, July 1988.
Radford, Tim. "Ecstasy 'Injures Brain For Life'." *Guardian*, 30 October
    1998
Randall, Colin. "Yuppies Fall For Promise Of 'Ecstasy'." *Daily Telegraph*,
    16 May 1987.
"Raving Mad." *Liverpool Echo*, 28 January 1992.
Raymond, Maria. "Ecstasy Wrecked My Life." *Sun*, 30 June 1989.
Real, David. "Ecstasy Slides Into Illegal Category." *Dallas Morning News*,
    1 July 1985.
Redhead, Steve. *The End Of The Century Party: Youth And Pop Toward
    2000*. Manchester: Manchester University Press, 1990.
Redhead, Steve, ed. *The Club Cultures Reader*. Oxford: Blackwell, 1997.
Rees-Mogg, William. "Who Breaks A Butterfly On A Wheel?" *Times*,
    1 July 1967.
Reidlinger, Thomas and June Reidlinger. "The 'Seven Deadly Sins' Of
    Media Hype Considered In Light Of The MDMA Controversy."
    In Lyttle, Thomas, ed. Psychedelics: *A Collection Of The Most
    Exciting New Material On Psychedelic Drugs*. New York: Barricade,
    1994.
Release Drugs And Dance Survey. *Release*, 1997.
Release Annual Review And Anthology 1967–1997. *Release*, 1997.
Reynolds, Simon. *Energy Flash: A Journey Through Rave Music And Dance
    Culture*. London: Picador, 1998.
    "Gathering Of The Tribes." Melody Maker, 6 June 1992.
    "Rave Culture: Living Dream Or Living Death?" In Redhead, Steve,
        ed. *The Club Cultures Reader*.
    "Technical Ecstasy." *The Wire*, November 1992.
Richardson, Lynda. "Study Finds HIV Infection Is High For Young Gay
    Men." *New York Times*, 16 February 1999.
Rietveld, Hillegonda. "The House Sound Of Chicago." In Redhead,
    Steve, ed. *The Club Cultures Reader*.
Roberts, Todd. "Built For Speed?" *Urb*, October 1995.

Robins, Cynthia. "The Ecstatic Cybernetic Acid Test." *San Francisco Examiner Magazine*, 16 February 1992.

Robson, Philip. *Forbidden Drugs: Understanding Drugs And Why People Take Them*. Oxford: Oxford University Press, 1995.

Romero, Dennis. "Sasha Shulgin, Psychedelic Chemist." *Los Angeles Times*, 5 September 1995.

"Spinning In The Spotlight." *Los Angeles Times*, 25 June 1995.

Rose, Cynthia. *Design After Dark: The Story Of Dancefloor Style*. London: Thames and Hudson, 1991.

"Turning The Tables On New Music." *Dallas Morning News*, 4 April 1986.

Rotello, Gabriel. *Sexual Ecology: AIDS And The Destiny Of Gay Men*. New York: Dutton, 1997.

Rowe, Mark and Tim Cornwell. "Women's Drinks Spiked With Date-Rape Drug." *Independent On Sunday*, 4 May 1997.

Rushkoff, Douglas. *The Ecstasy Club*. New York: Sceptre, 1998.

Sack, Kevin. "HIV Peril And Rising Drug Use." *New York Times*, 29 January 1997.

"The Saint Of Hotter Than Hell." *Blueboy*, January 1981.

Salamon, Jeff. "Aces In The Crowd." *Spin*, September 1996.

Sampson, Katie. "I Work For Ministry: Mark Rodol And James Palumbo." *Independent*, October 1997.

Samuels, David. "Woodstock 99: Rock Is Dead." *Harper's*, November 1999.

Samuels, Lennox. "Chicago Firm Agrees To Lease Starck Club." *Dallas Morning News*, 1 June 1989.

"Starck Club Closing Doors." *Dallas Morning News*, 31 May 1989.

"The State Of Nightclubs." *Dallas Morning News*, 3 September 1989.

Saunders, Nicholas. *E For Ecstasy*. London: Nicholas Saunders, 1993.

Ecstasy And The Dance Culture. London: Nicholas Saunders, 1995.

"E For Ecstasy." *Eternity*, July 1996.

Scarce, Michael. "A Ride On The Wild Side." *Poz*, February 1999.

Schoofs, Mark. "The AIDS Race: Can New Drugs Keep Up With The Wily Virus?" *Village Voice*, 10 February 1999.

"Shame Of Di Ecstasy Tabs." *Mirror*, 15 January 1998.

Sharrock, David. "Ecstasy Use Grows As Seizures Rocket." *Guardian*, 10 January 1992.

Shirer, William. *The Rise And Fall Of The Third Reich*. London: Pan, 1960.

Shulgin, Alexander and Ann Shulgin. *PiHKAL: A Chemical Love Story*. Berkeley: Transform Press, 1992.

Signorile, Michelangelo. *Life Outside: On Gay Men, Sex, Drugs, Muscles, And The Passages Of Life*. New York: HarperCollins, 1997.

"641,086 & Counting." *Out*, September 1998

"A Troubling Double Standard." *New York Times*, 16 August 1997.

"Bareback And Restless". *Out*, July 1997.

"Beyond The Good Gay/Bad Gay Syndrome". *Newsday*, 17 August 1997.

"Out At The New York Times". *Advocate*, 5 May 1992.

Silcott, Mireille. *Rave America: New School Dancescapes*. Toronto: ECW Press, 1999.

Smith, Andrew. "Raving Mad." *Melody Maker*, 14 July 1990.

"Safer House." *The Face*, October 1995.

Smith, Gill. "Life Support Switched Off For Ecstasy Boy, 13." *Scotsman*, 20 June 1997.

Smith, Russel. "Mistral Has Come Out Swinging." *Dallas Morning News*, 30 September 1985.

"Starck Club Dies, But What A Life It Had." *Dallas Morning News*, 6 April 1989.

"Starck Raving Madness." *Dallas Morning News*, 8 September 1985.

"Take Off Those Dancing Shoes." *Dallas Morning News*, 20 April 1987.

Staricco, Paul. "The Underground: Truth Or Trend?" *XLR8R*, issue 18.

"The Star Says." *Daily Star*, 29 January 1992.

Stevens, Jay. *Storming Heaven – LSD And The American Dream*. London: Flamingo, 1993.

Stolaroff, Myron. *The Secret Chief: Conversations With A Pioneer Of The Underground Psychedelic Therapy Movement*. MAPS, 1996.

Strauss, Neil. "All-Night Parties And A Nod To The 60's (Rave On!)." *New York Times*, 28 May 1996.

"Electronica 101." *Spin*, September 1996.

"Strife Of Brian." *NME*, 25 January 1997.

The Substance Of Youth: The Role Of Drugs In Young People's Lives Today. Joseph Rowntree Foundation report, 1997.

Summers, Owen. "Yard Stand-By As New Ecstasy Drug Arrives In Britain." *Daily Express*, 17 March 1986.

Sylvester, Rachel. "Tests Prove Ecstasy Harm Is Permanent." *Sunday Telegraph*, 7 April 1996.

Tackling Drugs To Build A Better Britain: The Government's 10 Year Strategy For Tackling Drugs Misuse. The Stationary Office, 1998.

Tanouye, Elyse. "Antidepressant Makers Study Kids' Market." *Wall Street Journal*, 4 April 1997.

Thomas, Rebecca. "Break, Rattle And Roll." *The Orlando Sentinel*, 17 July 1997.

Thompson, Hunter S. "The Hashbury Is The Capital Of The Hippies."
In Kureishi, Savage, *The Faber Book Of Pop*.

Thornton, Sarah. *Club Cultures: Music, Media And The Subcultural Capital*.
Hanover: Weslyan University Press, 1996.

Timms, Phil. "Empire Building." *DJ*, 10 November 1994.

Toop, David. *Ocean Of Sound: Aether Talk, Ambient Sound And Imaginary
Worlds*. London: Serpent's Tail, 1995.

"The Floyd." *Mixmag*, October 1993.

Travis, Alan. "Anti-Drugs Drive Fails To Stem Abuse." *Guardian*,
22 March 1999.

"The New Epidemic." *Guardian*, 26 May 1999.

Troup, John. "Baker Axes Funding For Drug Leaflet." *Sun*, 31 January
1992.

Tuck, Andrew. "Agony And Ecstasy." *Time Out*, 16 October 1990.

Turner, Ben and Rob Da Bank. "Clubs Of The Year '98." *Muzik*,
January 1999.

"TV Bob's Fury Over 'E For Ecstasy' Shirt." *Today*, 23 March 1992.

The UK Anti-Drugs Co-ordinator First Annual Report And National Plan.
The Stationary Office, 1999.

Underwood, John and Chris Blythe. "Crazed Acid House Mob Attack
Police." *News Of The World*, 6 November 1988.

Untitled *Melody Maker* news article, 12 November 1988.

Untitled *Soul Underground* news article, July 1988.

Untitled *Soul Underground* news article, November 1988.

US Naval Technical Mission In Europe. US Naval Technical Mission report,
1945.

*Verfahren Zur Darstellung Von Alkyloxyaryl-, Dialkyloxyaryl- Und
Lkylendioxyarylamino-Propanen Bzw. Deren Am Stickstoff
Monoalkylierten Derivaten*. Kaiserliches Patentamt Patentschrift
Number 274350, 1914.

Verfahren Zur Gewinnung Von Formylderivaten Sekundarer Basen. Deutsches
Reich Reichspatentamt Patentschrift Number 334555, 1921.

Ward, Christopher and Oonagh Blackman. "Dance Drug Crackdown."
Sunday Express, 29 December 1991.

Warhol, Andy and Pat Hackett, eds. *The Andy Warhol Diaries*. New
York: Warner Books, 1989.

Waxman, Sharon. "Starck: Portrait Of An Artist." *Dallas Morning News*, 7
August 1990.

Wells, Steven. "Get Right Off One Chummy." *NME*, 19 November
1988.

Welsh, Irvine. *The Acid House*. London: Jonathan Cape, 1994.

Weir, John. "Orlando: Hot Sound." *Rolling Stone*, 21 August 1997.

239

"Western States Battle Methamphetamine." *San Jose Mercury News*,
    6 September 1996.

White, Mark. "This Man Smuggled 25 Pills Through Customs (And Got
    Caught)." *Mixmag*, June 1998.

Whittow, Hugh and Jeff Edwards. "Dicing With A Cocktail Of Death."
    Daily Star, 2 November 1988.

Whittow, Hugh. "US Link In Huge Acid Drugs Haul." *Daily Star*,
    12 January 1989.

Wilmott, Ben. "Viva Agitate." *NME*, 30 April 1994.

Wurtzel, Elizabeth. "The Keepers Of Cool." *Dallas Morning News*,
    13 August 1987.

Wyburn, Claire. "Born Slippy." *Muzik*, May 1997.

Wynne-Jones, Ros. "Let Us Take Over 'Britannia', Says Ministry Of
    Sound." *Independent On Sunday*, 2 December 1997.

"Yard Stand-By As New Ecstasy Drug Arrives In Britain." *Daily Express*,
    17 March 1986.

Yardley, Jim. "Gay Charity Event Seen As Sending The Wrong
    Message". *New York Times*, 2 January 1997

Yates, Charles. "Dead Claire's Ecstasy Man Gets Six Weeks." *Sun*,
    1 September 1989.

Young, Francis. *Drug Enforcement Administration In The Matter Of MDMA
    Scheduling*. US Department Of Justice, 1986.

Young, Jock. *The Drugtakers – The Social Meaning Of Drug Use*. Boulder:
    Paladin, 1972.

Young, Sydney. "Eee Orville! Are You On Ecstasy?" *Daily Mirror*,
    2 October 1992.

Internet Resources

Addiction Research Foundation: www.arf.org
AIDS Treatment Information Service: www.hivatis.org
Albert Hofmann Foundation: www.hofmann.org
Another GHB Page: members.tripod.com/~ghb_info
The Art Of Deception: www.angelfire.com/ca3/jphuck
Bad Boy Club Montreal: www.bbcm.org
Big Brother's Virtual Underground: www3.l0pht.com/~bb
Biopark Foundation: www.biopark.org
Boston University Medical Center: www.bu.edu/cohis
Candy Kids Central: www.candykids.com
Central Intelligence Agency (CIA): www.cia.gov
Check It!: drugs.ort.org
The Circuit Dog: www.thecircuitdog.com
Circuit Noize: www.circuitnoize.com
Circuit Parties: www.circuitparties.com
Circuit Party Finder: www.partyfinder.com
Circuit Stud: www.circuitstud.com
City Of Amsterdam: www.amsterdam.nl
Cognitive Enhancement Research Institute (CERI): www.ceri.com
The Company Of Biologists: www.biologists.com
Cosmic Sales: www.nubrain.com
Crew 2000: www.2000c.freeserve.co.uk
Crimestoppers: www.worldserver.pipex.com/crimestoppers
Darmstadt: www.tu-darmstadt.de/city
DEMOS: www.demos.co.uk/
The Deoxyribonucleic Hyperdimension: www.deoxy.org
The Do It Now Foundation: www.doitnow.org
Drug Enforcement Administration (DEA): www.usdoj.gov/dea
Drug Free America: drugfreeamerica.org
The Drug Library: www.druglibrary.org
The Drug Reform Co-ordination Network: drcnet.org
The DXM Appreciation Page: www.ugmadness.com/Ledderson/DxM
Ecstasy Org: ecstasy.org
Ecstasy Survey: www.cia.com.au/aburton/Ecstasy
England FC: www.englandfc.com

eRave: www.erave.org
Federation Of American Scientists: www.fas.org
Freebass Society: www.freebass.com
Gatecrasher: www.gatecrasher.co.uk
The Gay Men's Health Crisis (GMHC): www.gmhc.org
Gay Wave: www.gaywave.com
The GHB: www.the-ghb.org
GHB FAQ Crisis Center: uts.cc.utexas.edu/~laborit
Happy 4 Beats: www.h4b.org
The Hedonistic Imperative: www.hedweb.com
Heffter Research Institute: heffter.org
HX Magazine: www.hx.com
Hyperreal: www.hyperreal.org
The Ibogaine Dossier: www.ibogaine.org
The Informed Drug Guide: www.infomed.org
International Anti-Aging Systems: www.smart-drugs.com
Internet Mental Health: mentalhealth.com
John C Lilly Homepage: www.garage.co.jp/lilly
Johns Hopkins University: www.jhu.edu/
The Joseph Rowntree Foundation: www.jrf.org.uk
Leicester Drugs Archive: area51.upsu.plym.ac.uk/infoserv/drugs
The Libra Project: www.brookes.ac.uk/health/libra
The Life Extension Foundation: www.lef.org
London Toxicology Group: ramindy.sghms.ac.uk
The Lycaeum: www.lycaeum.org
The Media Awareness Project: www.mapinc.org
Merck: www.merck.de/english/index.htm
Metropolitan Police: www.met.police.uk
Michelangelo Signorile Homepage: www.signorile.com
Ministry Of Sound: www.ministryofsound.co.uk
Multidisciplinary Association For Psychedelic Studies (MAPS): maps.org
The Musclesoft Online Store: www.musclesoft.com
National AIDS Treatment Advocacy Project: www.natap.org
National Center For Biotechnology Information: www.ncbi.nlm.nih.gov
National Institute On Drug Abuse: www.nida.nih.gov
Parascope: www.parascope.com
The Party List: www.partylist.com
Rave Data: www.ravedata.com
Rave Gear Store: www.ravegear.com
Rave Wave: www.geocities.com/SunsetStrip/Basement/2162
Rave World: www.raveworld.net
Raves R Us: www.maxpages.com/ravesrus

Reggie's Nootropic Archive: www.globalserve.net/~reggiec
The Saint: www.landofmakebelieve.com
The Saint At Large: www.saintatlarge.com
Sigma-RBI Homepage: www.callrbi.com
Smart Basics: www.smartbasic.com
Smart Bomb: www.smartbomb.com
The Smart Drink FAQ: www.globalserve.net/FAQ-Smart-Drink
Smart Publications: www.smart-publications.com
Sputnik Drug Information Zone: nepenthes.lycaeum.org
The Stationary Office: www.tsonline.co.uk
The Treatment Action Group (TAG): www.aidsinfonyc.org/tag
UK Cannabis Internet Activists: www.ukcia.org
UK Official Documents: www.official-documents.co.uk
US Army 90th Infantry Division: www.cris.com/~Patriot2/90th
US National Library Of Medicine: www.nlm.nih.gov/
The Vaults Of Erowid: www.erowid.org
Virtual Pines: www.fipines.com
Xtremesex: rampages.onramp.net/~tmike/xtremesex/xtreme.html